A Book Of

OPERATIONS AND SUPPLY CHAIN MANAGEMENT

For
MBA Semester - II
As Per New Syllabus
Effective from June 2013

Vijay Gaikwad
B.E. (Mech.), MMS

Pushkar Aurangabadkar
B.Com. DBF, MBA (Finance), EPAF (IIM Calcutta)

N2980

MBA - Sem. II : Operations & Supply Chain Management ISBN 978-93-83750-67-2

Second Edition : January 2016
© : Authors

The text of this publication, or any part thereof, should not be reproduced or transmitted in any form or stored in any computer storage system or device for distribution including photocopy, recording, taping or information retrieval system or reproduced on any disc, tape, perforated media or other information storage device etc., without the written permission of Authors with whom the rights are reserved. Breach of this condition is liable for legal action.

Every effort has been made to avoid errors or omissions in this publication. In spite of this, errors may have crept in. Any mistake, error or discrepancy so noted and shall be brought to our notice shall be taken care of in the next edition. It is notified that neither the publisher nor the authors or seller shall be responsible for any damage or loss of action to any one, of any kind, in any manner, therefrom.

Published By :
NIRALI PRAKASHAN
Abhyudaya Pragati, 1312, Shivaji Nagar,
Off J.M. Road, PUNE – 411005
Tel - (020) 25512336/37/39, Fax - (020) 25511379
Email : niralipune@pragationline.com

Printed By :
Repro Knowledgecast Limited,
Thane

☞ DISTRIBUTION CENTRES

PUNE
Nirali Prakashan : 119, Budhwar Peth, Jogeshwari Mandir Lane, Pune 411002, Maharashtra
Tel : (020) 2445 2044, 66022708, Fax : (020) 2445 1538
Email : bookorder@pragationline.com, niralilocal@pragationline.com

Nirali Prakashan : S. No. 28/27, Dhyari, Near Pari Company, Pune 411041
Tel : (020) 24690204 Fax : (020) 24690316
Email : dhyari@pragationline.com, bookorder@pragationline.com

MUMBAI
Nirali Prakashan : 385, S.V.P. Road, Rasdhara Co-op. Hsg. Society Ltd.,
Girgaum, Mumbai 400004, Maharashtra
Tel : (022) 2385 6339 / 2386 9976, Fax : (022) 2386 9976
Email : niralimumbai@pragationline.com

☞ DISTRIBUTION BRANCHES

JALGAON
Nirali Prakashan : 34, V. V. Golani Market, Navi Peth, Jalgaon 425001,
Maharashtra, Tel : (0257) 222 0395, Mob : 94234 91860

KOLHAPUR
Nirali Prakashan : New Mahadvar Road, Kedar Plaza, 1st Floor Opp. IDBI Bank
Kolhapur 416 012, Maharashtra. Mob : 9850046155

NAGPUR
Pratibha Book Distributors : Above Maratha Mandir, Shop No. 3, First Floor,
Rani Jhanshi Square, Sitabuldi, Nagpur 440012, Maharashtra
Tel : (0712) 254 7129

DELHI
Nirali Prakashan : 4593/21, Basement, Aggarwal Lane 15, Ansari Road, Daryaganj
Near Times of India Building, New Delhi 110002
Mob : 08505972553

BENGALURU
Pragati Book House : House No. 1, Sanjeevappa Lane, Avenue Road Cross,
Opp. Rice Church, Bengaluru – 560002.
Tel : (080) 64513344, 64513355,Mob : 9880582331, 9845021552
Email:bharatsavla@yahoo.com

CHENNAI
Pragati Books : 9/1, Montieth Road, Behind Taas Mahal, Egmore,
Chennai 600008 Tamil Nadu, Tel : (044) 6518 3535,
Mob : 94440 01782 / 98450 21552 / 98805 82331,
Email : bharatsavla@yahoo.com

niralipune@pragationline.com | www.pragationline.com

Also find us on www.facebook.com/niralibooks

Pushkar Aurangabadkar

Dedicated to,

My constant source of support and inspiration...
My parents

Mrs. Trupti Mangalmurti Aurangabadkar
and
Mr. Mangalmurti Kamlakar Aurangabadkar

Preface ...

With the liberalisation and opening up of the economy our country was thrown into a global system from its traditionally insular and self-reliant stance. Again with the new millennium, enabling technologies, especially information technology have created a whole new realm of virtual reality, which has changed many paradigms of how business is conducted globally.

India also faces the task of not only integrating itself with the rest of the world, but more importantly, of understanding future global trends to work towards finding a place among the leading economies. Countries like India can ill-afford any wastage in the industrial sector because of the resource constraints. Unfortunately, the productivity is a major concern in developing nations. Therefore, the development of skilled and dynamic managers has become a demanding need of the developing nations. These managers can perform great results if they are provided with proper working conditions that promote a creativity and innovative spirit in them. Managers, in turn, must develop the right type of shop-floor spirit and values based on professional leadership which gives an equal emphasis to productivity and personal job satisfaction of workers.

An acute dearth of good textbooks, written by Indian authors based on Indian philosophy and work culture is the real handicap for management students and professionals in India. This book **Operations and Supply Chain Management** is a humble attempt to overcome this handicap. The scope of Operations and Supply Chain Management is large and includes topics like Materials Management, Logistics, Inventory, Material Requirement planning, Purchasing Management, Stores, Inventory control and Cost Reduction techniques. The book is intended primarily for the students and faculty members of the management courses like MBA, PGDBM, BBA and correspondence courses in MBA. It will be equally useful for all the entrepreneurs as well as professionals in both the public and private sectors.

There are five theory chapters in this book, with each chapter dedicated to a particular area of the subject. These are arranged in a logical sequence for easy development and understanding of the subject. Numericals, Multiple Choice Questions and Case Study chapters have been separately added for the assessment purpose. We have made utmost effort for the book to be helpful to all the targets; however we would feel grateful to welcome suggestions for improving the quality of this book.

We would like to express our sincere appreciation and acknowledgements to Shri. Dineshbhai Furia, Shri. Jignesh Furia, our publishers and Nirja Sharma, Prasad Chintakindi, Ilyas Shaikh, Chaitali Takale, Ravindra Walodare and the entire staff of Nirali Prakashan for their encouragement and support in printing and publishing this book.

We are very grateful to our family members, Arpita Aurangabadkar, and sister Ketaki, our parents, in laws and relatives and friends, for their enduring support, encouragement and patience without which the publication of this book would have been a futile attempt.

This effort is just a part of the blessings granted to us by our divine 'sat-guru'. We are just a small medium to ensure social empowerment in the society.

Blessed..!!
Thanks a lot..!!!

Pushkar Aurangabadkar

Syllabus ...

Unit 1

INTRODUCTION TO OPERATIONS AND SUPPLY CHAIN MANAGEMENT

1.1 Introduction to Operations and Supply Chain Management : Definition, Concept, Significance and Functions of Operations and SCM. Evolution from Manufacturing to operations management, Physical distribution to Logistics to SCM, Physical Goods and Services Perspectives.

1.2 Quality : Definitions from various Perspectives, Customers view and Manufacturer's view, Concept of Internal Customer, Overview of TQM and LEAN Management, Impact of Global Competition, Technological Change, Ethical and Environmental Issues on Operations and Supply Chain Functions.

Unit 2

OPERATIONS PROCESSES

2.1 Process Characteristics in Operations : Volume Variety and Flow. Types of Processes and Operations Systems - Continuous Flow System and Intermittent flow systems.

2.2 Process Product Matrix : Job Production, Batch Production, Assembly line and Continuous Flow, Process and Product Layout

2.3 Service System Design Matrix : Design of Service Systems, Service Blueprinting

Unit 3

PRODUCTION PLANNING & CONTROL

3.1 Production Planning and Control (PPC) : Role and Functions

3.2 Demand Forecasting : Forecasting as a Planning Tool, Forecasting Time Horizon, Sources of Data for forecasting, Accuracy of Forecast, Capacity Planning

3.3 Production Planning : Aggregate production planning, Alternatives for Managing Demand and Supply, Master Production Schedule, Capacity Planning : Overview of MRP, CRP, DRP, MRP II.

3.4 Production Control : Scheduling, Loading, Scheduling of Job Shops and Floor Shops, Gantt Charts.

Unit 4

INVENTORY PLANNING AND CONTROL

4.1 Inventory Planning and Control : Continuous and Intermittent demand System, Concept of Inventory, Need for Inventory, Types of Inventory - seasonal, decoupling, cyclic, pipeline, safety - Implications for Inventory Control Methods.

4.2 Inventory Costs : Concept and behaviour of ordering cost, carrying cost, storage cost.

4.3 EOQ : Basic EOQ Model - EOQ with discounts.

4.4 Inventory Control : Classification of material - ABC Analysis - VED, HML, FSN, GOLF, SOS.

(Numericals expected on Basic EOQ, EOQ with discounts and ABC, Inventory turnover ratios, Fixed Order Quantity Model - Periodic Review and Re-order Point)

Unit 5

SUPPLY CHAIN MANAGEMENT

5.1 Supply Chain Management : Generalized Supply Chain Management Model-Key Issues in SCM - Collaboration, Enterprise Extension, responsiveness, Cash to Cash Conversion.

5.2 Customer Service : Supply Chain Management and Customer Service linkages, Availability, Service Reliability, Perfect Order, Customer satisfaction Enablers of SCM - Facilities, Inventory, Transportation, Information, Sourcing, Pricing.

Contents ...

1. **Introduction to Operations and Supply Chain Management**   1.1 - 1.62

2. **Operations Process**   2.1 - 2.30

3. **Production Planning and Control**   3.1 - 3.42

4. **Inventory Planning and Control**   4.1 - 4.66

5. **Supply Chain Management**   5.1 - 5.28

- **Case Studies**   C.1 - C.30

- **Numerical**   N.1 - N.56

- **Multiple Choice Questions**   M.1 - M.6

- **University Question Papers (April 2014 - April 2015)**   P.1 - P.2

Chapter 1...

Introduction to Operations and Supply Chain Management

Contents ...

1.1 Introduction to Operations and Supply Chain Management
- 1.1.1 Definitions
- 1.1.2 Concept
- 1.1.3 Significance and Functions of Operations and Supply Chain
- 1.1.4 Evolution from Manufacturing to Operations Management
- 1.1.5 Physical Distribution to Logistics to Supply Chain
- 1.1.6 Physical Goods and Service Perspectives

1.2 Introduction to Quality
- 1.2.1 Definitions of Quality
- 1.2.2 Customer's View and Manufacturer's View
- 1.2.3 Concept of Internal Customer
- 1.2.4 Overview of Total Quality Management and Lean Management
- 1.2.5 Impact of Global Competition
- 1.2.6 Technological Change
- 1.2.7 Ethical and Environmental Issues on Operations and Supply Chain Functions

- Points to Remember
- Questions for Discussion
- Questions from Previous Examinations

Learning Objectives:
- To study the significance and functions of operation and supply chain management
- To study the set of activities concerned with physical distribution
- To understand the two meaning of quality and customer satisfaction
- To study the ethical and environmental issues on operations and supply chain functions

1.1 Introduction to Operations and Supply Chain Management

Operations management is an area of management concerned with overseeing, designing, and controlling the process of production and redesigning business operations in the production of goods or services. It involves the responsibility of ensuring that business operations are efficient in terms of using as few resources as needed, and effective in terms of meeting customer requirements. It is concerned with managing the process that converts inputs (in the forms of materials, labour, and energy) into outputs (in the form of goods and/or services). The relationship of operations management to senior management in commercial contexts can be compared to the relationship of line officers to highest-level senior officers in military science. The highest-level officers shape the strategy and revise it over time, while the line officers make tactical decisions in support of carrying out the strategy. In business as in military affairs, the boundaries between levels are not always distinct; tactical information dynamically informs strategy, and individual people often move between roles over time.

A **supply chain** on the other hand is a system of organisations, people, activities, information, and resources involved in moving a product or service from supplier to customer. Supply chain activities transform natural resources, raw materials, and components into a finished product that is delivered to the end customer. In sophisticated supply chain systems, used products may re-enter the supply chain at any point where residual value is recyclable. Supply chains link value chains.

However, Operations Management is a narrower concept if compared with Supply Chain Management. Supply Chains link the Suppliers of the Manufacturer, the Materials, the Processes and the Customers as well. However, Operations management is concerned merely with the process of conversion of inputs into outputs within an organisation. Hence, Supply Chain is more dynamic as compared with operations management.

1.1.1 Definitions

Operations management is an area of management concerned with overseeing, designing, and controlling the process of production and redesigning business operations in the production of goods or services.

- **H A Hardings:** *"Manufacturing management is concerned with those processes which convert the Inputs into Outputs. Inputs are raw Material, Men, Machines, Methods and the outputs are finish goods and services."*
- **Edward Buffa:** *"Manufacturing management deals with decision making related to Production process so that the resulting goods and services are produced according to specifications, in the amounts and by the schedule demanded at minimum Costs."*

- The **Council of Logistics Management** defines Supply Chain Management as *"The process of planning, implementing and controlling the efficient, cost-effective flow and storage of raw materials, finished goods and related information from the point-of-origin to the point-of-origin consumption for the purpose of conforming to customer requirements"*.
- According to the **Journal of Business Logistics**, *"Supply chain management is the systematic and strategic co-ordination of various business functions and the tactics across them within the supply chain of a particular company."*
- **The Global Supply Chain Forum**, 1994 defines it as *"the integration of key business processes from the end user through original suppliers that provide products, services and information that add value for customers."*

1.1.2 Concept

According to the **U.S. Department of Education**, *"operations management is the field concerned with managing and directing the physical and/or technical functions of a firm or organisation, particularly those relating to development, production, and manufacturing."*

Operations management programmes typically include instruction in principles of general management, manufacturing and production systems, factory management, equipment maintenance management, production control, industrial labour relations and skilled trades supervision, strategic manufacturing policy, systems analysis, productivity analysis and cost control, and materials planning. Management, including operations management, is like engineering in that it blends art with applied science. People skills, creativity, rational analysis, and knowledge of technology are all required for success.

Operations Management

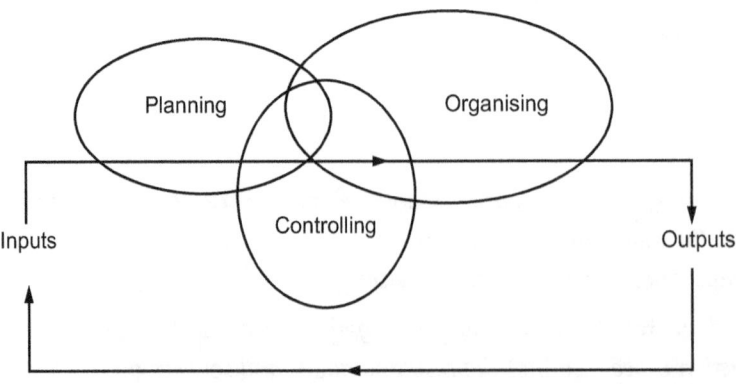

Fig. 1.1: Operations Management

The Council of Supply Chain Management Professionals defines supply chain management as follows: "Supply Chain Management encompasses the planning and management of all activities involved in sourcing and procurement, conversion, and all logistics management activities. Importantly, it also includes coordination and collabouration with channel partners, which can be suppliers, intermediaries, third-party service providers, and customers. In essence, supply chain management integrates supply and demand management within and across companies. Supply Chain Management is an integrating function with primary responsibility for linking major business functions and business processes within and across companies into a cohesive and high-performing business model. It includes all of the logistics management activities noted above, as well as manufacturing operations, and it drives coordination of processes and activities with and across marketing, sales, product design, finance and information technology."

A typical supply chain begins with the ecological, biological, and political regulation of natural resources, followed by the human extraction of raw material, and includes several production links (e.g., component construction, assembly, and merging) before moving on to several layers of storage facilities of ever-decreasing size and increasingly remote geographical locations, and finally reaching the consumer.

Many of the exchanges encountered in the supply chain are therefore between different companies that seek to maximise their revenue within their sphere of interest, but may have little or no knowledge or interest in the remaining players in the supply chain. More recently, the loosely coupled, self-organising network of businesses that cooperates to provide product and service offerings has been called the *Extended Enterprise*.

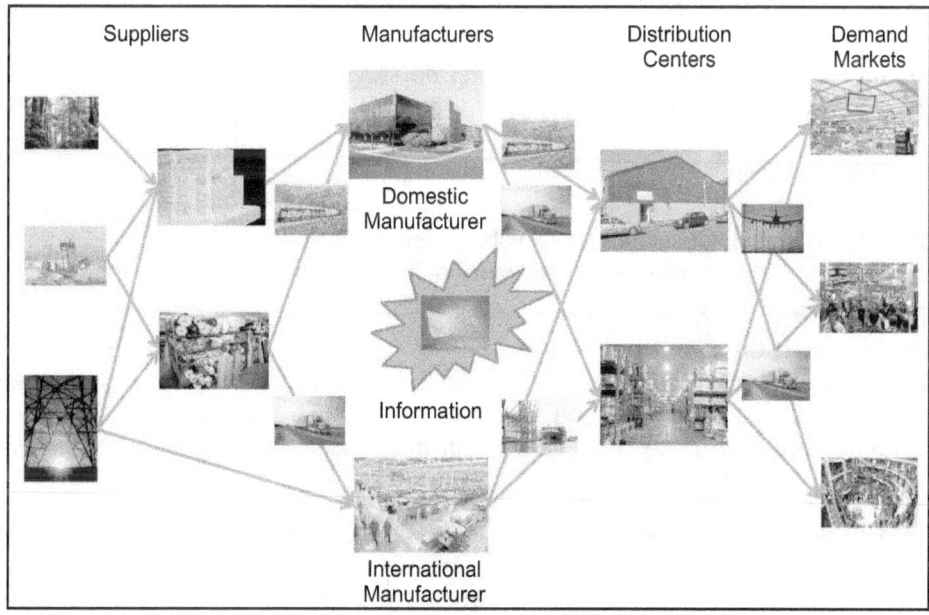

Fig. 1.2

Guaranteeing acceptable conditions in a global supply chain can be a complex challenge. As part of their efforts to demonstrate ethical practices, many large companies and global brands are integrating codes of conduct and guidelines into their corporate cultures and management systems. Through these, corporations are making demands on their suppliers (facilities, farms, subcontracted services such as cleaning, canteen, security etc.) and verifying, through social audits, that they are complying with the required standard.

In the 1980s, the term Supply Chain Management (SCM) was developed to express the need to integrate the key business processes, from end user through original suppliers. Original suppliers are those that provide products, services, and information that add value for customers and other stakeholders. The basic idea behind SCM is that companies and corporations involve themselves in a supply chain by exchanging information about market fluctuations and production capabilities. Keith Oliver, a consultant at Booz Allen Hamilton, is credited with the term's invention after using it in an interview for the Financial Times in 1982.

If all relevant information is accessible to any relevant company, every company in the supply chain has the ability to help optimise the entire supply chain rather than to sub-optimise based on a local interest. This will lead to better-planned overall production and distribution, which can cut costs and give a more attractive final product, leading to better sales and better overall results for the companies involved.

Incorporating SCM successfully leads to a new kind of competition on the global market, where competition is no longer of the company-versus-company form but rather takes on a supply-chain-versus-supply-chain form.

The primary objective of SCM is to fulfil customer demands through the most efficient use of resources, including distribution capacity, inventory, and labour. In theory, a supply chain seeks to match demand with supply and do so with the minimal inventory. Various aspects of optimising the supply chain include liaising with suppliers to eliminate bottlenecks; sourcing strategically to strike a balance between lowest material cost and transportation, implementing just-in-time techniques to optimise manufacturing flow; maintaining the right mix and location of factories and warehouses to serve customer markets; and using location allocation, vehicle routing analysis, dynamic, and traditional logistics optimisation to maximise the efficiency of distribution.

There is often confusion over the terms "supply chain" and "logistics". It is now generally accepted that "logistics" applies to activities within one company or organisation involving product distribution, whereas "supply chain" additionally encompasses manufacturing and procurement, and therefore has a much broader focus as it involves multiple enterprises (including suppliers, manufacturers, and retailers) working together to meet a customer need for a product or service.

Starting in the 1990s, several companies chose to outsource the logistics aspect of supply chain management by partnering with a third-party logistics provider (3PL). Companies also outsource production to contract manufacturers. Technology companies have risen to meet the demand to help manage these complex systems.

There are four common supply chain models. Besides the three mentioned above, there is the Supply Chain Best Practices Framework.

1.1.3 Significance and Functions of Operations and Supply Chain

Supply chain management systems are integrated partnerships among all links in the flow of goods and services to the customer. They are created for the purpose of improving quality, reducing costs and achieving competitive advantage in a world where lean manufacturing and specialisation force companies to rely on one another for valuable productive activities. All supply chain activities, including planning, sourcing, producing, delivering and providing for returns, are handled collaboratively within an integrated supply chain to ensure the maximum use of shared resources. In traditional supply chain systems, large companies found it beneficial to vertically integrate supplier functions and distribution activities to maximise production and logistical control. Many modern firms, however, rely heavily on outsourced services and suppliers that perform one or more functions of production. Reliance on third parties for important supply chain activities such as raw material procurement and distribution raises concerns related to quality assurance, timely delivery and adherence to responsible business practices. Supply chain management was introduced as a solution to these problems. When companies along a supply chain make a concerted effort to work together in the areas of procurement, production and distribution in an environment of teamwork and transparency, all of the firms involved can experience a greater competitive advantage.

Supply chain management influences your ability to satisfy the expectations of your customers and achieve competitive advantage. It determines the effectiveness and efficiency with which you handle ordering, production, storage and distribution activities. Any expected or unexpected supply chain disruptions may devastate your business aspirations. It is for these reasons that supply chain management has become such an important topic in business and strategic management issues. To remain competitive, small firms have to offer superior quality goods at the lowest prices possible. The need to minimise product costs makes effective supply chain management vital. There are costs involved in every process of the product life cycle, and it is the responsibility of management to ensure that these costs are kept low, so the company can continue to pass along these savings to the consumer.

1. **Reduced Costs:** Supply chain management involves identifying those processes that increase cost without increasing the value of the final product. These processes are wasteful and do not add value, and should be eliminated whenever possible.

2. **Increased Efficiency:** Resource wastage is a common source of increase production costs. Often this is due to improper planning. A company that employs supply chain management is able to achieve efficiency of its operations since only those value adding activities are encouraged. This ensures that the organisation's processes flow smoothly and output keeps inline with the company's needs.

3. Increased Output: A company that employs supply chain management can foster close-knit relationships with its suppliers and customers, ensuring the timely fulfillment of orders. A company known for its timeliness and responsiveness will attract more customers, and will grow as a result of increased output and sales.

4. Increased Profits: Businesses exist to make profits. One of the most efficient ways of increasing a company's profits is by ensuring that costs are kept as low as possible. The application of supply chain management by a small company leads to cost reductions due to elimination of wasteful processes. Since these are operating costs for the company, the savings on these costs reflect increased profits by the company.

5. Mitigation of Rising Costs of Operations: Rising costs of operations have influenced fundamental shifts in supply chain management. There is growing urgency for mitigating measures needed to inject efficiency and cut down the costs associated with supply chain activities. For instance, you may outsource some of your supply chain activities to avoid the high costs of warehousing, fleet operations and staff maintenance. The findings of PWC's "Global Supply Chain Survey 2013" revealed that some of the leading players in different sectors outsource as much as 60 percent of their warehousing and logistics operations.

6. Acknowledgement of Sustainability Issues: The impact of supply chain activities on climate change has been a subject of heated debate. There are concerns that the transportation of cargo by road, sea and air emit toxic gases to the atmosphere. Many business organisations are crafting and implementing appropriate strategies in response to these challenges. For example, Proctor and Gamble was edging closer to achieving its 2015 targets of cutting the total mileage traveled by its trucks by 30 percent in efforts to reduce carbon dioxide emissions. As such, you cannot underestimate the realities of global warming when crafting your supply chain management strategies.

7. Development of Information Technology: Widespread use of the internet has fundamentally transformed the world into a global village. A brick-and-mortar approach to business is no longer the norm as e-commerce platforms edge towards occupying the center stage of business procurement and supplies strategies. However, increased accessibility of international markets comes with greater challenges of managing expansive supply chain networks. You must harness your supply chain capabilities to achieve quick turnarounds in the procurement and distribution of stock items. It is equally important to reduce response times and make timely shipments of streaming customer orders.

8. Shortage of Skilled Labour Force: The growing complexity of global business operations has ignited unprecedented demand for skilled supply chain personnel in businesses across industries. This has resulted to a shortage of qualified personnel in the fields of inventory management, procurement and supplies management. This exposes you to the challenges of recruiting well-trained employees for your supply chain operations because they demand high salaries and are hard to come by.

1.1.4 Evolution from Manufacturing to Operations Management

Understanding evolution is a historic process and we need to go back to the early stages of the Industrial Revolution. We shall chronologically see how the function changed with time. Prior to the industrial revolution also there were goods such as agricultural equipment, arms/armaments, clothing and service providers such as blacksmiths, carpenters, and cobblers. However, these industries were on a very small scale and designed to support needs of a considerably small community. This condition prevailed in all the Asian and most of the European countries.

In India we had system of 12 craftsmen in each village (known as *Bara balutedar* in Marathi) who supported mainly agricultural economy mutually. These products were produced by individuals who had highly developed skills working with mainly wood and iron. This category of production is known as "Craft Production". It was capable of producing decent quality but "Non interchangeable" products.

There are many sound techniques and management tools contributed by many experts in this field, which have changed the way the function of conversion of resources is carried out, especially in last two centuries. Industrial revolution is supposed to have started with James Watt's steam engine (1764) which removed the restriction of using either man/animal power in the industry.

This industrial revolution quickly spread through European nations and U.S.A. Another contributing factor was spread of colonies from which raw materials were available at cheap rates in abundance and sure market was available for large amount of finish products. This was helped by opening of trade routes - both on land and through sea at relatively cheap transportation costs. Let us have a glance at this evolution.

In India industrial revolution started only after independence especially from Second Five Year Plan (1956- 61). The Second Five year Plan focused mainly on heavy industry as against the First Plan which was essentially an agricultural plan. This was done to boost domestic production and manufacturing of goods. The plan aimed primarily at developing the public sector.

Globally the concept of "Factory Production" is supposed to have started with Adam Smith.

- **Adam Smith**, 1776, was a Scottish economist who advocated Division of Labour in manufacturing through his book *'The Wealth of Nations'*. Major benefits from division were:
- If work is performed repetitively higher skills and more dexterity is achieved.
- Improvement in production method takes place when worker made to specialise on simple tasks.

Since this concept is foundation to many future concepts, Adam Smith is accepted as originator of production management concept.

- **Interchangeability:** In the early eighteenth century, factory as an organisation began to develop. It was started in England using water (kinetic energy) and steam power in textile mills. **Eli Whitney** (December 8, 1765 – January 8, 1825) was an American inventor best known for inventing the cotton gin. The cotton gin is a mechanical device that removes the seeds from cotton, a process that had previously been extremely labour-intensive. The word gin is short for engine. The cotton gin was a wooden drum stuck with hooks that pulled the cotton fibers through a mesh.

  Eli Whitney saw the potential benefit of developing "interchangeable parts" for the firearms of the United State army. In July 1801, he built ten guns, all containing the same exact parts and mechanisms, and then disassembled them before the United States Congress. He placed the parts in a mixed pile and, with help, reassembled all of the weapons right in front of Congress.

- **Charles Babbage (1832)** was a mathematician. In his book *'The Economy of Machinery and Manufacture'* he put forward "SPECIALISATION" as an additional advantage of Division of Labour and assignment of jobs by skill.-

- **Frederick W. Taylor (1900)** is called "Father of Scientific management". His concepts have developed into major scientific management tools namely Method study, Time study (Work Measurement) and gave rise to concept of "Selection, Training, Placement and Industrial relations" in the field of personal management. He also proposed dividing planning and doing of work between management and work force so each group takes responsibility for the work, for which it is best suited.

- **Frank and Lillian Gilbreth (1900)** are called inventor of Motion of study of jobs. Time and motion study (also referred to as motion and time study) is the scientific study of the conservation of human resources in the search for the most efficient method of doing a task.

A fascination with the word "efficiency" began in the late 19th and early 20th centuries when it was considered one of the most important concepts. Motion study was developed by Frank B. Gilbreth and Lillian M. Gilbreth and consists of a wide variety of procedures for the description, systematic analysis, and means of improving work methods. It is difficult to separate these two aspects completely. Therefore, the combined term usually refers to all three phases of the activity: method determination, time appraisal, and development of material for the application of these data.

Frank and Lillian also broadened scientific management by including the human element, therefore using psychology to gain the cooperation of employees.

- **Henry Ford (1913)** introduced the concept of mass production and organised work stations into a job sequential conveyor belt assembly line. Ford did not invent the automobile, but he developed and manufactured the first automobile that many middle class Americans could afford to buy. His introduction of the Model T automobile, revolutionised transportation and the American industry.

- **Henry L. Gantt (1910)** was an American mechanical engineer and management consultant who is best known for developing the Gantt chart in the 1910s. Gantt charts were employed on major infrastructure projects and continue to be an important tool in project management.

- **F.W. Harris (1915)** developed first Economic lot sizes model for inventory control.

- **Elton Mayo (1927)** is known as the founder of the Human Relations Movement, and was known for his research including the Hawthorne Studies. The research he conducted under the Hawthorne Studies of the 1930s showed the importance of groups in affecting the behaviour of individuals at work. He carried out a number of investigations to look at ways of improving productivity, for example changing lighting conditions in the workplace. What he found however was that work satisfaction depended to a large extent on the informal social pattern of the work group.

- **Walter A. Shewhart (1931):** Total Quality Management and continuous improvement trace back to a former Bell Telephone employee named Walter Shewhart. One of Deming's teachers, he preached the importance of adapting management processes to create profitable situations for both businesses and consumers, promoting the utilisation of his own creation - the SPC control chart.

He also developed the Shewhart Cycle Learning and Improvement cycle, combining both creative management thinking with statistical analysis. This cycle contains four continuous steps: Plan, Do, Study and Act.) Generally the period upto the World War II is called **Scientific Management era** where number of tools described above were put into practice but focus was on **Production**.

1940 to 1980 and widening the SCOPE: This was period of World War II and subsequent cold war between western nations and Soviet block. This was also a period of massive rebuilding of economies of war torn nations like Japan. Major developments were emergence of "Operations Research" outside defense field and introduction of "Value Engineering" by L. D. Miles.

Operations Research is the application of scientific methods and development of Mathematical models to study and devise solutions to managerial problems like resource allocation, product mix, inventory control, location lay out etc.

Value Analysis is a systematic approach to identify waste of product and processes by analysis of the function, without affecting quality, reliability and service. Introduction of computers made it possible to use many Industrial engineering and Operation Research techniques which earlier would have been too time consuming.

By 1958 to monitor and control large projects, techniques of PERT and CPM were introduced. By 1960 the scope of Production was widened to include organisations like Transport, Banks, Hospitals, Warehouses etc., which **brought in concept of "OPERATIONS MANAGEMENT"** so as to include both production of goods (manufacturing organisations) as well as services (service organisations).

1980 to 2012: In this period there was emergence of Asian economies like Japan, South Korea and in later part China and India. Compared to western countries their products were not only cheaper but many times equal or better in quality. Hence there was rush to find out what made it possible. Notable techniques introduced were Quality and Inventory control applications from Japan which were actually originated by **W. E. Deming and J. Juran.** Techniques like Zero Defect Production, Just-In-Time inventory, TQM, TPM are popular amongst them.

Present Trend: Economic reforms and liberalisation have established the importance of customer and market. This is a long way especially in India because after independence for 50 years we operated under "Planned Economy" where focus was on building infrastructure and Production. Customer choices were limited. Here a major realignment is necessary to change the Focus and traditional mind set. Today's priorities are:

- Match operations systems to customer/ market requirements.
- Build up capabilities to accept big increase in number of product and service variety.
- To maintain CIP (Continuous Improvement Programme) develop systems and procedures which promote learning.
- Develop sustainable GREEN manufacturing practices.

1.1.5 Physical Distribution to Logistics to Supply Chain

The working of the economic system by which goods and services are supplied to consumers involves four basic market functions:

- Production
- Distribution
- Exchange
- Consumption.

Logistics assists in the efficient performance of each of these functions. Production transfers raw materials into finished goods (i.e. it creates form utility). In doing so, a long and intricate logistical chain is activated to bring the material together in the proper quality and quantity at the right time in support of the production process.

The function of distribution, places raw materials in the hands of the producers, and finished goods in the hands of the consumers when and where wanted (i.e. it creates time and place utility). Transportation comes into play as a key element in this chain, but getting goods where and when involves much more than just the services of carrying products from here to there.

Physical distribution is the set of activities concerned with efficient movement of finished goods from the end of the production operation to the consumer. Effective physical distribution involves addressing the issues of inventory, transportation, warehousing/ storage, and communication. It thus bridges the gap between consumer demand and producer supply, although the consumer can include both the individual user of a product and the user of raw materials or finished goods produced by someone else.

Physical distribution takes place within numerous wholesaling and retailing distribution channels, and includes such important decision areas as customer service, inventory control, materials handling, protective packaging, order procession, transportation, warehouse site selection, and warehousing.

Physical distribution is part of a larger process called "distribution," which includes wholesale and retail marketing, as well the physical movement of products.

Physical distribution is defined as handling, movement, and storage of goods from the point of origin to the point of consumption or use, via various channels of distribution.

Physical distribution is the art and science of determining requirements, acquiring them, distributing them and finally maintaining them in an operationally ready condition for their entire life.

Physical Distribution Management:

The term 'Physical distribution management' is employed in manufacturing and commerce to describe the broad range of activities (like freight, warehousing, material handling, protective packing, inventory control, selection of site for various activities, marketing, forecasting) concerned with the efficient movement of finished products from the end of production line to the consumer and in some cases, includes the movement of raw materials from the sources of supply to the beginning of the production line.

Physical Distribution

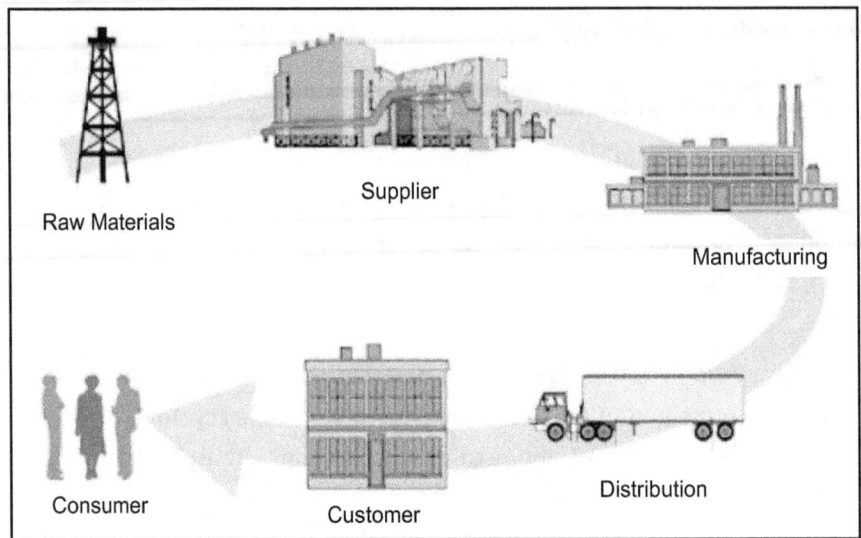

Fig. 1.3: Physical Distribution

'Physical distribution management' is specifically concerned with the flow of goods through the economic system.

The primary participants of the physical distribution process are Producers, Wholesalers, Distributors, Retailers and End-users. However, the physical distribution process also involves management (planning, action and control) of the physical flows of raw materials and finished products from the point of origin to the points of use/consumption to meet the customer needs at a profit. It covers all the activities in the flow of goods between the producer and consumer.

The following are thus the participants or the components in the physical distribution process:

- Distribution planning and accounting,
- In bound transport,
- Receiving,
- Inventory management,
- In-plant warehousing,
- Order processing,
- Packaging/repackaging where applicable,
- Dispatch of goods,
- Outbound transport,
- Field warehousing.

These participants or components are dissimilar but they all are related by the common bond of an efficient flow of goods. The major ones are Transportation, Warehousing and Inventory management.

Participants of physical distribution can be used as elements of marketing strategy. Reorganisation of physical distribution service/process can bring about better customer service, increase in sales, cost reduction and higher profit margin.

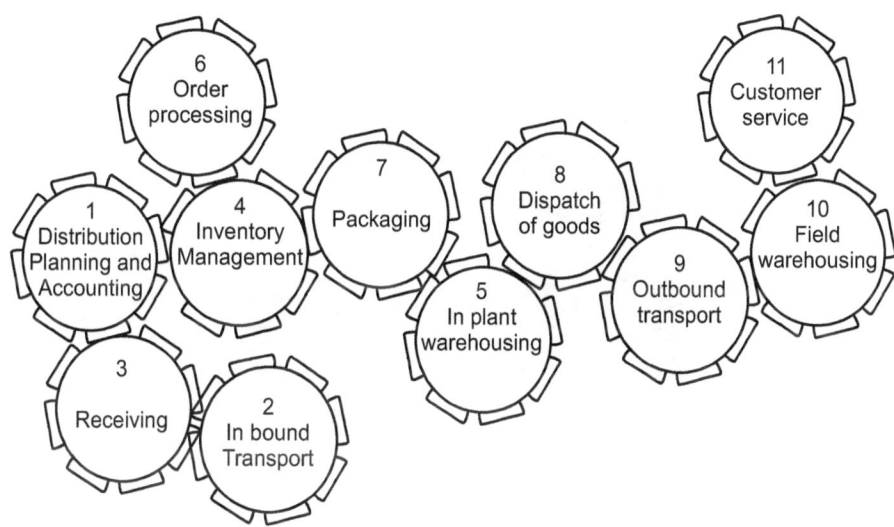

Fig. 1.4 : Participants of the Physical Distribution Process

Fig. 1.4 depicts the participants of the physical distribution process. All these constantly interact with each other. They often interact in an inverse way with one another.

Definition of Logistics

According to **Council of Supply Chain Management Professionals Logistics** is *"the process of planning, implementing and controlling the efficient, effective flow and storage of goods and services and related information, from the point of origin to point of consumption for the purpose of conforming to customer requirements."*

Difference between Logistics Management and Supply Chain Management over time has become blurred. Logistics basically consists of movement and storage of goods between businesses and not within the business. Logistics and Supply chain Management are two areas which often overlap. Different companies define them differently.

This is one of the main differences between logistics and supply chain management.

Logistics

Supply chain management include factors relating to inventory, materials and production planning in its concept. On the other hand logistics includes factors relating to demand management and forecasting in its concept. This is also a difference between logistics and supply chain management.

In order to understand Supply Chain Management, let us study a schematic diagram showing Bearing Industry. Bearings consist of Outer Ring, Inner Ring, Ball/ Roller and cage. These components can be procured from vendors and after processing can be assembled by a bearing manufacturer. Customer places an order with the "Customer Service dept." over the telephone, by e-mail or entering directly into the ERP (enterprise resource planning) system. This is processed by manufacturing, planning and requirements of components are placed with vendors with appropriate schedules. This part is INFORMATION FLOW.

Vendors plan the manufacture accordingly and supply components to Manufacturing. Manufacturing plant in turn processes the components through processes like heat treatment, grinding, honing and assemble the components to manufacture bearing as per customer requirements. These bearings are then forwarded to the customer using the distribution network of plant warehouse and distribution centers.

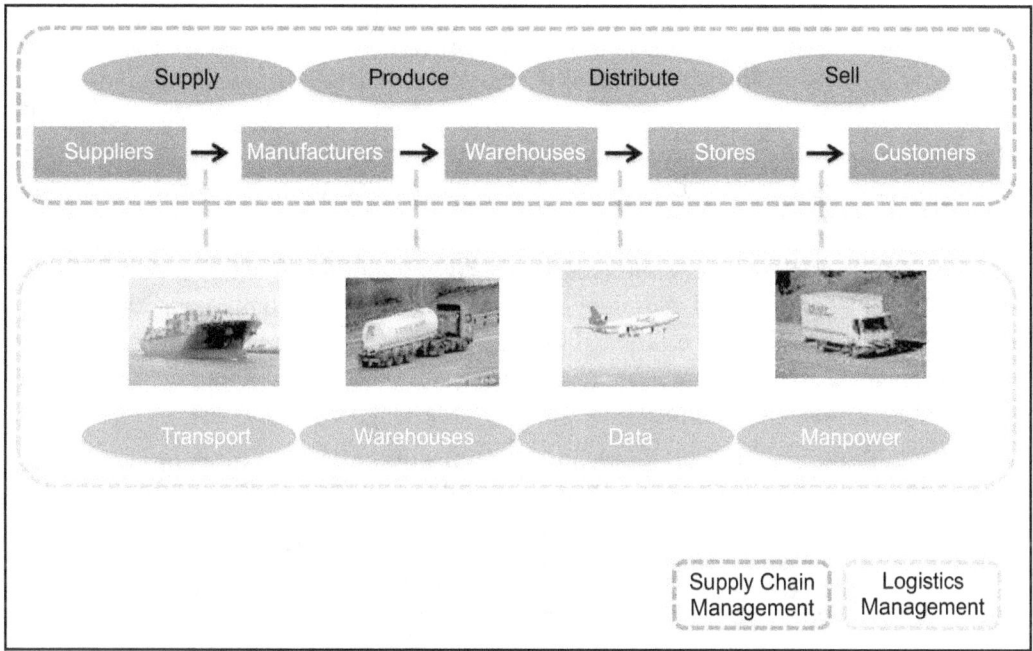

Fig. 1.5: Example of Supply Chain Management Vs. Logistics Management

Difference between Logistics and Supply Chain Management (SCM)

Logistics	Supply Chain Management
Logistics management is a narrower concept.	Supply chain management is a broader concept.
Logistics management is relatively old.	Supply chain management concept is relatively new.
It is concerned with getting goods and services where they are required and when they are desired.	SCM includes all those activities associated with movement of goods from raw material stage to the end user customer.
Logistics is used by a single organisation.	Supply chain management requires coordination and implementation through various organisations in the supply chain.
Logistics is a part of Supply Chain management.	Supply chain management is an extension of Logistics management.
Logistics adds value when inventory is correctly positioned to facilitate sales.	Effective SCM helps in reducing operating costs, improves asset productivity and reduces order cycle time.

1.1.6 Physical Goods and Service Perspectives

As earlier mentioned, in India the **service sector** has grown in recent past at a very fast rate. The service sector is a vital element in the wheel of the Indian economy. The sector, accounting for 60 percent of the gross domestic product (GDP), grew 5 percent in the Financial Year 2013. The Indian service industry has emerged as one of the largest and fastest-growing sectors on the global landscape and hence has made substantial contribution towards global output and employment.

Growing at faster pace as compared to agriculture and manufacturing sectors, Indian service segment comprises of wide range of activities, such as trading, transportation and communication, financial, real estate and business services, as well as community, social and personal services. The following table gives a comparison of the contribution to growth of the three sectors namely the agriculture, the industry and the service sector.

Table 1.1: Comparison of the Contribution to Growth of Agricultural, Industry and Service Sector

SECTOR/Year	Contribution to Growth		
	Agriculture	Industry	Service
1997	15.84	23.88	60.92
1998	13.64	25.27	61.8
1999	14.28	21.97	64.44
2000	10.21	21.7	69.05
2001	10.27	21.55	69.09
2002	10.28	24.35	66.15
2003	9.36	26.18	65.28
2004	8.93	27.89	64

Supply Chain for Goods Vs. Supply Chain for Services:

The end goal of any company is a satisfied customer. The process of locating, obtaining and transporting the inputs needed to do this is the core function of supply chain management. Supply chain design in the manufacturing industry requires a great deal of focus on physical product and a broader supplier base, while service firms typically have little need for physical inputs other than office supplies, and often work with a much smaller group of suppliers. The differences however can be identified on the following main areas;

 (1) Inputs: Both the service and the manufacturing industries require an input of labour to complete the processing necessary to satisfy their promise to the end customer. Additionally, companies in both industries require inputs from suppliers of various types. Finally, both industries require capital investment in equipment that allows their employees to do their work. The primary difference is that most of the cost of manufacturing labour is involved in procuring, transporting and manipulating physical material, while almost all service industry labour is expended on manipulating information and developing relationships. Because of this difference, capital investments in machinery and equipment are typically much higher in the manufacturing industry.

(2) **Logistics:** Traditional manufacturing supply chain management focuses on logistics in terms of moving physical material from one location to another. The size and weight of objects being shipped and the distance from the supplier to the manufacturing facility can play a major role in the cost of the product. In service organisations, particularly in the financial sectors, these factors are irrelevant because no physical product is moving except perhaps a few sheets of paper. While the manufacturing industry tries to negotiate better shipping rates and fill containers with product to reduce unit cost, the service industry upgrades servers and installs new software to speed the flow of communication, thereby reducing the labour costs necessary to produce a finished product.

(3) **Finished Goods:** Traditionally, a finished good is a product that has been completely transformed from a raw material form to a form that is ready to sell to the customer. It's a physical unit that has been assembled, tested and packaged, and is now sitting on a shelf at a warehouse or a store, ready to be sold. In the service industry, a finished good equals a closed file. The loan has been booked, the home sale has closed, or the class has been completed, leaving no physical evidence except a few sheets of paper. However, the goal of either finished product is a customer who is satisfied with the product or service she paid for.

(4) **Optimisation:** In a manufacturing organisation, optimisation of the supply chain is accomplished primarily by improving speed of delivery and reducing cost. Companies work to reduce physical bottlenecks and inventory, and negotiate better pricing on raw materials. The main way to speed production is to find a faster way to move or manipulate the components. A research paper published by Eastern Illinois University points out that the main drivers of optimisation in a service model are relationships and information flow. By building partnerships with companies whose strengths complement its own, a corporation can reduce costs. By eliminating virtual bottlenecks caused by duplicate approval loops or other intangible delays, a service company can realise the same goal as the manufacturing company: a lower-cost finished product, delivered to the customer more quickly.

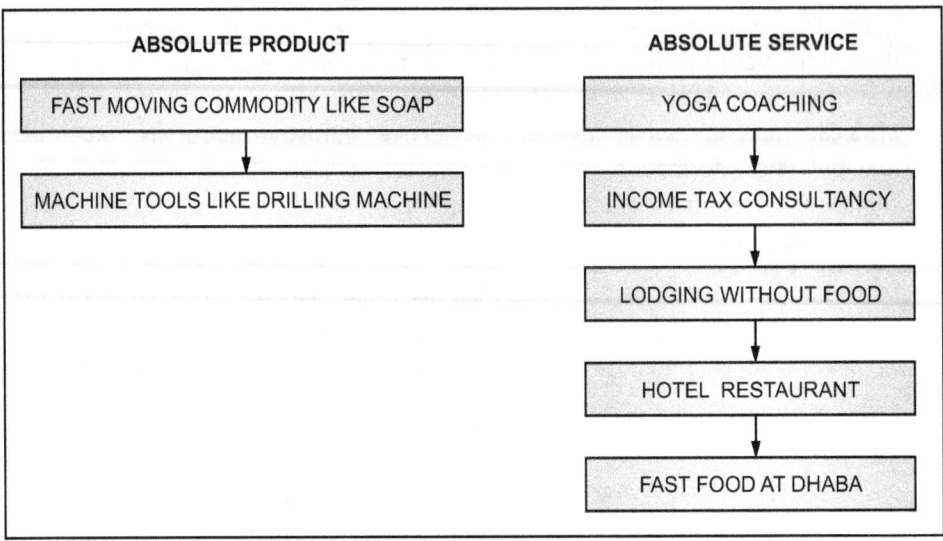

Fig. 1.6

Here it can be seen that Yoga teaching has hardly any product attribute, whereas a Machine tool like lathe or drilling machine has hardly any service attribute. However, in the case of food services, there is a different mixture of product- service as seen in case of Dhaba and Restaurant. Dhaba focuses more on actual food served as its customers do not care much about service/ cutlery and need cheap quick food whereas in restaurant the customers are ready to pay for the air conditioning, ambience and service.

Having seen the differences now we can see some of the similarities of product and Service organisations also. Here is a list of similarities:

- Both have focus on Quick response to Customer, Quality and Productivity.
- Both type have to PLAN their capacity, Location and Lay out.
- Model of Vendor – Organisation- Customer is common.
- Have to organise resources, plan operations and draw schedules.
- Make demand forecast.
- Need to do capacity balancing with demand by planning resources carefully.

DIFFERENCES:

However, services differ from goods mainly on the base of the four "I"s. These 4Is which differentiate a good from a service are;

- Intangibility,
- Inconsistency,
- Inseparability,
- Inventory.

Let us now see the meaning of each of these 4 Is.

(a) Intangibility: Anything which cannot be seen, touched, eaten or consumed, or which is not present in any physical form, is called intangible. Intangibility is an inherent characteristic of a service. Unlike a physical product, a service cannot be touched, eaten or consumed.

Intangibility indicates that a service has no physical attributes, and hence, it is impossible for a customer to taste, eat, hold or touch a service. The service can only be experienced.

For example, you cannot hold air travel.

Products, on the other hand, are tangible and have a physical form. Some examples are soap, pen, chair, etc.

(b) Inconsistency: Inconsistency is also referred to as **Variability** or **Heterogeneity**.

Inconsistency in the service occurs mainly on three counts. These are:

1. Different service providers perform a given service on different occasions.
2. The service provided by an individual provider may also differ from time to time.
3. Interaction between the customer and the provider may vary depending on the customer.

Every time a service is performed, the process and the customer experience are different. Services that are provided by individuals (rather than by machines), will vary depending upon:

- Who is providing the service (different individuals or the same individual);
- When it is being provided (time when the service is being provided);
- Degree to which the customers are involved in the production of the service.

For example, if a customer goes to a hotel, the same dish may taste different on different occasions because of any of the following reasons:

- Different chefs have prepared it;
- The same chef has prepared it but at varying times;
- The customer has asked for a modification in the taste, for example, lesser spices to be used in the dish.

Products are comparatively more consistent. If chemical A and B are mixed to prepare soap in the right proportion, then every time the process is repeated, the output will be the same.

(c) Inseparability: This characteristic of a service indicates that it cannot be separated from the creator/seller/service provider.

In case of goods, they are generally produced in a factory, then they are distributed, then they are sold, and lastly they are consumed.

As against this, most of the services are created, delivered, and consumed simultaneously through interaction between customers and service providers.

For example, the dentist and the patient have to be present to treat the patient for a dental problem.

(d) Inventory: It is also known as **perishability**. Inventory basically involves maintaining a stock to meet the demand. Services cannot be saved, stored or inventoried.

For example, a bus seat that is vacant today cannot be used tomorrow when there are more passengers than the capacity.

Products can be inventoried and stocked as per the demand or requirement. Excess stock can be carried over for later use.;

Problems faced in Marketing a Service as compared to a Good:

(a) Intangibility: Problems that a marketer faces because of intangibility are:
- Since services are intangible, the customer perceives a risk while purchasing the service, that is, if the service cannot be seen, touched or consumed, how does the customer know that he is paying for the right kind and quality of service?
- Secondly, since services do not have a physical form, they cannot be displayed directly.
- Thirdly, services cannot be patented.

(b) Inconsistency: Problems that a marketer faces because of inconsistency are:
- In the age of quality consciousness, where standardisation is a key word, inconsistency acts as a barrier to standardisation.
- This also makes it hard to set up quality control.
- Quality can only be predicted or determined after the service has been performed.

(c) Inseparability: Problems that a marketer faces because of inseparability are:
- It is extremely difficult to mass produce a service.
- Efficiency of production of the service is dependent on the service provider and hence, it is less efficient than production of goods.
- The customer's presence is inevitable, and this makes the service provider-customer interaction very important.

(d) Inventory: Problems that a marketer faces because of inventory are
- Value of the service product is short-lived.
- Capacity is finite.
- The time period may be limited.
- Adjusting delivery to demand becomes very difficult.

1.2 Introduction to Quality

The importance of quality, be it in product or service, cannot be over-emphasised.

Quality is the buzzword these days and everybody talks about it, the politicians from public platforms, the company executives from business forums, and of course, the common man on the street. Nevertheless, few understand the true meaning of the word quality and fewer still are able and willing to put quality in its true perspective in the changing context of the liberalisation and globalisation where the national boundaries for free trade and commerce are slowly, but surely, breaking down. In the earlier times, quality had a simple definition — a product or service should fit the purpose for which it was intended. For example, a part should fit another part without much effort.

This resulted in making the customer a secondary objective to be satisfied. "Fitness for use" was the predominant concept, to the exclusion of everything else. This went on for quite sometime and consumers did get a raw deal when confronted with statements like "Our product/service is fit for the purpose for which it was intended. If that does not satisfy you, you have tough luck. We can do very little about it," would be the bland statement. Strangely, often it was the producer/manufacturer who decided such a 'fitness for the purpose' to the exclusion of the customer.

Fortunately, we have come a long way by now in understanding the true meaning of quality and customer satisfaction. Consequently, the all-encompassing meaning of the word quality is: *"Total and continuous satisfaction"* while using a product or service. Such a holistic concept for quality is universally accepted and benefits the customers since they are the focus of attention by everyone in the organisational distribution chain.

Quality means the product has, preferably, all or most of the under mentioned characteristics as detailed below:

- It has the right quality.
- Is safe, reliable, and long lasting.
- It's economical to the customer to use it till it lasts.
- It's delivered on time.
- Its price is right.
- Its customer support is good, polite, quick and responsive.
- Its after-sales service is polite and competent with availability of genuine spare-parts and repair cost is affordable.
- Disposal of product/service presents no problem and is environmentally friendly.
- 'Buy-back' schemes of used items for new are user-friendly.
- The total life-cycle cost to the customer (the 'cradle-to-grave' cost) is optimum.

- Conforms to norms of ethics and does not infringe on any trademark or patent laws and is genuine. Its potential for pollution is within acceptable limits.
- No unethical practices like underhand dealings, employment of child labour, exploiting the employees/workers are used as business practices.

As stated earlier, quality is the driving force in the market. The race is on to capture a bigger slice of the market pie with competition heating up from domestic as well as international business. More and more industries are re-orienting their focus on customers' needs to make them satisfied and to maintain their loyalty. Quality is thus the golden mantra for salvation for both the customers and businesses. It should be clearly understood that quality is an attitude of mind and a way of life where "excellence is a journey, not a destination."

Every manufacturing organisation is concerned with the quality of its product. While it is important that quantity requirements be satisfied and production schedules met, it is equally important that the finished product meet established specifications, as customer's satisfaction is derived from quality products and services. Stiff competition at national and international level and consumer's awareness require production of quality goods and services for survival and growth of the company.

Quality and productivity are more likely to bring prosperity into the country and improve quality of work life. However, the management looks to achieve customer satisfaction by running its business at the desired economic level. Both these can be attained by properly integrating quality development, quality maintenance and quality improvement of product. The integration of these three aspects of a product can be achieved through a sound quality control system.

1.2.1 Definitions of Quality

It is not easy to define the word Quality since it is perceived differently by the different set of individuals. If experts are asked to define quality, they may give varied responses depending on their individual preferences. These may be similar to following listed phrases.

- Fitness for use or purpose,
- To do a right thing at first time,
- To do a right thing at the right-time,
- Find and understand what consumer wants,
- Features that meet consumer needs and give customer satisfaction,
- Freedom from deficiencies or defects,
- Conformance to standards,
- Value or worthiness for money.

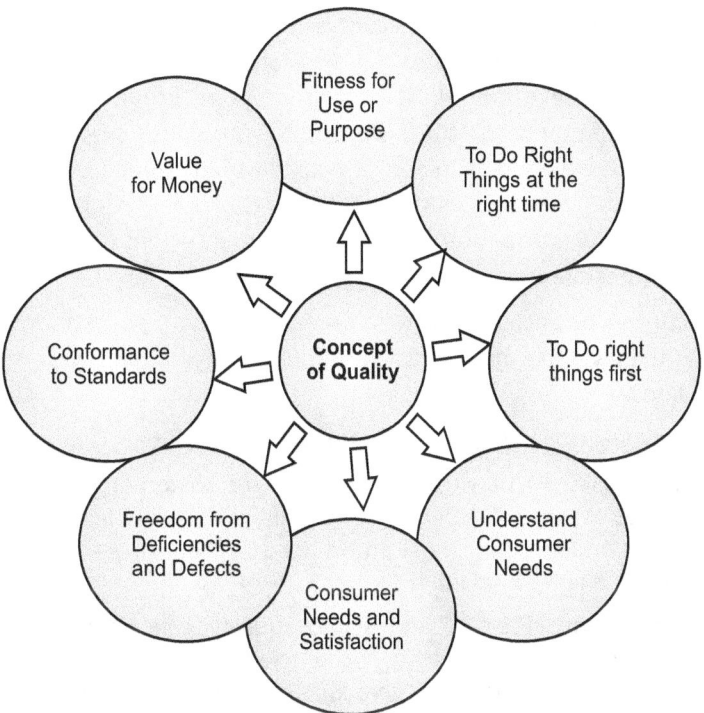

Fig. 1.7

Dr. Joseph Juran coined a short definition of quality as; "Product's fitness for use."

Juran's definition of quality is quite simple and popular one. However, it doesn't directly convey an in depth meaning of quality needed by managers who are faced to decide on selecting a right course of action.

As per **British Standard 4778(10)** quality is defined as *"Totality of features and characteristics of a product or service that bears on its ability to satisfy the customer"*. Quality has been defined in different ways from various perspectives. Some of these are as follow:

- **Product Oriented:** Quality is precise and measureable variable and differences in quality reflects differences in quantity of some attribute of the product. E.g. percentage amount of fat in milk, 22 carat gold.

- **Universal:** Quality is absolute, innate and universally recognisable and often related to comparison of features and characteristics of products. E.g. two brands of cameras or motor cycles or mobile hand sets.

- **Deming:** Defined quality based on how efficient the management circle is in planning, implementing and making improvements in the project. Deming further defined quality as **dynamic**. Customers' needs and expectations are always changing, thus definition of quality also changes. It is very important that the management team is able to adapt and respond to the changes in expectations and needs of the customers.

- **Quality is multidimensional:** Quality is defined by the satisfaction of the customers. A product with good quality does not only satisfy the customers but also makes the customers patronise the product, wherein they are proud about the product and encourage their friends to try it. Depending on whose perspective, definition of quality varies. A worker's definition of quality would depend on how he is proud of his accurate work. Manager would see quality depending on how specifications and number of products produced are met. Customers would gauge quality by his/her needs and expectations.

- **Manufacturing oriented:** Quality is "Conformance to Specifications". Conformance measures the level the manufactured product/service attains with respect to design specifications.

- **Variability:** Quality is inversely proportional to **variability**.

- **Perception:** Quality is the value perceived by the customer. Quality as representing all the features of a product or service that affect its ability to meet customer needs. If the product or service meets all those needs - then it passes the quality test. If it doesn't, then it is sub-standard.

- **A. V. Feigenbaum:** Product and service quality can be defined as, *"The total composite product and service characteristics of marketing, engineering, manufacturing, and maintenance through which the product and service in use will meet the expectations of the customer."*

- **Juran** defines quality as *"fitness for use in terms of design, conformance, availability, safety, and field use."* Thus, his concept more closely incorporates the viewpoint of customer. He is prepared to measure everything and relies on systems and problem-solving techniques. Unlike Deming, he focuses on top-down management and technical methods rather than worker pride and satisfaction.

- **Genichi Taguchi** defines quality in a negative manner. Quality is the loss imparted to society from the time the product is shipped. This **"loss"** would include the cost of customer dissatisfaction that leads to the loss of company reputation. This differs greatly from the traditional producer-orientated definition which includes the cost of re-work, scrap, warranty and services costs as measures of quality. The customer is the most important part of the process line, as quality products and services ensure the future return of the customer and hence improves reputation and increased market share.

Meaning of the term "Quality":

Quality is a relative term and it is generally used with reference to the end use of the product. For example, a gear used in sugarcane juice extracting machine may not possess good surface finish, tolerance and accuracy as compared with the gear used in the head stock of a lathe, still it may be considered of good quality if it works satisfactorily in the juice extracting machine. The quality is thus defined as die fitness for use/purpose at the most economical level.

The quality depends on the perception of a person in a given situation. The situation can be user-oriented, cost-oriented or supplier-oriented. Since, the item is manufactured for the use of the customer, the requirements of the customer dictates the quality of the product. Quality is to be planned, achieved, controlled and improved continuously.

The word "Quality" has variety of meanings:

- **Fitness for purpose:** The component is said to possess good quality, if it works well in the equipment for which it is meant. Quality is thus defined as fitness for purpose.
- **Conformance to requirements:** Quality is the ability of the material/component to perform satisfactorily in an application for which it is intended by the user. Quality of a product, thus, means conformance to requirements. Customer needs have to be assessed and translated into specifications depending upon the characteristics required for specific application. Just as every human has his own characteristics every application has its own characteristics.
- **Grade:** Quality is a distinguishing feature or grade of the product in appearance, performance, life, reliability, taste, odour, maintainability etc. This is generally called as quality characteristics.
- **Degree of preference:** Quality is the degree to which a specified product is preferred over competing products of equivalent grade, based on comparative test by customers, normally called as customer's preference.
- **Degree of excellence:** Quality is a measure of degree of general excellence of the product.
- **Measure of fulfillment of promises:** The quality of a product is a measure of fulfillment of the promises made to the customers.
- **Suitability:** For specific application.
    - **Reliability:** It should give efficient and consistent performance.
    - **Durability:** It should have desired life.
    - **Safety:** Safe and foolproof workability.
    - **Affordability:** It should be economical.
    - **Maintainability:** It should be easy to maintain.
    - **Aesthetic look:** It should look attractive.
    - **Satisfaction to customers:** It should satisfy the customers' requirements.
    - **Economical:** It should have reasonable price.
    - **Versatility:** It should serve number of purposes.

A product is said to possess good quality if all the above requirements are properly balanced while designing and manufacturing it.

1.2.2 Customer's View and Manufacturer's View

The various definitions of quality are as follows:

- "A pragmatic system of continual improvement, a way to successfully ORGANISE men and machines".
- "The meaning of excellence".
- "The unyielding and continuing effort by everyone in an ORGANISATION to understand, meet, and exceed the needs of its customers."
- "The best product that you can produce with the materials that you have to work with."
- "Continuous good product which a customer can trust."
- "Producing a product or service that meets the needs or expectations of the customer."
- "Not only satisfying customers, but delighting them, innovating and creating."

Producers / Providers view

Meeting requirements.

Customers view

Fitness for purpose.

Crosby

Conformance with requirements (producers' view).

Juran

Fitness for use or purpose (customers' view.).

Taguchi

The (minimum) loss imparted by the product to society.

ISO 9000 (old definition)

The totality of characteristics of an entity (product or service) that bear on its ability to satisfy stated and implied needs.

ISO 9000 : 2000 (New Definition)

Degree to which a set of inherent characteristics fulfil requirements.

Note 1 : The term quality can be used with adjectives such as poor, good or excellent.

Note 2 : Inherent, as opposed to assigned, means existing in something, especially as a permanent characteristic.

Characteristic : distinguishing feature,

Requirement : need or expectation that is stated, generally implied or obligatory.

Industry accepted definitions of quality are "conformance to requirements" (from Philip Crosby) and "fit for use" (from Dr. Joseph Juran and Dr. W. Edwards Deming). These two definitions are not inconsistent.

Customer's/Consumer's View of Quality

Quality is what customers expect in the products/services they buy. If a customer expects 'excellence' in everything they purchase, then their expectations are high. However, this could prove to be elusive to a customer when he actually gets a product/service that he has paid for.

For example, a passenger travelling in an economy class on a flight or sleeper class in train cannot expect service like a passenger who is travelling in the first class. We should appreciate the fact that a first class passenger has paid two to three times more for the fancy first class and that person has every right to get optimum service pampered on the flight.

This applies to hotels where a five star hotel guest expects and wants star treatment unlike a budget hotel occupant who is satisfied with basic amenities. A customer who receives something more than he has paid for would be delighted.

This is how a brand loyalty is built up where the product/service provider puts in that little extra effort to make the life of a customer better and happier.

On the same lines, what quality can a Mercedes Benz luxury car owner expect? He would look to safety, smooth noiseless ride, many features like GPS, luxury fittings like leather upholstery, top class music system and the list is endless. On the other hand, a Maruti 800 car owner has fewer expectations. Yet he too expects some features that would make his drive smooth. We have to remember that a Mercedes Benz vehicle costs many times more than a simple Maruti 800 car.

So the quality as perceived by a customer depends upon the money he has invested. The higher the investment, the higher is the expectation on quality. Though a customer has invested modest money, he still has every right to expect quality as perceived by him. If it falls below what he had expected, he becomes an aggrieved dissatisfied customer looking for a better quality of product/service than what he got from a particular organisation.

The relation between quality and price might be seen from Fig. 1.8 on next page.

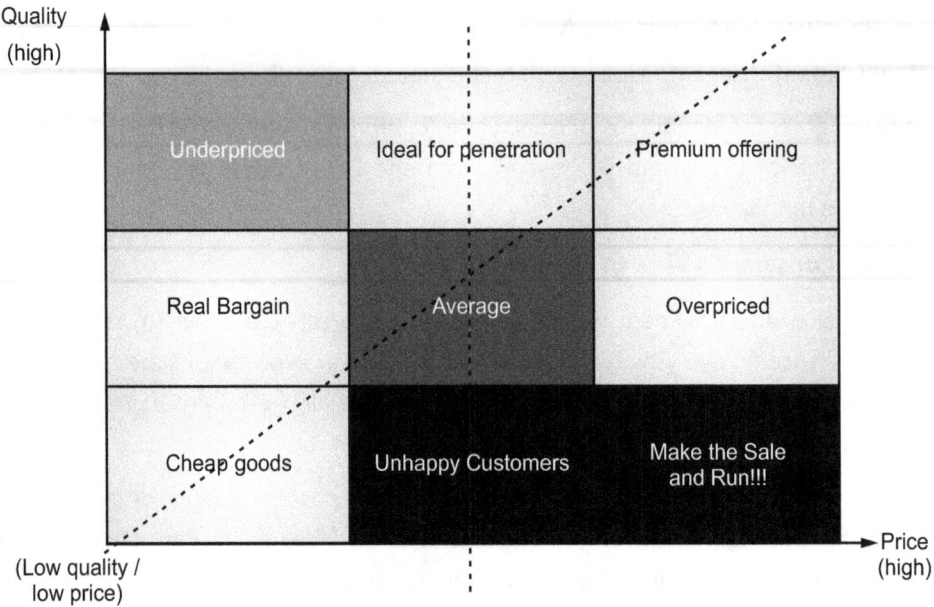

Fig. 1.8: Relation between Quality and Price

> Higher price = Higher quality

When a customer pays a higher price for a service/product, he is paying for not only quality which he can see, feel, or judge, known as 'tangibles', but also the 'intangibles' such as the 'esteem' value. While a standard Maruti 800 car and a Mercedes Benz limousine perform more or less the same function, with some difference in 'tangibles', both perform the same function of transporting people, the difference between the two being that the latter has a higher 'esteem' value.

Another example could be a meal in a modest dhaba costing ₹ 20 whereas a regular meal in a five star hotel, even without drinks, could run up to ₹ 1500 or more. It is not that the food in that starred hotel is superior, though to some extent that is true, but the customer is paying for the 'intangibles' such as the exotic food menu, ambience, the music, the air-conditioning, the décor, the fine plates and cutlery, as well as liveried attendants. It is quite possible that a modest dhaba food could be tastier and more like home food than a fine restaurant. However, the rich and the mighty would like to shell out more money to be seen in such splendid hotels and posh restaurants.

> Quality = Tangible + Intangible (esteem) value

It is interesting to note that a customer attaches various values to the product/service he purchases. These are defined as given below:

- Cost value
- Use value

- Exchange/Resale value
- Esteem value.

Meeting requirements is a producer's view of quality: This is the view of the organisation responsible for the project and processes, and the products and services acquired, developed, and maintained by those processes. Meeting requirements means that the person building the product does so in accordance with the requirements. Requirements can be very detailed or they can be simple, but they must be defined in a measurable format, so it can be determined whether they have been met. The producer's view of quality has these four characteristics:

- Doing the right thing.
- Doing it the right way.
- Doing it right the first time.
- Doing it on time without exceeding cost.

"Being fit for use" is the customer's definition: The customer is the end user of the products or services. Fit for use means that the product or service meets the customer's needs regardless of the product requirements. Of the two definitions of quality, fit for use, is the more important. The customer's view of quality has these characteristics:

- Receiving the right product for their use.
- Being satisfied that their needs have been met.
- Meeting their expectations.
- Being treated with integrity, courtesy and respect.

In addition to the producer and customer views of quality, the organisational infrastructure also includes a provider and a supplier view. These views are as follows:

- **Provider view:** This is the perspective of the organisation that delivers the products and services to the customer.
- **Supplier view:** This is the perspective of the organisation (that may be external to the producer's company, such as an independent vendor) that provides either the producer and/or the provider with products and services needed to meet the requirements of the customer.

The Two Quality Gaps: Most Information Technology (IT) groups have two quality gaps: the producer gap and the customer gap as shown in the figure below. The producer gap is the difference between what is specified (the documented requirements and internal standards) versus what is delivered (what is actually built). The customer gap is the difference between what the producers actually delivered versus what the customer wanted.

Closing these two gaps is the responsibility of the quality function. The quality function must first improve the processes to the point where the producer can develop the products according to requirements received and its own internal standards. Closing the producer's gap enables the IT function to provide its customers consistency in what it can produce. This has been referred to as the "McDonald's effect" - at any McDonald's outlet in the world, a Big Mac burger should taste the same. It doesn't mean that every customer likes the Big Mac or that it meets everyone's needs, but rather, that McDonald's has now produced consistency in its delivered product. In Indian context we can say "Thums Up effect"- the soft drink. Whether it is drunk in Kashmir or Kanyakumari, it will taste the same, even though it is bottled in number of plants throughout the country.

Closing the second gap requires the quality function to understand the true needs of the customer. This can be done by customer surveys, Joint Application Development (JAD) sessions, and more user involvement through the process of building information products. The processes can then be changed to close the customer gap, keeping consistency while producing products and services needed by the customer.

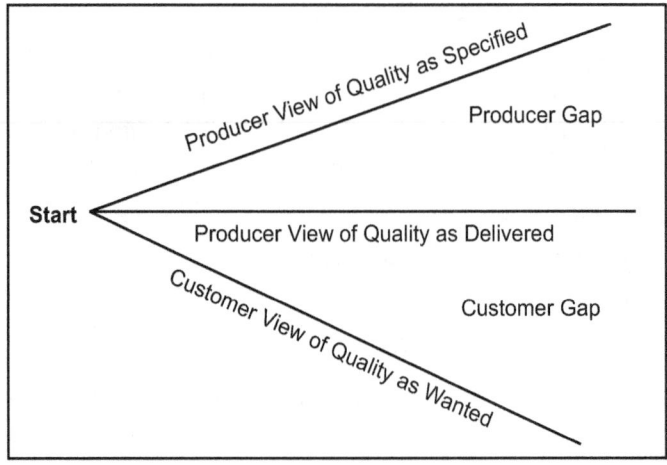

Fig. 1.9

The Role of Quality: Japan Story

The importance of quality in every walk of life cannot be overemphasised in this global economy. Dr. J. M. Juran, an international expert in quality and management put it succinctly: "We live behind the dykes of quality". It may be recalled Dr. J. M. Juran and Dr. W. E. Deming were responsible for the quality revolution in Japan, which had the pre-war, dubious distinction of a producer of poor quality and shoddy goods. All that changed after Dr. Juran and others taught the Japanese the importance of quality in the goods and services they produced. Dr. Juran's prediction that one day Japan would surpass the advanced countries like Germany, UK, and USA, in quality has been proved right. During our daily life we presume so many things: milk is not adulterated, the food we consume does not contain harmful substances, vegetables do not have pesticides and herbicides, the transportation is safe and reliable, we can occupy the seat as indicated in the railway reservation chart and a flight on a particular day and time would take off as scheduled, our money is safe in the banks we trust so much, investment in a sound mutual fund is not risky but will give attractive returns, the refrigerator which we bought by investing a hefty amount would produce ice and keep the stuff inside cold at all times without consuming too much power or making too much noise.

All these suppositions would go awry if something goes wrong. For example, an unscrupulous trader mixes a dangerous substance in cooking oil that turns deadly and results in serious sickness or death. Air travel is generally safe but a minor pilot error could prove disastrous with the tragic loss of hundreds of passengers. Thus, we have taken quality as being reliable and safe in whatever activity we are involved.

Take for example, the gym equipment we exercise. If a minor problem exists unnoticed, then someone sometime is bound to face a serious injury. In these days of technological inventions, supposed to improve the quality of life, quality is given a high degree of importance as one mistake could put an end to that invention in which millions of rupees have been invested.

For instance, the new passenger Airbus 380, supposed to carry five hundred and more passengers, has yet to prove its reliability and so its official launch has been delayed by a couple of years. A few product inventions have been hastily introduced, though without wide field trials, while the customers' feedback forced the manufacturer to recall the products prematurely with consequent financial losses and loss of reputation. There cannot be any short cut to quality despite offer of attractive schemes, low prices and freebies.

A responsible and intelligent customer will always choose quality and reliable products as he/she knows the quality of a product/service will endure as long that customer has it, whereas the price paid is forgotten within a short time.

It is wise to be reminded what W. A. Foster stated some years ago:

"Quality is never an accident. It is always the result of high intention, sincere effort, intelligent direction and skilful execution. It represents the wise choice of many alternatives."

No doubt there are still people who would like to go back to the *'good old days'*—no vehicles but only bullock carts, no telephone, no electricity, and no processed food. They would like, if possible, to turn the clock back. But these diehard 'conservatives' have to realise the world is moving towards a technological society.

For instance, e-mail has almost replaced the traditional 'snail mail'. Bank clerks and tellers are being made redundant by increasing use of automatic ATMs, which work 24 hours a day throughout the year. If some people are reluctant or unhappy with the rapid changes, tough luck on them as some of these changes are irreversible. Either you try to catch up with the changes or you would be isolated and left far behind.

However, a point to remember is that any technological change has to be user-friendly, safe and reliable. This is where quality counts. For instance, if a person wants to draw cash from an ATM, all that he needs his credit/debit card, the password which only he/she knows, the amount to be drawn. If that person wishes to draw ₹ 1000, then he/she should get it without fail. That customer cannot be short-changed due to a glitch in the system. Of course, the customer cannot be given extra cash by machine error either.

Evolution and Historical Developments of Quality

Great civilisations all over the world have built monuments that have stood the test of time. It is well to remember that, "Excellence is not a skill. It is an attitude." It is remarkable that those civilisations, with such low technology, could fashion out great structures like the Pyramids, Great Wall of China, and Taj Mahal.

Taj Mahal, a poem in marble

The Pyramids were built about 3000–5000 years ago but have weathered the intense heat and the dust of the desert storms raging around these for centuries. The Cheops Pyramid at Giza, near Cairo, which is one of the seven wonders of the ancient world was so carefully built during 3000 B.C. with a height of 481 feet 4 inches and the sides of its square base 775 feet 9 inches vary by no more than an inch.

A great deal of thinking and planning must have gone into the design of the pyramid and the chief designer must have been a genius. One is awestruck even to think of the tremendous efforts that must have gone into the planning and execution of the Pyramid. Contrary to what was thought to be cruel employment of slave labour, research indicates that the workers were devoted to their task, were supplied tools, food and drinks and put up in housing colonies near the construction site. They took pride in their work and wanted to make the final resting place of their Pharaoh memorable so that he can have an easy passage to the next world.

A few countries like France, Germany, Switzerland, UK and USA, have a high reputation for quality. They dominated the global market for a number of years till China, Japan and Korea, and India too in some fields like IT, are posing serious challenge to the dominance of the western countries.

Post-war Japan transformed itself to become an international producer of high quality and low cost products and services. It rose like a Phoenix from the ashes of two atomic devices unleashed during the fag end of World War II. Japan became known for its quality of goods like automobiles, cameras, photo-copiers, video-cameras, low cost watches and audio and video electronic goods like two-in-one radio/recorder and TV sets of high definition. Not to be left behind, Asian Tigers like Singapore, South Korea and Taiwan challenged Japan and have now won a slice of the global pie.

Quality in the last 100 years has undergone six distinct stages which are described as under :

1. **Stage 1: Inspection and Quality Control**

    This stage is refereed to as "Inspection phase" and has the following features :

    - This stage employs simple inspection based systems.
    - Teams of inspectors are employed to examine, measure or test a product and compare it with the product standards.
    - Inspection is conducted at various stages of manufacture such as incoming materials, semi-finished and finished goods.
    - Non-conforming products (i.e. products of poor quality) are segregated from good ones.
    - Often, lots of products are subjected to hundred percent inspection.
    - Non-conforming products are subsequently scrapped, reworked or sold at lower prices.

    Inspection based systems often fail to find poor quality items (1005 inspection is also never fool proof) and are costly as :

    - Persons are employed to look for faulty work and persons are employed to repair/rectify it.
    - They usually employ 100 percent inspection.

2. **Stage 2: Acceptance Sampling**

    This stage has the following distinguishing features:

    - Acceptance function (i.e. accepting good ones by rejecting and segregating defectives) is replaced by corrective function i.e. utilising inspection results for the prevention of defectives in future lots.

- Data on defects is generated from the inspection results of product testing done at various stages of manufacturing.
- Sampling inspection plans are adopted for product control thereby replacing 100% inspection by sampling inspection.
- Statistical Quality Control (control charts) are employed for process control.

3. **Stage 3: Quality Assurance**

    Quality Assurance can be gained through the following features :

    - Quality Control (inspection based) is substituted by Quality assurance (prevention based).
    - Emphasis is placed on quality of processes.
    - Quality planning and quality manuals are prepared with an object to build quality into the manufacturing process.

    Quality assurance (prevention based) however pays little or no alteration to service industries and soft areas of quality such as delivery, customer satisfaction etc.

4. **Stage 4: Statistical Process Control**

    Principles underlying Statistical Process Control are as follows:

    - Variability is necessarily inherent in any process.
    - Total variability is composed of two parts: one internal to the process i.e. chance variations and the other external to the process (caused due to assignable reasons which can always be traced to the operating conditions of the process and corrected).
    - Variation pattern of an industrial process when under control (process being influenced only by inherent causes) fits into a normal curve.
    - Every quality characteristic has certain specification and the manufacturing process is expected to produce within this specification (called design tolerance) which is the range within the specification limits.
    - The arithmetic means of sample drawn from the population which is normal with mean μ and standard deviation σ if plotted also yield normal distribution with mean X (X being the average of the sample averages) being equal to the mean of the population ($X = \mu$) and standard deviation being the sample size n.

5. **Stage 5: Quality Management Systems**

    Principles underlying Quality Management Systems are :

    - Consistent quality can only be achieved by devising, implementing and adhering to sound procedures, methods and controls (i.e. implementation of standardised systems/procedures) in all functional areas (e.g. design, purchasing, production, inspection etc.) in the manufacturing or service set up.

- Once all these systems are strengthened and become effective the customers will always get consistent quality of the product thereby avoiding the need to inspect the products every time they purchase.
- Further, for the system to be effective, it is necessary to evaluate it at periodic intervals. Evaluation gives rise to the need for a suitable yardstick or benchmark against which the system elements can be evaluated or compared.
- To have a uniform benchmark, International Organisation for Standardisation has brought out asset of international standards called ISO-9000 series which provides necessary guidelines for manufacturing and service organisations in formulating quality systems for themselves.

6. Stage 6: Six Sigma

Principles underlying the six sigma concept are :

- Variability is necessarily inherent in any process.
- Total variability is the result of two types of causes : chance causes and assignable causes. Chance causes can't be identified and hence cannot be eliminated while assignable causes can be identified and be avoided/removed.
- Variation pattern of a process influenced by only chance causes fits into (yields) a normal distribution and process mean and standard deviations can be estimated (i.e. each process parameter is characterized by normal distribution).
- Process mean in real life (in practice) can shift from the nominal mean by 1.5 times standard deviation (i.e. 1.5 sigma).
- Defects are normally distributed throughout the units, and parts and processes are individual.
- For execution of any operation (manufacturing or non manufacturing), certain standard is specified for the output and some variations are allowed from the ideal measure. These requirements are usually stated in terms of :

  USL = Upper Specification Limit, LSL = Lower Specification Limit.
- Since process mean in real life can shift from nominal by 1.5 times the standard deviation (i.e. 1.5 standard deviation) due to gradual drift (e.g. tool wear) or as a result of sudden drift, the defect rates in practice expected at different sigma levels are higher than in the mean centered process.

7. Stage 7: Total Quality Management (TQM)

TQM is the current stage in quality and has the following distinguishes features:

- TQM covers all kinds of industries manufacturing as well as servicing.
- TQM implementation requires clear and unambiguous vision of top management and gradual removal of inter-departmental barrier.
- TQM believes that good training based on the identification of the needs of systematic training is essential to attain greater quality.
- TQM lays greater thrust on business processes, advocates continuous improvement in every business activity.

1.2.3 Concept of Internal Customer

Customers don't only include people who interact or place orders through telephone or the internet. Customers also include those who work every day with the company to make the operation a success. While external and internal customers may fulfil different roles, both are critical to the viability of the business.

- **Identification:** An external customer is someone who uses the company's products or services but is not a part of the organisation. If you own a retail store, for example, an external customer is an individual who enters your store and buys merchandise. An internal customer is any member of your organisation who relies on assistance from another to fulfil the job duties, such as a sales representative who needs assistance from a customer service representative to place an order.

- **External Customer Significance:** External customers are essential to the success of any business, as they provide the revenue stream through their purchases that the enterprise needs to survive. Satisfied external customers often make repeat purchases as well as refer your business to other people they know. A customer who suffers through a negative experience with a business, such as being treated rudely by an employee, can also hinder a business by dissuading others from patronising it.

- **Internal Customer Significance:** While internal customers may not necessarily purchase the products or services offered by their employer, the internal customer relationship also plays a key role in the business's success. In the sales example, the salesperson who does not work well with customer service may have greater difficulty placing orders or obtaining answers to his external clients' questions, resulting in a poor level of service. Strained internal relationships can also adversely affect company morale.

- **Considerations:** As a business owner, you may have a natural tendency to focus on the relationship with external customers, as they are the ones who purchase your products and services. Still, seeking ways to improve internal customer relations can lead to a healthier work environment. You can take steps to improve internal relations by training employees to think of co-workers in the same manner as external customers and provide the same high level of service. Set an example by showing appreciation for your employees' efforts and encouraging their feedback.

The concept of Internal Customer has developed out of a need to build quality into the product rather than inspect the product for quality. The earlier practice was to inspect the product thoroughly just before it left the factory so that only the product meeting specifications could reach the customer. The meaning of customer now has been expanded. Even within an organisation the product is processed in various stages. After each stage the product goes to the next stage for further processing. Now each stage is seen as a supplier to the next stage and a customer to the preceding stage. This way the product is sought to be inspected and the process controlled at each stage to ensure that the next stage gets a quality product.

Each department also continuously communicates with other related departments within the organisation about its requirements and capabilities. This control at each stage ensures that the organisation itself works as an integrated whole. It also ensure that there are fewer regradings, rejects, reworks or scrap due to mistakes committed by the previous stage.

The internal customer concept works through a system of communication between the supplier and customer departments as illustrated below:

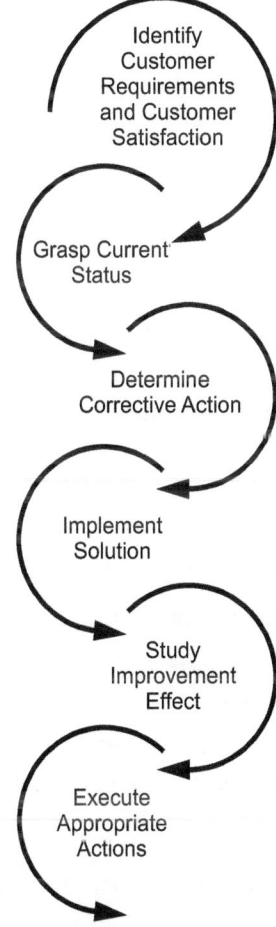

Fig. 1.10: Steps for Implementation of the Internal Customer Concept

Step-1: Identify Customer Requirements and Measures of Customer Satisfaction Department's:

Clear identification of internal customer needs is a test for the efficiency of the communication process within the organisation. The need of the internal customer must be unambiguously stated because this forms the basis on which the supplier can improve himself. All means of communication are acceptable for this purpose. Measures should be as the customer measures them. Based on the situation and need a combination of the following could be used.

- Forms and Formats
- Suggestion Schemes
- Inter-Department Meetings
- KAIZEN Groups
- Project Teams
- Project Postmortems
- Specifications/Instructions
- QFD, etc.

Step-2: Grasp the current Status:

The objective of this step is to understand the current position vis-à-vis the requirement of the customer. Here, after collecting data about the current status we analyse it so that we can pin-point where we are lagging and by how much, e.g., if components are being delayed from our department alone we can analyse where they are being delayed and for how long. We can also analyse the causes for the delay and segregate them based on their importance. Process flow charts, pareto-charts, trend charts, control charts, histograms, process capability indices, etc., may be used.

Step-3: Analyse the Cause and Determine the Corrective Action:

Once the problem area has been identified, we have to find out the root cause so as to plan the corrective action. The item to examine is selected. This can be the first two or three bars in a pareto diagram, the outcome of a control chart or trend chart, etc. Tools such as a cause and effect diagram and pareto chart can be employed in this step.

Step-4: Implement the Solution:

The objective here is to implement the plan and eliminate the root causes of the problem. Employees who execute the correction must understand the corrective action. Good communication and training will be necessary.

Step-5: Check the Effect of the Improvement:

The effect of the improvement can be analysed on two inputs.

(a) Self Analysis

(b) Customers' Feedback

In the process of Self Analysis, the overall results before and after implementation are compared. The before and after results should be compared on all the items selected for study during Step-3 using the same tools as those used in that step. Tools such as Bar Graphs, Paired Pareto Diagrams, Trend Charts, Control Charts, Histograms and Process capability indices may be used.

In the case of failure due to improper implementation, we must go back to Step-5, otherwise we go to Step-4, and again analyse the cause for the problem.

In case the result is as good or better than the existing conditions, we should also check to ensure that there are no adverse side-effects, particularly, with respect to other departments.

Customer Feedback in various forms such as Feedback Forms, Review Meetings, Project Postmortems, etc., can also be a source of improving the service of the department with respect to other departments.

Step-6: Take Appropriate Action:

There are two alternative courses of action to be taken up:

(a) Standardise and Institutionalise.

(c) Further Improve (Go to Step-3).

The improvement in the Method or Process has to be standardised and institutionalised so that the benefits of the improvement are maintained. For this the new method should be documented in operating procedures or standards. Poor documentation can result in recurrence of the problem in future. The information about method or process change must also be shared with other connected departments so as to ensure that they can tailor their operations to suit the new method.

In implementing the improvement, the implementing department must also identify critical parameters to be controlled. The intention is to monitor the appropriate parameters and to detect any deviation from the new standards with a view to analyse and correct them at the earliest. Trend Charts, Control Charts or Check sheets may be used as appropriate.

The documentation should be reinforced with training of employees wherever appropriate.

In case we find that there is further scope for improvement, we should go back to Step-3 and then follow the procedure outlined above.

1.2.4 Overview of Total Quality Management and Lean Management

Quality control is the system a set of tools and techniques by which products are made to comply with the specifications at minimum cost to the firm. According to one definition : "Quality control is the mechanism by which products are made to measure upto the specifications determined from the customer's demand and transformed into engineering and manufacturing requirements. It is concerned with making things right than discovering and rejecting those made wrong".

Another dimension to the quality control is the control of manufacturing process which has been brought out very clearly in the following definition :

"Quality control refers to the systematic control of those variables encountered in a manufacturing process which affect excellence of the end product. Such variables result from application of materials, machines and manufacturing conditions. Only when these variables are regulated to the extent that they do not detract unnecessarily from the excellence of the manufacturing process as reflected in the quality of the finished product, can the control of quality said to exist."

Three Basic Aspects of Quality Control

Quality control function must be looked upon as an integrated function because the quality of a product can be directly traced to the quality of raw materials and components purchased from vendor; the quality of production aids-(tools, jigs and fixtures, measuring instruments); the quality of manufacturing process and manufacturing facilities employed; quality of workmanship; and the quality of system set to regulate and control work on the shop floor. To ensure quality of the products, scientific quality control recognises three distinct functions:

(a) **Acceptance function** refers to the inspection of goods to ensure that they are up to the specifications thereby segregate and reject those which are defective. Acceptance function of quality is called "inspection" and it includes elements like receiving, inspection, process inspection, finished goods inspection, gauge maintenance, disposition on non-conforming materials, day-to-day trouble shooting etc.

(b) **Preventive function** refers to the identification of defectives thereby avoiding or minimising occurrence of defectives. Preventive function of quality is called "Quality Control" and it includes elements like process, capability studies, failure statistic analysis, training of inspectors, methods and studies to reduce defectives, etc.

(c) **Assurance function** refers to verification that every quality characteristic or a product is assured to meet a pre-determined performance standards at each stage in the manufacturing cycle. The assurance function includes elements like customer's complaints, quality audit, quality determination, accuracy of inspection, executive reports on quality, etc.

There are many approaches in the business domain in order to achieve and exceed the quality expectations of the clients. For this, most companies integrate all quality-related processes and functions together and control it from a central point. As the name suggests, Total Quality Management takes everything related to quality into consideration, including the company processes, process outcomes (usually products or services) and employees.

Total Quality Management is a management approach that originated in the 1950's and has steadily become more popular since the early 1980's. Total Quality is a description of the culture, attitude and organisation of a company that strives to provide customers with products and services that satisfy their needs. The culture requires quality in all aspects of the company's operations, with processes being done right the first time and defects and waste eradicated from operations.

Total Quality Management, TQM, is a method by which management and employees can become involved in the continuous improvement of the production of goods and services. It is a combination of quality and management tools aimed at increasing business and reducing losses due to wasteful practices.

Some of the companies who have implemented TQM include Ford Motor Company, Phillips Semiconductor, SGL Carbon, Motorola and Toyota Motor Company.

TQM is a management philosophy that seeks to integrate all organisational functions (marketing, finance, design, engineering, and production, customer service, etc.) to focus on meeting customer needs and organisational objectives. It views an organisation as a collection of processes. It maintains that organisations must strive to continuously improve these processes by incorporating the knowledge and experiences of workers.

The simple objective of TQM is "Do the right things, right the first time, every time". TQM is infinitely variable and adaptable. Although originally applied to manufacturing operations, and for a number of years only used in that area, TQM is now becoming recognised as a generic management tool, just as applicable in service and public sector organisations. There are a number of evolutionary strands, with different sectors creating their own versions from the common ancestor. TQM is the foundation for activities, which include:

- Commitment by senior management and all employees,
- Meeting customer requirements,
- Reducing development cycle times,
- Just In Time/Demand Flow Manufacturing,
- Improvement teams,
- Reducing product and service costs,

- Systems to facilitate improvement,
- Line Management ownership,
- Employee involvement and empowerment,
- Recognition and celebration,
- Challenging quantified goals and benchmarking,
- Focus on processes / improvement plans,
- Specific incorporation in strategic planning.

This shows that TQM must be practiced in all activities, by all personnel, in Manufacturing, Marketing, Engineering, RandD, Sales, Purchasing, HR, and so on.

The core of TQM is the customer-supplier interfaces, both externally and internally, and at each interface lie a number of processes. This core must be surrounded by commitment to quality, communication of the quality message, and recognition of the need to change the culture of the organisation to create total quality. These are the foundations of TQM, and they are supported by the key management functions of people, processes and systems in the organisation.

TQM is mainly concerned with continuous improvement in all work, from high level strategic planning and decision-making, to detailed execution of work elements on the shop floor. It stems from the belief that mistakes can be avoided and defects can be prevented. It leads to continuously improving results, in all aspects of work, as a result of continuously improving capabilities, people, processes, and technology and machine capabilities.

Continuous improvement must deal not only with improving results, but more importantly with improving capabilities to produce better results in the future. The five major areas of focus for capability improvement are demand generation, supply generation, technology, operations and people capability.

A central principle of TQM is that mistakes may be made by people, but most of them are caused, or at least permitted, by faulty systems and processes. This means that the root cause of such mistakes can be identified and eliminated, and repetition can be prevented by changing the process.

There are three major mechanisms of prevention:

1. Preventing mistakes (defects) from occurring (Mistake - proofing or Poka-Yoke).
2. Where mistakes can't be absolutely prevented, detecting them early to prevent them being passed down the value added chain (Inspection at source or by the next operation).
3. Where mistakes recur, stopping production until the process can be corrected, to prevent the production of more defects. (Stop in time).

The basis for TQM implementation is the establishment of a quality management system which involves the organisational structure, responsibilities, procedures and processes. The most frequently used guidelines for quality management systems are the ISO 9000 international standards, which emphasise the establishment of a well- documented, standardised quality system. The role of the ISO 9000 standards within the TQM circle of continuous improvement is presented in the following figure.

Continuous improvement is a circular process that links the diagnostic, planning, implementation and evaluation phases. Within this circular process, the ISO 9000 standards are commonly applied in the implementation phase. An ISO 9000 quality system also requires the establishment of procedures that standardise the way an organisation handles the diagnostic and evaluation phases.

However, the ISO 9000 standards do not prescribe particular quality management techniques or quality-control methods. Because it is a generic organisational standard, ISO 9000 does not define quality or provide any specifications of products or processes. ISO 9000 certification only assures that the organisation has in place a well-operated quality system that conforms to the ISO 9000 standards. Consequently, an organisation may be certified but still manufacture poor-quality products.

Lean Management:

The most significant production management approach of the past 50 years is just-in-time (JIT) production the logic of which evolved in Japan at Toyota and later extended to other companies in Japan and other countries.

Lean Production is an integrated set of activities designed to achieve high volume production using minimal inventories of raw materials, work-in-process, and finished goods. Parts arrive at the next work station just-in-time and are completed and move through the operation quickly. Just-in-time is also based on the logic that nothing will be produced until it is needed. Need is created by actual demand for the product. When an item is sold, in theory, the market pulls a replacement from the last position in the final assembly which triggers an order to the factory production line, where a worker then pulls another unit from an upstream station in flow to replace the unit taken. This upstream station then pulls from the next station further upstream and so on back to the release of raw materials. To enable this pull process to work smoothly, JIT demands high levels of quality at each stage of the process, strong vendor relations, and a fairly predictable demand for the end product.

When "JIT viewed colloquially as big JIT and little JIT (now often termed as lean production), is the philosophy of operations management that seeks to eliminate waste in all aspects of a firm's production activities: human relations, vendor relations, technology and the management of materials and inventories. Little JIT focuses more narrowly on scheduling good inventories and providing service resources where and when needed".

Lean manufacturing is an inventory-management and manufacturing strategy that companies implement to reduce costs, increase productivity and gain a competitive advantage. The techniques lean manufacturing-organisations use to move materials through the company result in significant reductions in cost and time. Developing lean strategies in an organisation requires involvement of all employees from the top down.

Reduced Inventory Costs

A lean organisation maintains just enough stock to complete orders. Customer orders trigger purchases of materials to meet the requirements of the order. Large inventories of materials and supplies ties up funds, that a company could use to grow and drive itself forward.

Reduced Lead Time

Lean organisations use a pull method to move materials and products through the production process. A pull system requires the next step in a production process to pull the product through only when it is prepared. For example, some organisations use a batch system to move materials through the production process. Only when a batch is completed at the next workstation can product be moved forward. The ideal in lean manufacturing is a single-piece process with one product moving through the production line at a time. This eliminates bottlenecks in the process and reduces lead-time. A reduction in lead-time improves customer service, which can give a company a competitive advantage in the market.

Quality Improvements

Lean manufacturing systems focus on making small quality improvements in company processes to improve the overall quality of the product. Improving the quality of the product and the process improves reliability and customer satisfaction. In a lean manufacturing system, employees have the power to make improvements at any stage in the process.

For example, employees at each workstation must ensure the product meets quality standards before moving it on to the next workstation. Workers can send a product back to the previous station if it does not meet specifications. The system builds quality checks and inspections into the process instead of inspecting the product at the end of the line.

Employee Involvement and Morale

Quality improvement techniques allow workers to participate in changes to processes and production methods. Empowering workers to participate in change increases morale, which increases productivity. A productive and empowered workforce increases production rates and reduces costly employee turnover.

When organisations begin their journey towards creating a lean enterprise through a process of continuous waste elimination, they make several changes in the organisation. This includes changing the structural elements in the system, simplifying operations

Category	Manufacturing organisations	Service organisations
Inventory-related waste	<ul><li>Accumulating inventory</li><li>Waiting for material to work on</li><li>Stock verification</li><li>Counting the number of parts</li><li>Temporary storage</li><li>Parts shortage</li></ul>	<ul><li>Overflowing "in baskets"</li><li>Duplication of work</li><li>Excessive paper work</li><li>Incomplete information leading to pending decisions</li></ul>
Waste due to processes	<ul><li>Defects and rework</li><li>Machine breakdowns</li><li>Watching the machine run</li></ul>	<ul><li>Payments not made on time</li><li>Wrong service delivery (service failure)</li><li>Proposals not completed on time for the bid</li><li>Customer orders taking too long to be filled</li></ul>
Waste due to planning	<ul><li>Looking for tools</li><li>Carrying heavy pieces</li><li>Transferring parts over long distances</li><li>Overproduction and double handling</li></ul>	<ul><li>Complicated office layouts</li><li>Poorly planned meetings</li><li>Documents handled many times before a decision is taken</li><li>Extra signature needed that holds up completion</li><li>Team with incomplete or no direction</li></ul>

Why Lean Management:

The world was in the focus of a severe global economic slowdown after 2007, and all major economies underwent a slowdown, shrinkage, or even severe depression during this period. If we carefully analyse the trends during the five years preceding this recession, we will find that there were enough signals. Organisations in some sectors of the industry made intensive efforts to respond to the emerging scenario. Some of the trends during this period and their impact are worth mentioning:

(a) The "Big Three", the three large automobile manufacturers in the United States, along with other global auto majors, faced severe problems due to the economic slowdown. The inventory of vehicles was mounting and the companies had to cover high structural costs. General Motors had lost USD 82 billion since 2004, its last profitable year. In order to stay alive, GM announced a USD 10 billion cut in costs in July 2008 and a further USD 5 billion in November 2008. These included a dramatic cut in its 2009 capital expenditures and additional cuts for its white-collar workforce.

(b) Due to the mounting cost of crude and the competition in the civilian aerospace market, Boeing and Airbus began working with the central theme of enhancing efficiency and cost-cutting. Their new models (the Dreamliner of Boeing and the A380 of Airbus) emphasised these aspects in product development and production. There was increased competition from low-cost economies.

(c) In the textile sector, Indian companies suffered from longer lead times, lower productivity, and smaller plants compared to Chinese ones. Therefore, the Indian textile industry was not able to benefit much from the multi-fibre agreement that promotes free global trade in the garment sector.

In the light of the recent economic slowdown, it has become very important for organisations to improve productivity and response time and cut costs so that they can stay competitive. Manufacturing and service organisations are required to first understand how to develop better operational systems and deliver better quality products and services using fewer resources. The underlying requirement to be more competitive in the market is to ensure that less is more productive. Lean management principles address these issues directly and efficiently.

1.2.5 Impact of Global Competition

With the dawn of the era of liberalisation followed by globalisation in 1991, there emerged a totally new concept — that competition is good for the economy and is a better way to deliver quality goods and services to the customer more efficiently. We have seen how in the post-1991 period has seen a sea change in the availability of goods and services. Long waiting periods are a thing of the past. Now the consumer has a wide range of choices; for example, he can choose shiny cars in a variety of colours, various capacity engines, shapes, sizes, with additional fittings, with no waiting period. He also has a choice of loans with a small down payment, the rest in easy instalments at low interest rates. There is also an exchange programme to trade in an old car for a brand new one.

New advertisements and marketing strategies are being evolved to woo customers. For instance, 'scratch and win a car' or a 'free ticket to Singapore' and so on. There are offers of attractive prizes including overseas trips for one or two persons after buying a car and if lucky to win a prize in a draw held at random. Gifts and freebies are offered if one chooses to a buy a car during festival seasons when the manufacturers would like to increase their sales. Other consumer durables, 'white goods' are also offered for sales, of international brands at competitive rates by promising gifts, freebies, lottery et al. It is now possible to buy most of the foreign label goods within the country without having to step out of it, such is the choice before a consumer of today. Even there is an incentive for subscription to some of the popular journals and magazines by offer of prizes and free gifts with a chance to win a mega prize like a car in a lottery.

The present-day consumer had never had it so good. He is often confused about the choice that he has to make. He has come a long way from the problem of scarcity and no choice. Obviously, some of these consumers have a problem with a plethora of choices. "Market-driven quality starts with making customer satisfaction an obsession and empowering people to use their creative energy to satisfy and delight customers," so stated John F. Akers, Chairman and CEO, IBM some years ago. Companies will be forced to focus on quality, which will be dictated by the likes and dislikes of consumers. The strategy for companies in such a business milieu is to try to understand customers' perception of quality, monitor it regularly, measure it and use the data for enhancement of performance to retain the competitive edge over others. Thus, customer focus is the new strategy for the success of a business.

While there is good news on the number of products offered for sale, where there is plenty of choice, the service sector has yet to absorb the culture of service, which is needed to make customers happy and delighted. Unfortunately, the customer is not always right as far as a dealer/ serviceperson is concerned. 'Customer is King', 'Customer Focus', and 'Customer-friendly' are mere slogans left behind in the management/business school. Hardly any service organisation is putting into practice what it has learnt. On the other hand, such slogans are just part of overused corporate parlance. Every time one encounters pathetic demonstrations of these values, more from the private sector, one has reason to conclude that these are terms just to lure the customers. Some instances where the private sector fares badly:

(1) A private sector ATM is not working and the other machine runs out of cash.

(2) Set-up box on the TV malfunctioning.

(3) Cable operation faulty.

It takes a long time to get the complaints redressed and that too after follow up.

Surprisingly, the public sector is becoming more responsive and accountable like never before. They have realised that if they were not responsive they would lose business and may have to be shut down. Thus, the employees of such organisations are realising with all seriousness that unless they try to make peace with their customers there is a good chance of losing business to the private sector. Such a healthy change in outlook is welcome. For instance, the time taken to attend to complaints has been much reduced. In India we have transitioned from an era of face-to-face communication to faceless communication and in this bargain have lost the meaning of customer service. Call centres are welcome but they are too impersonal and it takes a long time before we can communicate with a human operator. Most of the time it's frustrating to be put 'on hold' listening to some music.

There is a ray of hope for the harassed Indian consumers. Politicians have slowly realised that the voter, the common man, is voting as per his judgment whether a particular government is responsive to his needs or not. He is no longer fooled by tall promises or inducements like cash, sari, cloth, freebies, liquor on the eve of elections. The common man, thanks to the information revolution spawned by satellite TV channels, e-mail, magazines and newspapers, is increasingly becoming aware of his duties and responsibilities. He has access to information that is often instantaneous and knows what is happening in some corner of the world. He is definitely influenced by global trends while keeping his feet firmly on the local soil. So manufacturers/producers/retailers are beginning to realise that customers can no longer be taken for granted despite inducements and low prices. He wants value for his hard earned money. The more value he gets for his money the better. Thanks to the availability of foreign goods/ services, he has set his benchmark on international standards which he expects at domestic prices. However, he has a problem while choosing a particular TV channel to view inspite of showing popular soaps. Though each channel touts its own popularity rating, he has no independent authority like the 'Nielsen' in the USA for a TV show guide. This is expected to change in the future, if the government takes interest in setting up such an independent TV channel viewership rating authority.

COMPETITION AND QUALITY

Everyone is realising, barring diehard manufacturers who have yet to change their mindset, that competition is good for everyone, customer as well as producer. This means the production is cost-effective and benefits the producer as well as customer with better quality and that too with quicker delivery. Survival of the fittest is becoming truer and truer. Just look at the open sky policy of the government that has opened the sky to competition. A number of airlines in the private sector are giving a run for the money for the nationalised carrier Indian and Air India, which is now forced to upgrade its service to survive the challenge of the many private carriers. However, 'survival of the fittest', the law of the jungle, is true even in the business world and there will be consolidation to stay competitive.

Sometimes a customer is enticed with half prices, and 'take one and the other free' type of offers which are hard to resist. In the end, it is possible that the customer is led up the garden path and would regret his decision to go in for a certain product or service which he could do without. It is possible that at the first glance, an offer might look very attractive but it could also prove in the long run to be 'too good to be true'. Deals which claim: 'Export rejects', 'seconds', 'half prices', 'everyday low prices', 'lottery', 'freebies', 'no interest or no deposit' need to be examined carefully and not fall into a trap unwittingly by the spur of the moment decision which one might regret later on.

It is possible for a customer in certain instances that he could be the judge to decide the quality of a product/service. At other times, the product features could be too complicated for the uninitiated to make a considered judgment about the product. In such cases, the customer would refer to the catalogue, ask friends and relatives about their experiences vis-à-vis a product and its performance. The 'word-of-mouth' publicity, both good and bad, plays an important role in decision-making. Another factor is the brand loyalty. You tend to purchase products from the same company (brand) unless you have come across something else, which is equally good. While it takes several good measures to get the seal of approval of a customer, one bad experience can ruin the brand name forever. And it is a difficult job regaining that trust and confidence.

The trend of multiple choices will continue and the regime of liberalisation and globalisation cannot be reversed as the customers are used to it by now. They know it is good for them as well as the nation. However, a problem faced by customers is the lack of reliable ratings for products/services though a few consumer organisations like the consumer voice are trying to fill the gap. That is the problem in a situation of multiple choices compared to zero choice of the past.

Liberalised/Globalised market → Multiple choice for customers

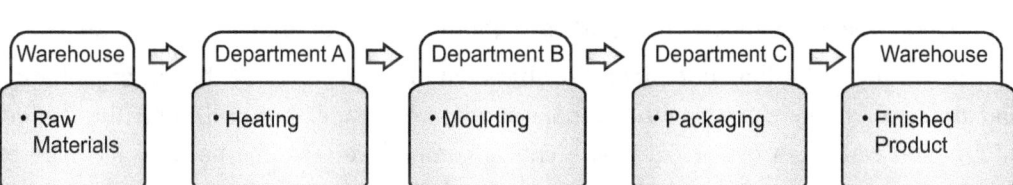

Fig. 1.11: Multiple Choice

As seen in the above figure, the output of the supplier department (Dept. A), be it a product or a service is received as an input by the customer department (Dept. B). The customer department uses this input for further processing. Depending on his experiences with the input and its suitability, the customer gives a feedback to the supplier about how to improve the input so as to make it more suitable to his need. This feedback is used by the supplier to further improve his output resulting in an improved input to the customer. This cycle is repeated over and over again to continuously improve the input to the customer. This whole process is dependent on free flow of unambiguous communication between the supplier and the customer.

1.2.6 Technological Change

Around 1990, a combination of factors began to change the role of logistics in major corporations. Quality initiatives and re-engineering were forcing companies to evaluate entire processes, rather than individual components. Supply-chain management, the integrated control over goods, information, and money, became the key facilitator in this new approach.

In essence, supply-chain management represented an attempt to develop a unified process by which goods and services would be produced for customer sale and consumption. Furthermore, logistics was now being considered as more than simply an opportunity to minimise cost – it was developing into a core component of corporate profitability.

More recently, the Internet has become part of people's daily lives, and has seen a steady progression of Internet innovations. Commercialisation of the Internet, initially Business-to-Consumer, spawned online shopping. Search engines morphed into portals, adding content, shopping, and other items. Finally, e-commerce came into its own with online auction leading the way, illustrating what potential the technology posed for organisations with regards to purchasing. Therefore suppliers quickly warmed up to the Internet, with the aim of fulfilling supplier expectations.

Technology impacts can be ineffective without necessary internal support. One challenge is the high cost of initial development and implementation. Systems can become outdated (for example, compare Windows 95 and Windows 2008). Another issue regards information sharing, as supply chain parties might be hesitant or unwilling to provide data.

Before the 1980s the information flow between functional areas within an organisation and between supply chain member organisations, were paper based. During this period, information was often over looked as a critical competitive resource because its value to supply chain members was not clearly understood. IT infrastructure capabilities provide a competitive positioning of business initiatives like cycle time reduction, implementation, implementing redesigned cross-functional processes.

One important impact of technology is to the quality of information available within the supply chain. Companies can develop Web-based programs or intranets to distribute information, such as information about new products, delays or changes. Technology allows everyone in the supply chain to be integrated and thus, stay informed. This translates into management efficiency and reduced risks.

Technology creates many financial impacts too for supply chains. Management teams can leverage technology to develop cost-effective supply chains. For example, suppliers, manufacturers and wholesalers can receive orders and payments electronically through secure connections.

Costs, such as shipping, can be reduced by establishing optimal networks, by using possibly suppliers located within a few miles of a manufacturer.

Another impact involves troubleshooting. Technology allows parties within the supply chain to identify challenges, such as delays in manufacturing or shipment.

For example, if a supplier is unable to meet a scheduled delivery of materials to a regional manufacturer, then he risks creating a bottleneck or constriction in the supply chain. Bottlenecks can lead to lost sales revenues and devalued materials or supplies.

Market changes too can be readily addressed when technology is used in supply chain management. If economic conditions change and inventory levels grow because of little or no sales, then adjustments can be made to decrease manufacturing.

Supply chain organisational dynamics:

All enterprises participating in supply chain management initiatives accept a specific role. They also share the joint belief that they and all other supply chain participants will be better off because of this collaborative effort. Power within the supply chain is a central issue. There has been a general shift of power from manufacturers to retailers in the recent past. Retailers are in a very important position in terms of information access for the supply chain. This they have managed through modern technologies.

The development of Interorganisational information system for the supply chain has also been possible as a result of modern technology. It provides three distinct advantages like cost reduction, productivity, improvement and product/market strategies.

Barrett and **Konsynsik** have identified five basic levels of participation of individual firms with in the inter-organisational system.

1. **Remote Input/Output mode:** In this case the member participates from a remote location within the application system supported by one or more higher-level participants.

2. **Application processing node:** In this case a member develops and shares a single application such as an inventory query or order processing system.

3. **Multi participant exchange node:** In this case the member develops and shares a network interlinking itself and any number of lower level participants with whom it has an established business relationship.

4. **Network control node:** In this case the member develops and shares a network with diverse application that may be used by many different types of lower level participants.

5. **Integrating network node:** In this case the member literally becomes a data communications/data processing utility that integrates any number of lower level participants and applications in real times.

Information and Technology: Application of SCM:

In the development and maintenance of Supply chain's information systems both software and hardware must be looked into. Hardware includes computer's input/output devices and storage media whereas software includes the entire system and application programme used for processing transactions management control, decision-making and strategic planning.

Some recent development in supply chain management software is:

1. Base Rate, Carrier select and match pay (version 2.0) developed by Distribution Sciences Inc. which is useful for computing freight costs, compares transportation mode rates, analyze cost and service effectiveness of carrier.
2. A new software programme developed by Ross systems Inc. called Supply Chain planning which is used for demand forecasting, replenishment and manufacturing tools for accurate planning and scheduling of activities.
3. Procter and Gamble distributing company and Saber decision Technologies resulted in a software system called Transportation Network optimisation for streamlining the bidding and award process.
4. Logitility planning solution was recently introduced to provide a programme capable of managing the entire supply chain.

Electronic Commerce:

It is the term used to describe the wide range of tools and techniques utilised to conduct business in a paperless environment. Electronic commerce therefore includes electronic data interchange, e-mail, electronic fund transfers, electronic publishing, image processing, electronic bulletin boards, shared databases and magnetic/optical data capture. Companies are able to automate the process of moving documents electronically between suppliers and customers.

Electronic Data Interchange:

Electronic Data Interchange (EDI) refers to computer-to-computer exchange of business documents in a standard format. EDI describe both the capability and practice of communicating information between two organisations electronically instead of traditional form of mail, courier, and fax.

The advantages and benefits of EDI are as follows:

1. Quick process to information.
2. Better customer service.
3. Reduced paper work.
4. Increased productivity.
5. Improved tracing and expediting.
6. Cost efficiency.
7. Competitive advantage.
8. Improved billing.

Bar coding and Scanner:

Bar code scanners are most visible in the check-out counter of super market. This code specifies name of product and its manufacturer.

Other applications are tracking the moving items such as components in PC assembly operations and automobiles in assembly plants.

Data warehouse:

Data warehouse is a consolidated database maintained separately from an organisation's production system database. Many organisations have multiple databases.

A data warehouse is a collection of informational processes rather than specific business processes. Data held in data warehouses are time dependent and historical data may also be gathered and stored.

Enterprise Resource Planning (ERP) tools:

Many companies now view ERP system as the core of their IT infrastructure. ERP system have become enterprise wide transaction processing tools which capture the data and reduce the manual activities and task associated with processing financial, inventory and customer order information. ERP system make it possible to achieve a high level of integration by:

- utilising a single data model,
- developing a common understanding of what the shared data represents,
- establishing a set of rules for accessing data.

1.2.7 Ethical and Environmental Issues on Operations and Supply Chain Functions

Ethics can be best described as "the science of behaviour, in the context of conscious and deliberate action to attain a goal. It is the basic principles of correct behaviour". Furthermore, ethics in business is the way in which these individual behaviours affect the decision-making of an organisation. More succinctly put, "business ethics comprises the principles and standards that guide behaviour in the workplace".

In today's world a shift in the role ethics can be seen in the business world. In the past, the concept of ethics seemed to be taken for granted, and may have been assumed to be operational in the actions and decisions of people and businesses. Ethical behaviour was left up to individuals to implement in their organisations in an ad hoc fashion.

In reality however, recent events have focused attention on ethics and, unfortunately, on unethical behaviour on the parts of some very well-known and respected organisations and individuals. Older examples include the 1980 check kiting scandal by E. F. Hutton as well as the 1985 unethical dealings by the Bank of Boston with a well-known Massachusetts mobster family, the Angiulos.

More recent examples include the scandals that surrounded stars like Kathy Lee Gifford and Jaclyn Smith in 1996 when it was discovered that their clothing lines were produced in sweatshops using child labour. Around the same time, Nike was exposed for violating the labour rights of employees in their Indonesian factories. Public attention to these production conditions shed light on a need to put an end to unlawful cheap labour.

More recently, and on a larger scale, Enron, WorldCom and Tyco were exposed for fraudulent behaviour in 2002 after being hailed as some of the world's most successful companies run by token "business heroes". Globally recognised individuals have also been cited for unethical behaviour in the recent years.

Businesses and organisations have also been known to act unethically in their dealings with customers. Examples include the bait-and-switch promotional tactics used by Hoover in late 1992 as an attempt to clear a backlog of stock, in 2003 British Gas' failure to mail bills to several customers for more than a year, and in the mid-1990s speculations that The Body Shop did not uphold their animal testing policy and were deceitful in the origins of a number of the "natural" ingredients used in their products. The most recent and widely publicised example of unethical treatment of customers stems from the sub-prime mortgage crisis that began in 2007.

As a result of the many business scandals that have been in the news in recent years, more academic attention is being given to the role of ethics in business. However, throughout these numerous scandals, the focus has been on the accounting and financial functions, probably because of the visibility of these high monetary impacts. Even for those cases exposing a company's questionable operations such as child labour, the main focus is on the unethical accountants who falsified numbers on their books in an attempt to hide the use of illegal workers, not on the fact that the use of child labour is unethical in itself.

The growing concern about the role of ethics in business provided a major push to the introduction of the Sarbanes Oxley Act of 2002. With Sarbanes Oxley, companies were required to shift from a principles-based method of accounting to a rules-based method. The introduction of this act to address the accounting function coupled with the public's awareness of the seemingly increasing number of unethical business behaviours may be contributing to a change in the perception of ethics and its role in business.

The concept of ethics has shifted from being based on personal principles and moral character to an environment of compliance to set ethical standards and rules for the behaviours of individuals and businesses.

For many years the ethical component has been ignored or pushed aside for the sake of profit.

However more attention is now being given to the tenancy of ethical behaviour in the business environment and, therefore, no company can seek a competitive position without due consideration about the ethical implications of their actions.

The recent events on Wall Street that contributed to the current economic crisis in the U.S. suggest that problems with unethical behaviours by individuals and businesses still exist, suggesting the need for a paradigm shift with respect to the role of ethics in businesses and business decision-making.

Such a shift may not be easy and may require a clear understanding of culture and values existing in a company and its people. Academics may play a major role in facilitating such a paradigm shift by thoughtful research, revealing the impact of ethical behaviour on the overall well-being of the organisation.

The roles of ethics and ethical behaviour must also be addressed within the heart of the organisation, in its operations and supply chain decisions.

Few companies set out deliberately to commit unethical practices. But the quest for competitive advantage can have a serious impact on the way products are made, and how workers are treated.

The problem of unethical behaviour is common to global supply chains, in good times and bad. Companies don't always understand the impact of their actions, and if consumers are unaware of how products get to market, there won't be a price to pay for cutting corners.

The situation is changing, however, as companies do a better job of auditing their global operations and working environments. Consumers today are becoming better educated about overseas working conditions, and the unfair treatment of workers can seriously harm sales and brand identity. The public's growing awareness of environmental issues also puts pressure on companies to build more sustainable supply chains.

The law is yet another powerful motivator. Trading blocs such as the European Union and North American Free Trade Agreement have generated a lively dialogue about issues such as poor working conditions and the use of child labour in factories. Industry groups have formed to address the issue, as governments clamp down on violations of fair labour standards. And when one company is caught, others scramble to reevaluate their own policies and practices.

The supply chain is a prime location for taking action. It encompasses many if not most of the processes that are subject to unethical behaviour.

Environmentally Conscious Supply Chain Management (ECSCM) refers to the control exerted over all immediate and eventual environmental effects of products and processes associated with converting raw materials into final products. While much work has been done in this area, the focus has traditionally been on either: product recovery (recycling, remanufacturing, or re-use) or the product design function only (e.g., design for environment).

Environmental considerations in manufacturing are often viewed as separate from traditional, value-added considerations. However, the case can be made that professional engineers have an ethical responsibility to consider the immediate and eventual environmental impacts of products and processes that they design and/or manage.

Organisations now aim to develop both their products and operations to be as environmentally friendly as possible. They focus both on improving the energy efficiency of chargers and on reducing stand-by consumption. In addition, they also place emphasis on improving the efficiency of their production facilities and operations.

Supply Chain Management and the Environment

For years, the producers' responsibilities were finished when the product was on the shelves in the shop or when the guarantee period was over.

Supply chain (SC) management was perceived as the planning and control of the flow of goods from the sourcing base to the final consumers, accompanied with the necessary information and money for the independent entities along that chain. Traditional supply chain management focuses on low cost, high quality, reduced lead time and high service level.

The introduction of the Extended Producer Responsibility in a number of countries and industries has changed the rules of the market behaviours. Nowadays manufacturers need to take into consideration the post-consumption phase of their products, the so called end-of-life phase (EOL): the environmental burdens incurred during different stages of the product transfer from manufacturer to final user and then to the disposal site.

The interest in environmentally friendly supply chain management has risen considerably in recent years. This can be seen by the number of initiatives taken by companies. Brand-owners are very often perceived to be responsible for environmental problems in the entire supply chain from to the sourcing base to end-of-life recovery issues. It is expected that the manufacturers reduce sources of waste and pollution throughout their entire SCs, across multiple entities, upstream (suppliers) and downstream (distributors and consumers).

An environmentally friendly supply chain connects with partners who should make managerial decisions with regard to environmental consequences. It enhances competitiveness and creates better customer service, resilience and increased profitability.

"Green SCM can reduce the ecological impact of industrial activity without sacrificing quality, cost, reliability, performance or energy utilisation efficiency, meeting environmental regulations to not only minimise ecological damage but also to ensure overall economic profit."

Companies are forced to adopt ecologically responsive practices to meet legislative requirements but they can also benefit from "green" behaviour.

For example, building the technological and organisational capacity to collect, recycle and reuse waste or returns stream can enhance the availability of materials as well as clear up the supply channels. According to Srivastava (2007), green SCM can reduce the ecological impact of industrial activity without sacrificing quality, cost, reliability, performance or energy utilisation efficiency, meeting environmental regulations to not only minimise ecological damage but also to ensure overall economic profit.

Environmentally friendly supply chain management requires a continuous course of actions in order to decrease the environmental impact of products and technology used by a manufacturer and its pre-chain (supplies) and post-chain (collection, inspection and reprocessing activities).

There are a number of problems covered within the framework of environmentally friendly supply chain management. The two main issues that need to be addressed by managerial decision-making are:

- Greening the supply chain operations by reducing the total carbon footprint of products' delivery process. From a logistics perspective, the main contributor of carbon footprint and greenhouse emissions besides the manufacturing operations is transport
- Closing the materials flow loops: including issues related to the collection of used products, their recovery and reuse

POINTS TO REMEMBER

- The term 'supply chain management' originated in the early 1980s, and is used to define those inbound processes and the management of a network of interconnected businesses involved in delivering goods and services to the ultimate customer.
- The **retailer** is the final organisational point in the supply chain, providing services and products to the consumer.
- **Operations management** is an area of management concerned with overseeing, designing, and controlling the process of productionand redesigning business operations in the production of goods or services.
- **Operations Research** is the application of scientific methods and development of Mathematical models to study and devise solutions to managerial problems like resource allocation, product mix, inventory control, location lay out
- **Manufacturing management** deals with decision making related to Production process so that the resulting goods and services are produced according to specifications, in the amounts and by the schedule demanded at minimum Costs.
- In SCM, Information flows in both directions. Information is related to all the reports, records which get generated to let all concerned know about the status of the materials as they move.
- The pace of change and the uncertainty about how markets willevolve has made it increasingly important for companies to be aware ofthe supply chains they participate in and to understand the roles thatthey play.
- **A supply chain** is the network of organisations that are involved through upstream and downstream linkages in the different processes and activities that produce value in the form of products and services in the hands of ultimate customers. It is also called as a value chain.
- Key factors in successful supply-chain management include:

- The selection and consolidation of the number of suppliers used by the retailer, enabling the retailer to focus on the development of the business and create administrative efficiencies.
- The coordination of prices and inventory policies to avoid short-term demand created by promotional and trade deals.
- More confident and sustained use of EDI enables retailers and suppliers to reduce delivery times and stock levels, and to develop processes such as warehouse cross-docking.
    - Successful supply-chain management requires joint problem-solving, and partnerships must involve joint decision-making, planning and operations.
    - In India industrial revolution started only after independence especially from second 5 year plan (1956- 61).
- **Physical distribution** is the set of activities concerned with efficient movement of finished goods from the end of the production operation to the consumer.
- Physical distribution is part of a larger process called "distribution," which includes wholesale and retail marketing, as well the physical movement of products.
- The term **'Physical distribution management'** is employed in manufacturing and commerce to describe the broad range of activities concerned with the efficient movement of finished products from the end of production line to the consumer and in some cases, includes the movement of raw materials from the sources of supply to the beginning of the production line.
- The primary **participants** of the physical distribution process are Producers, Wholesalers, Distributors, Retailers and End-users.
- **Logistics** deals with strategy and coordination between marketing and production.On the other hand supply chain management focuses more on purchasing and procurement but also sees that customer needs and production scheduling are synchronised.
- The word **quality** means *"Total and continuous satisfaction"* while using a product or service.
- Quality is a relative term and it is generally used with reference to die end use of the product and depends on theperception of a person in a given situation.
- When a customer pays a higher price for a service/product, he is paying for not only quality which he can see, feel, or judge, known as 'tangibles', but also the 'intangibles' such as the 'esteem' value.
- **Customers** don't only include people who interact or place orders through telephone or the Internet. Customers also include those who work every day with the company to make the operation a success - employees.

- The concept of Internal Customer has developed out of a need to build quality into the product rather than inspect the product for quality.
- Customer Feedback in various forms such as Feedback Forms, Review Meetings, Project Postmortems, etc., can also be a source of improving the service of the department with respect to other departments.
- **Total Quality** is a description of the culture, attitude and organisation of a company that strives to provide customers with products and services that satisfy their needs.
- **Total Quality Management**, TQM, is a method by which management and employees can become involved in the continuous improvement of the production of goods and services. It is a combination of quality and management tools aimed at increasing business and reducing losses due to wasteful practices.
- **Lean manufacturing** is an inventory-management and manufacturing strategy that companies implement to reduce costs, increase productivity and gain a competitive advantage.
- IT infrastructure capabilities provide a competitive positioning of business initiatives like cycle time reduction, implementation, implementing redesigned cross-functional processes.
- Technology allows parties within the supply chain to identify challenges, such as delays in manufacturing or shipment.
- Market changes too can be readily addressed when technology isused in supply chain management.
- The development of Inter organisational information system for the supply chain has also been possible as a result of modern technology.
- **Ethics** can be best described as "the science of behaviour, in the context of conscious and deliberate action to attain a goal. It is the basic principles of correct behaviour".
- As a result of the many business scandals that have been in the news in recent years, more academic attention is being given to the role of ethics in business.
- The concept of ethics has shifted from being based on personal principles and moral character to an environment of compliance to set ethical standards and rules for the behaviours of individuals and businesses.
- Trading blocs such as the European Union and North American Free Trade Agreement have generated a lively dialogue about issues such as poor working conditions and the use of child labour in factories.
- **Environmentally Conscious Supply Chain Management (ECSCM)** refers to the control exerted over all immediate and eventual environmental effects of products and processes associated with converting raw materials into final products.

- Nowadays manufacturers need to take into consideration the post-consumption phase of their products, the so called end-of-life phase (EOL): the environmental burdens incurred during different stages of the product transfer from manufacturer to final user and then to the disposal site.
- An environmentally friendly supply chain connects with partners who should make managerial decisions with regard to environmental consequences. It enhances competitiveness and creates better customer service, resilience and increased profitability.
- There are a number of problems covered within the framework of environmentally friendly supply chain management. The two main issues that need to be addressed by managerial decision-making are:
    - Greening the supply chain operations by reducing the total carbon footprint of products' delivery process. From a logistics perspective, the main contributor of carbon footprint and greenhouse emissions besides the manufacturing operations is transport
    - Closing the materials flow loops: including issues related to the collection of used products, their recovery and reuse

Questions for Discussion

1. What is meant by Supply Chain Management?
2. Explain in brief the concept of SCM.
3. What is the significance of operations and SCM?
4. Explain in brief the evolution of Manufacturing to Operations Management.
5. What is Quality? Explain the customers and the manufacture's view regarding it.
6. What does TQM mean?
7. Explain the concept of Lean Management.
8. How has technology impacted SCM?
9. Explain the importance of ethics and environment friendly practices in Supply Chain functions.
10. Write a brief note on:
    (a) TQM
    (b) Lean Management
    (c) Internal customer
    (d) Impact of Global competition on SCM
    (e) Manufacturer's view of quality
    (f) Similarities and differences between physical goods and services.

Questions from Previous Examinations

1. Trace the historical development of Manufacturing Management Beginning from Division of Labour to Quality Revolution and Environmental Control. **[April 2006]**

2. Explain all the Functions of Manufacturing Management. **[April 2006]**

3. Enlist the Functions and Objectives of Manufacturing Management and Explain each briefly. **[April 2006]**

4. State the Contributions Made by F. W. Taylor and Adam Smith in Development or Manufacturing Management. **[December 2006]**

5. Discuss Various Phases in Evolution from Manufacturing to Operation Management with the Contribution Given by Operation Management Philosophers there in. **[April 2009]**

6. List the Functions of Operations Management and Explain Contributions made by Henry Ford and Taguchi in Development of Production Management. **[December 2009]**

7. State the Scope of Operations Management and Explain Contributions made by Crossby and Taguchi in Development of Production Management. **[April 2010]**

8. Which Factors Accounts for the Resurgence of Interest in Operations Management ?
[December 2010]

9. What is Manufacturing Management ? Explain the contribution made by Henry Ford, Deming, Crossby and Taguchi in the development of Production Management.

[April 2011]

10. Explain briefly the Inter-management Functional Relationship of Operations Management and Other Functions. **[December 2011]**

    (a) Marketing (b) Finance (c) Personnel and administration.

11. Write Short Notes : **[April 2009, 2011]**

    (a) Lean Production System.

Chapter 2...

Operations Process

Contents ...

2.1 Process Characteristics in Operations
    2.1.1 Three Important Aspects of Designing Processes
    2.1.2 Types of Processes
2.2 Process Product Matrix
2.3 Service System Design Matrix
- Points to Remember
- Questions for Discussion
- Questions from Previous Examinations

Learning Objectives:

➢ To study the process characteristics of an organization under the co-ordinance of Operations Management
➢ To define and design the process product matrix for different styles of production
➢ To define and design the system matrix for an effective supply management

Introduction

A process based viewpoint facilitates a complete understanding of the various aspects of operations management. A process view point essentially involves identifying the input, output, and the processing and feedback mechanisms in a system. The basic inputs in a system are labour, material and capital. Processing involves the various activities that an operating system utilises to convert raw material into useful products for customers. The conversion process enhances the value of the product and enables the organisation to sell it in the market.

In the case of service organisations, the conversion process involves committing the various resources at its disposal to deliver useful services to the customer. Irrespective of whether it is a manufacturing or a service organisation, there are a set of activities to be performed in the conversion process.

One of the important decision-points in the design and operational control of an operations system, concerns the capacity to be deployed in the system. We often hear about excessive delays and waiting time in service systems such as a teller counter in a bank.

Similarly, we hear that some factories work with almost 100 per cent utilisation of their resources. All these relate to certain decisions taken with respect to the nature and capacity that an operating unit builds into the system. Improper choice of capacity deployed and poor planning of the existing capacity will lead to loss of productivity. It will also mean reduction in the profitability of the operating system. Therefore, a set of tools and techniques are required to take care of these issues.

In this chapter, we shall look at various issues related to capacity planning. The basic building block of capacity analysis is *process analysis*. After all, the process design determines the capacity of a system. Therefore, we shall begin with an understanding of processes before we address the issue of capacity planning.

2.1 Process Characteristics in Operations

Understanding any operations systems without doubt begins with an understanding of the processes that are integral to the operations system. A process is the basic building block of operations. It is made up of a set of activities that need to be carried out by combining resources and time.

This combination ultimately determines the performance of the operations systems in terms of time, productivity, profitability and other similar factors.

- Take for example a restaurant. When the customer goes to the counter and places an order for the food items he or she would like to eat, the outcome is determined by the process employed to satisfy this customer demand. The steps involved in serving the demand, the number of people involved, the nature of resources consumed and the time taken to serve this customer will all depend on the process design.
- The process design will in turn determine other things such as the time taken to serve the customer, the cost involved, the productivity of the people and the utilisation of the resources. These are the performance characteristics of the process in question. Viewed from this perspective, the performance of the processes finally dictates the performance of an operations system itself.
- Consider an automobile garage that deals with all angles of repairs. Here, too, one will encounter a set of issues similar to those at a restaurant. The design of the process will determine the performance of the automobile garage. One can extend this logic to larger manufacturing and service systems.

An operations manager will want to understand some of the following issues in the process design:

- Does the organisation have adequate resources to meet the demand? If they need to add some extra resources, where should they be added?
- What is the extent of the utilisation of the resources?
- If the organisation needs to increase the capacity of their system, how should they modify the process? Should some more resources be added? What would then happen to the cost of operations?

Answers to these questions can be found using process analysis. In this, some analytical mechanisms are used in order to understand the impact of process design on the output, cost, or any other performance parameter. It also results in understanding the impact of alternative process configurations on the chosen parameters.

PROCESS FLOW-CHARTING

The success of designing a process depends on the extent of detailing gathered by the Operations Manager. Each activity that constitutes a process must be identified. It is also important to know the time taken for each activity and the nature of flow of materials/information in the process.

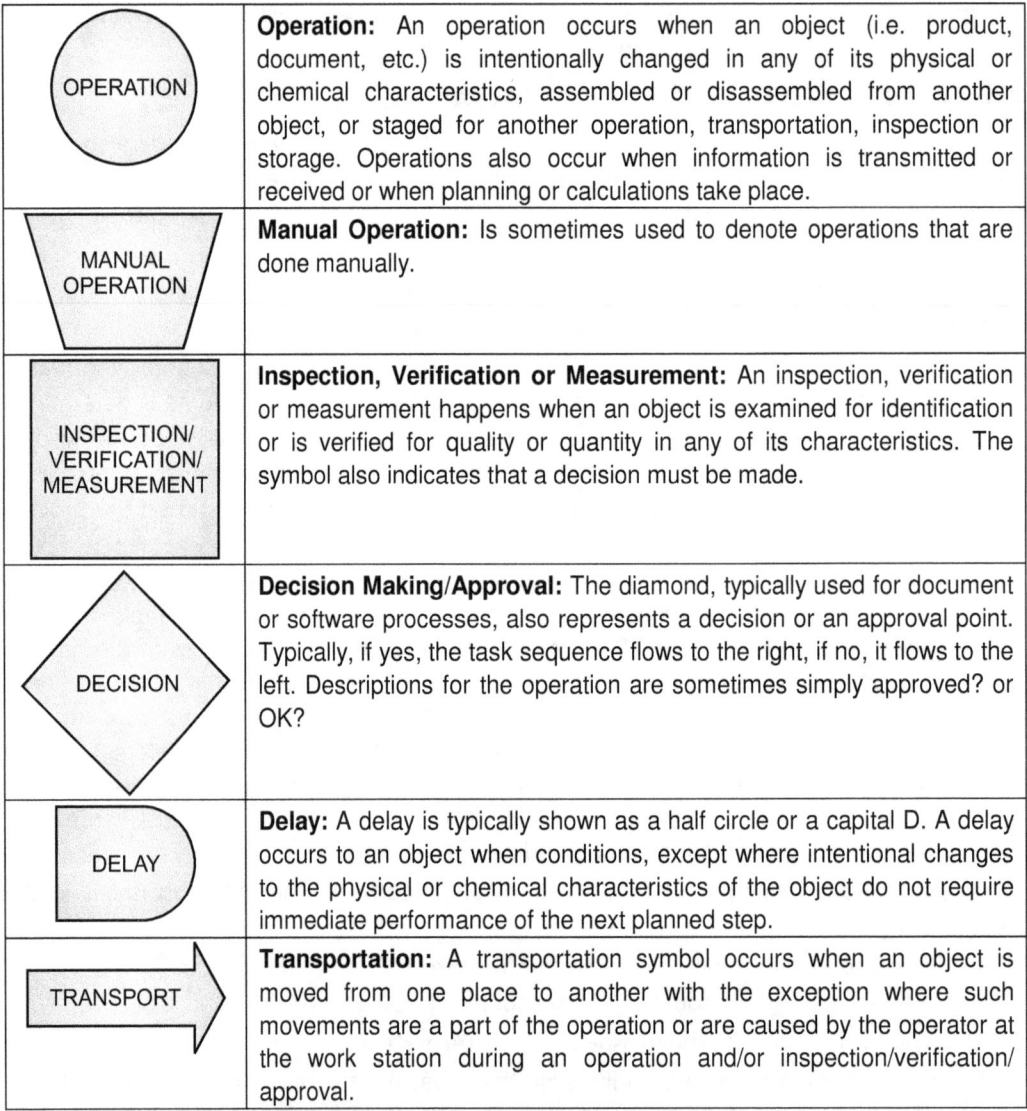

OPERATION	**Operation:** An operation occurs when an object (i.e. product, document, etc.) is intentionally changed in any of its physical or chemical characteristics, assembled or disassembled from another object, or staged for another operation, transportation, inspection or storage. Operations also occur when information is transmitted or received or when planning or calculations take place.
MANUAL OPERATION	**Manual Operation:** Is sometimes used to denote operations that are done manually.
INSPECTION/ VERIFICATION/ MEASUREMENT	**Inspection, Verification or Measurement:** An inspection, verification or measurement happens when an object is examined for identification or is verified for quality or quantity in any of its characteristics. The symbol also indicates that a decision must be made.
DECISION	**Decision Making/Approval:** The diamond, typically used for document or software processes, also represents a decision or an approval point. Typically, if yes, the task sequence flows to the right, if no, it flows to the left. Descriptions for the operation are sometimes simply approved? or OK?
DELAY	**Delay:** A delay is typically shown as a half circle or a capital D. A delay occurs to an object when conditions, except where intentional changes to the physical or chemical characteristics of the object do not require immediate performance of the next planned step.
TRANSPORT	**Transportation:** A transportation symbol occurs when an object is moved from one place to another with the exception where such movements are a part of the operation or are caused by the operator at the work station during an operation and/or inspection/verification/approval.

Fig. 2.1: Process Flow Chart Symbols

A pictorial representation of all this information should be developed using a process flow-charting methods. Process flow-charting employs a set of standard symbols and graphical tools to represent all the information about the process. The symbols typically used are as follows:

A process flow chart helps an operations manager in many ways. Some of these are follows:

- It provides a pictorial and compact representation of the process.
- It ensures faster and better understanding of the various aspects of the process.
- By superimposing additional information such as the time taken for each stage of the process, certain useful measures can be computed.
- For example, the management may be able to estimate the time required to complete the process.
- Using this information, the management can also identify the bottlenecks in the process and the productive capacity of the process.
- The management can also assess the amount of resources that need to be deployed at each stage in order to meet the projected requirements.

These aspects are what make up a process analysis. We shall see in some of these in detail ahead.

Designing of processes is an important and early step in operations management. The designing of manufacturing processes essentially consists of certain choices we make with respect to the flow of parts in a manufacturing system.

For example, we need to decide on the types of machines to use, the number of machines of each type, and their placement on the shop floor (factory shade).

As a prerequisite to this, a detailed analysis of how each component will be manufactured in the system is required. This implies determining the number of steps involved in manufacturing, the machines used, and the time spent in each of these steps. It is more commonly referred to as process planning.

Process design is defined by the nature of the activities that we pursue in an operating system. If the manufacturing system is designed for a wide range of products, it demands a certain type of process design, as opposed to one that mass-produces just one or two variations of a product.

By choosing an appropriate process, it is possible to streamline the product flow and deploy appropriate operations management practices commensurate to the process design.

2.1.1 Three Important Aspects of Designing Processes

Understanding the importance of designing a process for the effectiveness of an operations system of a company, the three major forces which influence the design and the its effectiveness are as follows:

1. Volume: Volume indicates the quantity of products produced in a manufacturing system. For example, turnkey project management organisations will usually have a production volume of just one system at a time, at a place. At the other extreme, organisations catering to the FMCG (Fast Moving Consumer Goods) sectors have high volumes of production that require continuous production. Examples include the manufacture of spark plugs, electric bulbs, soaps, standard electrical fittings, and common household utilities. Many chemical process industries also belong to this category.

Between these two extremes, we have mid-volume manufacturers who offer several versions of products. There are numerous examples of mid-volume manufacturing in the consumer durables, which include several industrial products. Hindustan Motors, for instance, manufactures several types of earth-moving equipment that belong to the mid-volume category.

In manufacturing there is a wide variety. On the one hand most of our daily consumption items such as tooth paste, soap, and detergents are consumed and manufactured in huge quantities. On the other Mazgaon docks manufacture one submarine in two years. Or to manufacture a big boiler for process industry or a turbine for hydroelectric project it takes months. In between these two extremes there are number of products which are required in smaller quantities and require a day or a week to manufacture. Typical of these mid volumes are large generators or earth moving equipment, textile machinery and so on.

2. Variety: Variety refers to the number of sub categories of products and variants of each product produced in a manufacturing system. For example, a watch company has more than five thousand varieties of watches. These varieties arise not only from alternative product lines but also from variants in each product line. Similarly, consider a car manufacturer such as Maruti Suzuki Limited. The Maruti Swift is available in several models. Basically, there are the petrol and diesel versions. However, within the petrol and the diesel versions, there are variations based on the features offered by the company. While one version will have power steering only, the second will offer power steering and power windows, the third may have automatic transmission, and so on. A choice of colours adds another dimension of variety to passenger car manufacturing.

An increase in the variety of product offerings is likely to introduce variety in the manufacturing processes. More variety may mean alternative production resources, materials, skill of workers, and an increase in the number of stages of production. It may need better operations management practices. Planning and scheduling may become more complex on account of these added choices in the manufacturing system.

We can study a similar phenomenon in service systems too. Suppose that a travel agency was earlier engaged only in selling tickets for bus journeys from Delhi to Pune. In the course of time, if the agency added booking of bus tickets to multiple destinations, rail tickets, air tickets for domestic travel, and air tickets for international travel, one can imagine how many alternative choices of processes, skill sets and resources are required by the travel agency.

Operations management in the case of additional services is far more involved and complex.

Henry Ford had said in his autobiography about his model T, *"my customers can have any colour as long as it is black!"* Gone are those days and customers demand more and more customisation. Each of this variety will require some change in the manufacturing process. It will require different machines, different skill workers and more complex planning and control system.

A similar phenomenon has occurred in Service sector also. Earlier air lines were selling only travel tickets. Now they offer you advance seat booking, advance meal booking, advance check in facility and all on internet with credit card facility. All this requires additional processes, skill sets, training resources, auditing and also a different type of management!

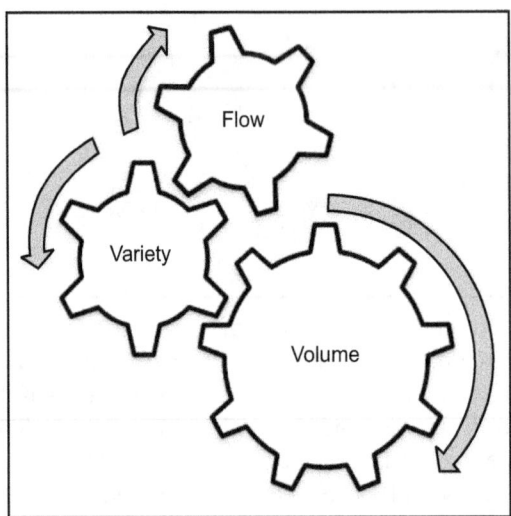

Fig. 2.2: The Important Aspects of Designing Process

3. **Flow:** Irrespective of the nature of activities involved, all manufacturing systems require some input material where the processes start. The material undergoes a conversion process from the raw material phase to the finished goods phase. Flow indicates the nature and intensity of this phenomenon.

Knowledge of flow provides important clues to the operations manager about production planning and control issues that need to be looked into. It also gives useful information about the complexities of operations management in an operations system.

Volume, variety, and flow are linked to one another.

In general, volume and variety will have an inverse relationship. When the volume of production is very high, the firm is likely to be engaged in manufacturing fewer varieties of products.

On the other hand, if the firm caters to a wide range of products and services, then the production volume of each of these variations is likely to be very low. Volume and variety also influence the flow patterns in a manufacturing system. Therefore, process design choices available to an operations manager could be understood by analysing alternative flow patterns.

In short, Volume, Variety and Flow are interconnected. The smaller the variety higher is the volume of that product and vice versa. Then volume and variety together influence the Flow of the manufacturing system.

So, to understand Process Design choices available to operations manager, we need to analyse alternate flow patterns.

2.1.2 Types of Processes

Process characteristics are largely determined by the flow of products in a manufacturing system. Therefore, it is important to first understand the nature of flow in operations and then identify the process choices available to the operations manager for each category of flow.

Generically, two types of flows are identified in manufacturing systems:

Continuous and Intermittent

1. **Continuous Flow Systems:** A continuous flow system is characterised by a streamlined flow of products in the operating system. Usually in such systems, the conversion processes begin with the input of raw materials at one end. It progresses through the system in an orderly fashion to finally get converted into finished goods.

The production process is sequential and the required resources are organised in stages. Continuous flow is largely a result of technological constraints and a high volume of production.

In the manufacturing of petrochemicals, steel, pharmaceuticals, cement, and glass, the reason for continuous flow is technological constraint.

For example, in a glass manufacturing unit, once the manufacturing process begins, it cannot be stopped until finished glass components come out of the system. On the other hand, in a discrete manufacturing industry, the high volume of production of very few varieties results in a reorganised flow.

Consider the case of manufacturing spark plugs. Due to fewer variations and large volume of production, the production system is laid out in such a manner that an orderly flow is possible. Similarly, in a fast-food outlet offering very few variations for breakfast during peak hours in a busy locality, the system will have a highly reorganised flow.

Despite the similarity of streamlined flow in process industries and mass production systems, there are important differences with respect to operations management practices between the two. Therefore, it is useful to discuss these issues separately for these two categories.

Process Industries: Process industries have peculiar characteristics compared to discrete manufacturing industries. Process industries have a closed manufacturing set-up and finished goods are usually got at the end of the manufacturing process. In some cases, it is possible to get products during the intermediate stages of the process in the form of by-products.

An example of a process industry is the paper manufacturing industry. An analysis of the paper-manufacturing process will reveal many features of a process industry. As shown in the figure, there are three main stages in the paper-manufacturing process:

- ❖ Step 1: Preparatory stage
- ❖ Step 2: Pulp making stage
- ❖ Step 3: Paper making stage

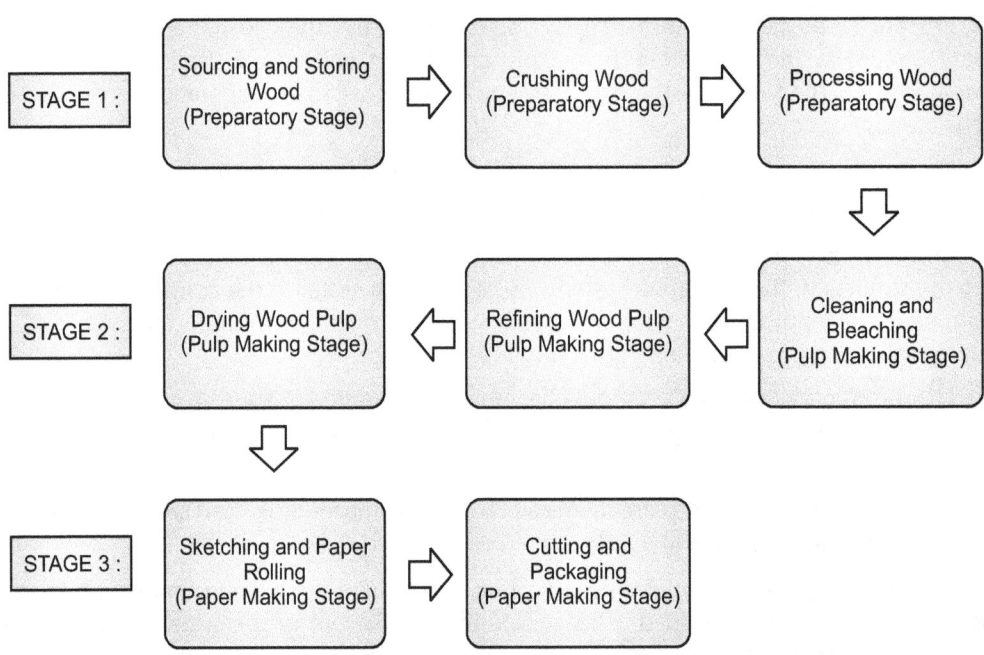

Fig. 2.3: 3 Stages in Paper Manufacturing Process

Phase 1:

During the preparatory stage, logs of wood and chips of various sizes are first put into the system, and are broken into smaller and uniform pieces in a crusher. After they are cut into uniform pieces, they are processed in a huge chamber where some chemicals are also added.

During this process, the pieces are digested and the fibers are laid in a uniform pattern. This is done with the help of a chemical process. After this process is complete, the extract is ready for making wood pulp.

Phase 2:

The pulp-making process is nothing but further refining of the wood fiber and cleaning and bleaching of the material.

Finally, excess moisture is taken out of the pulp. At this stage, the pulp is almost devoid of moisture and is in a near-solid state. Therefore, it is possible to press it into the required thickness and remove remaining moisture.

This is the last stage of the process known as papermaking.

Phase 3:

The dried and processed paper is then rolled into reels and cut to required lengths and shapes.

The papermaking example illustrates certain distinctive features of process industries:

- Once the logs (raw materials) are put into the system, it is not possible to stop the system until the dried wood pulp reaches the paper-rolling and cutting (final) stage.
- Since the process is continuous, there should be a balance of capacity between all the stages in the manufacturing process to maintain an even flow of the material from the raw-material stage to the finished-goods stage. Otherwise, there will be a capacity mismatch, which may result in gross underutilisation of resources.
- The productivity of the system is directly related to the flow rate (or throughput) of the product.
- Process industries require huge capital investments in the manufacturing system as incremental addition at a later stage is not possible. Due to this, high productivity implies lower production costs and vice versa.
- An important operations management task in process industries is making continuous process improvements and capacity de-bottlenecking to maximise the flow rate in the system.
- As the flow rate directly determines productivity, it also implies that failure of any intermediate stage in the system will have an adverse effect on the cost as the entire system will have to be stopped.

The need to keep the production facilities continuously running in a process industry directly points to a need to be good in maintenance management. Therefore, process-industry firms invest more time in developing good maintenance practices.

The amount of spare-parts inventory that they carry will be a significant portion of the overall inventory in the system. Owing to the continuous and closed-loop nature of the entire manufacturing process, process industries tend to have very little work-in-process inventory.

Although not evident from the paper-manufacturing example, process industries benefit greatly from the upward integration of their operations as well as from the addition of several secondary conversion facilities. This is because, at certain intermediate stages of processing, by-products are released from the manufacturing system. Having the facilities to process these by-products into useful products will lower the overall cost of the production system and increase revenue generation opportunities.

Mass Production: The mass production system in the discrete manufacturing industry is another example of continuous and streamlined flow in the manufacturing system.

Here, the volume of production is very high and the number of variations in the final product is low. Therefore, it is possible to organise the entire process by dedicating the required manufacturing resources for each product variant and arranging the resources one after the other, as per the manufacturing sequence.

Such a structure is usually known as a product line structure. As a result of this arrangement, a reorganised flow is possible. Automobile and two-wheeler manufacture, the manufacture of electrical components (such as switches), and that of healthcare products (such as disposable syringes)—all are typical examples of high-volume production. Other examples include the manufacturing of several consumer non-durables.

Process design for streamlined flow can be visualised at two levels in a mass production system. Overall, each product would flow across departments in a streamlined fashion. Further, within each department, there would be an orderly flow of components and materials.

In operations management terminology, the manner in which the manufacturing resources are arranged for mass production is referred to as a *flow shop*.

As in the case of process industries, balancing of capacity across various stages of the manufacturing system is required to maximise output and productivity. Also, line work stoppage due to breakdown and asynchronous production practices would also be disadvantageous to the working of the system. Therefore, better maintenance management practices and appropriate design of product-based layouts are important operations management practices in a mass-production system.

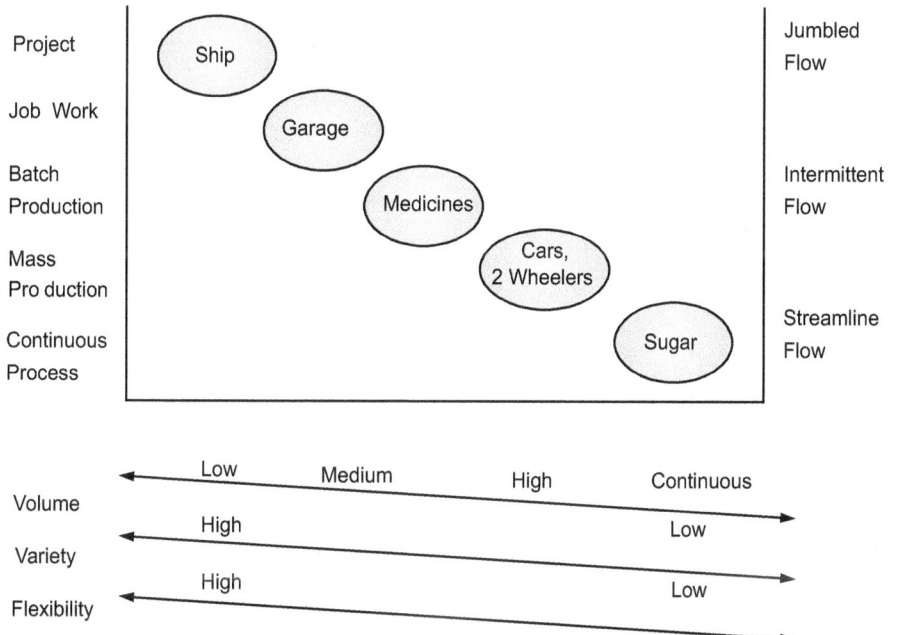

Fig. 2.4

Job Production: Job production is used to create one-off orders or 'jobs' especially made for the purpose. This might be a relatively small job such as a tailoring a suit or a sandwich made to order in a café, or it could be a massive job such as a building cruise liner. Job production helps ensure that the product or service matches the customer's exact needs, as closely as the firm is able, because it is literally 'custom-made'.

In many cases, skilled or specialised staff makes products of very high quality, or which have individual character that might have less appeal if they were mass-produced. Job production is a relatively expensive process because it requires specialised and skilled staffs who concentrate on the individual job or project. It is therefore labour intensive, although some projects–such as the cruise liner–may also need a lot of expensive capital equipment. Small businesses that are built on the skills of the owner, such as a window cleaner or a hairdresser, use job production techniques.

Batch Production: As the name suggests, products are produced in small or large batches. This process is useful to a firm that makes a number of different variations of basically similar products. Examples could be; a bakery, a car exhaust pipe factory or a toothpaste manufacturer.

If the sandwich shop mentioned above wanted to speed up production, instead of making sandwiches to order, it might be able to benefit by making the day's sandwiches in batches of all the different types and have them available for sale, pre-packed. A toothpaste manufacturer will set its weekly batches of production of each product according to the orders from the supermarkets and wholesalers. The same machinery is used for each product but the ingredients, packaging and/or size is changed for each batch as required.

It is very important that the machinery can be quickly cleaned and reset for each new batch, to reduce unproductive time. In a factory that uses flow production, it is quite common for component parts to be made in batches that are enough for a week's production.

Flow production: This is a production line method, where the product is continuously produced, flowing from one stage of production to the next. Workers and many a times robots, carry out individual repetitive tasks aiming to work as quickly as possible without loss of quality. This method was pioneered by Henry Ford for his Model T car, and the efficiencies he gained enabled him to produce large numbers of cars at low cost.

Any product made in high volumes will almost certainly be made on a flow production line. This approach to production has close links with F.W. Taylor and his 'Scientific School of Management'. Taylor's motivational theories were all about creating the workplace and forms of reward to maximise efficiency. This in turn led to very boring work and added to industrial unrest over the years. More modern, lean production techniques have at least partly recognised the fact that this type of work can be extremely boring. Ideas such as cell production and quality circles can help improve the workplace as workers become multi-skilled, take more responsibility for quality and can contribute their ideas for improvements.

Flow production systems are usually capital intensive and it is important to keep them running smoothly with high levels of capacity utilisation, so that these high overhead costs are spread over as many units as possible. Once set up properly, flow production lines can in some cases produce millions of consistently high quality products.

Intermittent Flow

All manufacturing firms do not enjoy the benefit of high volume and low variety such as a mass production system. As customer preferences increase, the need for creating more variety also increases and firms respond to this need by increasing the product line. Moreover, as competition increases, organisations try to retain their market share by introducing new products.

An example of this is the passenger car segment in the country. The passenger car segment was de-licensed in 1993. Until then, there were very few car manufacturers. They offered very few variations. However, as the competition increased and customer expectations rose, product variety also increased.

When variety increases, the volume of production for each variation would be less compared to a mass production system. Therefore, allocation of manufacturing resources for each variation may not be a possible option. The manufacturing resources would be shared by a group of products. Since each product may have different processing requirements and sequences of operations, the flow will become complicated. Therefore, the manufacturing process is characterised as mid-volume, mid-variety systems and process design for this type of system must look into issues arising out of intermittent flow.

Discrete and process industries have other ways by which they can look into the flow complexities. In the case of process industries, one way to minimise this flow complexity is to work the system in batches. In one batch, one set of variations is manufactured and in the next batch, another set of variations is manufactured. In between these two batches, the necessary set-up and changeover of resources are made to make possible smooth production and maximise productivity. Such an arrangement results in intermittent flow systems.

In the case of discrete manufacturing systems, the entire manufacturing set-up can be split into units in which similar processing requirements can be combined and manufacturing resources arranged to work in favour of these requirements. One batch of components maybe produced in one of these units and another batch in yet another unit. In each batch, components of different product variations may be combined since they share the same processing requirement.

By now, it is evident that operations management issues in intermittent flow systems are very different from those of continuous flow systems. The concept of flow balancing is not an issue in the case of intermittent flow systems.

However, capacity planning for catering to the overall requirements of the various varieties is important. Capacity estimation is difficult in an intermittent flow system as compared to a continuous flow system. The major problem pertaining to the overall working of an intermittent flow system is the issue of switch from one variety to another.

Production planning and scheduling must critically analyse the impact of alternative changeovers and develop an optimal changeover sequence while planning for production.

Comparative Study

Parameters	Continuous Flow System	Intermittent Flow System
Product Attributes	High volume but very low variety	Medium volume and medium variety
Examples	Mass Production Systems	Batch production in process
Important Issues	Flow balancing, maintenance, capacity utilisation and debottlenecking, backward integration	Manufacturing system and layout design, changeover management, capacity planning and estimation
Operations management tools and techniques	Line balancing, maintenance management, process optimisation planning and product layout design, flow shop scheduling, pull type scheduling, single piece flow design	Forecasting, capacity planning and estimation, optimised production optimisation sequencing, group technology layout design, materials management

2.2 Process Product Matrix

Job production, sometimes called **jobbing** or **one-off production**, involves producing custom made work, such as a one-off product for a specific customer or a small batch of work in quantities usually less than those of mass-market products. It is the oldest form of production. Individual products are made, with probably not a lot of standardised parts in it.

Job production is often associated with classical craft production such as small firms:

- Making railings for a specific house.
- Building or repairing a computer for a specific customer.
- Making flower arrangements for a specific wedding.

Large firms also use job production. Examples include:

- Designing and implementing an advertising campaign
- Auditing the accounts of a large public limited company.
- Building a new factory.
- Installing machinery in a factory.

Fabrication shops and machine shops whose work is primarily of the job production type are often called job shops. The associated people or corporations are sometimes called **jobbers**.

Job production is manufacturing on a contract basis, and thus forms a subset of the larger field of **contract manufacturing**. But the latter field also includes, in addition to jobbing, a higher level of outsourcing in which a product-line-owning company entrusts its entire production to a contractor, rather than just outsourcing parts of it.

There are many advantages as well as disadvantages to this process. Job production work is generally of a high quality and a high level of customisation is possible to meet the customer's exact requirements. Besides this significant flexibility in product design is possible, especially when compared to mass production. On the other hand, customisation may lead to higher cost of production and sometimes engineering drawings or an engineering assessment, including calculations or specifications, need to be made before the work can be done. It also requires the use of specialist labour to complete a job.

Batch production is a technique in which the object in question is created stage by stage over a series of workstations, and different batches of products are made.

Batch production is most common in bakeries and in the manufacture of sports shoes, pharmaceutical ingredients, purifying water (APIs), inks, paints and adhesives.

There are several advantages of batch production; it can reduce the initial capital outlay or the cost of setting up the machines, because a single production line can be used to produce several products. Batch production can be useful for small businesses who cannot afford to run continuous production lines. Batch production is also useful for a factory that makes seasonal items, products for which it is difficult to forecast demand, a trial run for production, or products that have a high profit margin.

Batch production also has some drawbacks. There are inefficiencies associated with batch production as equipment must be stopped, re-configured and its output tested before the next batch can be produced.

Product and process designs make up an integral part of the conversion process. Every operations system has to make important decisions with respect to the type of products and services to be offered. Once the right mix of products and services are identified, correct processes for manufacturing and delivering them to the customers need to be identified.

This involves:

- Deciding on the technology to be used,
- The machines to be used in the conversion process,
- The exact method of creating the products and services.

These steps are known as product and process design.

Once the product and process designs are finalised, an operations system must focus on ensuring that the demand for products and services is met. Here, the organisation may also require operations planning to ensure the availability of enough material and capacity to meet the targeted production. This is known as operations planning.

The operations system also requires methods for real-time control of operations as there may be many deviations from the plan. For example, there might be a breakdown of machinery or rejection of a lot of material supplied by a vendor. In another cases, some customer might change their order quantities or cancel the order. The operations control activity takes care of these changing needs in an operations system.

Another important activity in the conversion process relates to ensuring enough supply of materials for the operations system. This means that the suppliers of various materials are identified and a relationship established with them. With such an arrangement, it would be possible to place orders for material with the suppliers and receive them within the given time. This activity is called purchasing and inventory control.

From an operations management perspective, the processing part of the system primarily focuses on identifying the nature of resources required, planning for material and capacity, and ensuring that such changes are addressed. The output of an operations system consists of goods and services. An organisation that manufactures passenger cars will provide many variants of the passenger car. On the other hand, a fast-food restaurant may provide various options of food for breakfast, lunch and snacks as per its process and product design. In several manufacturing organisations, services are also offered in the form of after-sales support and warranty.

So far we have discussed various aspects of the alternative process choices that an operations manager possesses and the relationship between process choices and flow patterns in a manufacturing system. The culmination of all these ideas is the process-product matrix. A process—product matrix depicts all these relationships in a compact form. One dimension of the matrix represents product characteristics and the other process characteristics.

Product characteristics essentially indicate the degree of customization and the volume of production. On the other hand, process characteristics indicate the complexity and divergence in the process. When organisations have a high volume of production, the flow will be streamlined. Similarly, when the variety is high, the flow will be jumbled.

Process based Factors: A process or a functional layout is an arrangement of resources on the basis of the process characteristics of the resources. Consider a machine shop consisting of Turning Machine, Heat Treatment, Grinding Machine, and Assembly Line.

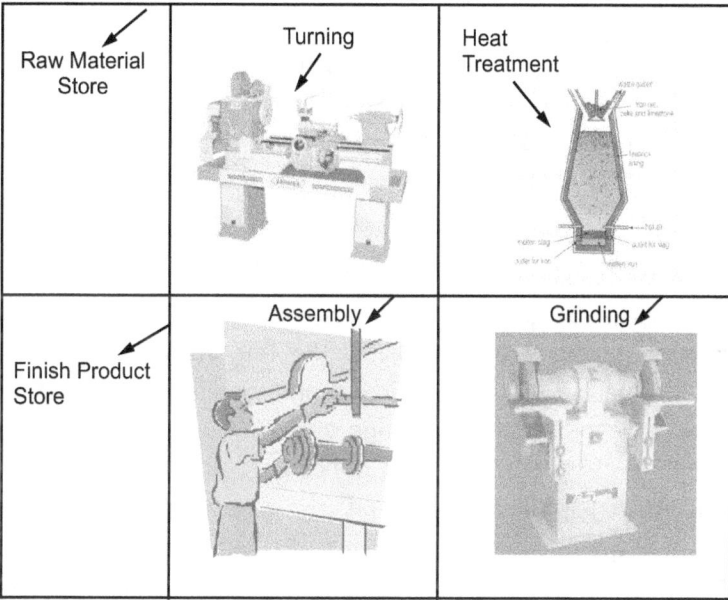

Fig. 2.5

For example, components belonging to this product first visit Turning Machine, then a Heat Treatment, a Grinding Machine, and finally Assembling is done. The sequence of visits is a function of the process plan and is available in a route card.

The main implication of this design is that when the number of components manufactured is large, there will be enormous overlapping of systems and processes in the shop, as components need to visit machines in multiple combinations. This increases material handling options and places challenges for controlling production activities.

Each department in a **process layout** is organised into functional groups. Thus, all the turning machines will be organised into a Turning department. Similarly, there will be a Grinding department, a milling department, and so on. In the fabrication area a similar arrangement would be a welding department, a fitting department, a Heating department, and so on. All manufacturing support areas are also arranged on a functional basis. Examples include a maintenance department, quality control department, procurement, stores, and production planning.

Product based Factors: A product layout is another design for the arrangement of resources. In this case, the order in which the resources are placed exactly follows the process sequence expressed by a product. As a result of this, the resources are arranged in the order of the machining requirements. This results in a smooth component flow in the shop. Since each product will have its own set of resources, material handling is simpler. It is also possible to invest in fixed-path material-handling systems to speed up material transfer between successive terminals. The production control issues are much simpler in a product type of layout compared to the process layout.

Very often the final assembly in several manufacturing plants follows a product layout. The assembly workstations are designed in such a manner that at each terminal a part of the job is completed. The feeder stations are linked to the assembly terminals to confirm material availability.

As the product moves through the assembly line, the process is completed. Testing, final inspection, and even packing can be part of this layout.

If you visit the Chinchwad plant of Tata Motors at Pune, you will notice that there are nearly 180 workstations in the final assembly of the Tata Indica. As the chassis moves through these stations, the car is assembled in a progressive fashion and finally the car is ready for dispatch. In product layouts, the design of the layout is far more important as it results in a certain degree of operational control. Once the design of individual workstations is properly made, many complications are resolved.

The idea of product and process layouts applies not only to manufacturing settings but also in a service setting. A classic example is the banking system. For several years, the layout in the banking operation was process based with the resources arranged on the basis of their function they do. Thus, we have savings bank clerks, current account clerks, cashiers, tellers and so on. However, in recent times, the layout is more product or customer based. In this arrangement, manpower and resources are organised on the basis of customer segments that need to be catered to.

Both process layouts and product layouts have certain advantages and disadvantages. Therefore, one needs to choose an appropriate layout depending on the specific circumstances. The table given below, lists some of the main advantages and disadvantages of both these types of layouts.

A product layout simplifies production planning and control problems. It also enables smooth production and high production rate. However, since a high level of dedication of resources is required it may increase the cost of operation and may be an unfeasible option in most cases. Only in the case of high-volume manufacturing can an organisation justify the dedication of several resources.

Table 2.1: Advantages and Disadvantages of Process and Product Layout

	Process Layout	Product Layout
Advantages	• Sharing of specialised and costly equipments • More flexibility • Less vulnerable to breakdown	• Standardised product/process routing • Operational control is simpler • High output rate is possible
Disadvantages	• Large inventory build-up • Operational control difficult • Excess material handling	• Low tolerance for breakdowns • Duplication of equipment leading to high cost • Lower flexibility due to dedication of resources

The advantages of process layouts include greater flexibility and optimum utilisation of resources. However these are more than offset by several drawbacks.

Organisations using process layouts often experience problems, which include the following:

➢ Enormous overlapping of the jobs, resulting in poor visibility of flow of jobs. This makes progress chasing a difficult task.

➢ Heavy load on material handling, leading to bottleneck situations in the material-handling system.

➢ Difficulty in production planning, scheduling, and control of the jobs.

➢ Very high output at times, which in turn increase the investments in stocks, stock holding costs, damages, and material obsolescence.

➢ Poor delegation of work and poor accountability.

➢ Low motivation and low job satisfaction for the workforce.

On account of these issues, another type of layout that combines the benefits of both process and product layouts is being widely adopted by organisations today. This is known as Product Process Matrix.

2.3 Service System Design Matrix

Designing operations systems involves making choices for the location, technology, capacity, and layout of the system. These decisions directly influence other aspects of the operations, such as the people and skills to be deployed and the planning methodology to be put in place.

However, designing a service system is immensely different from designing a manufacturing system. In a manufacturing system, the customer is rarely part of the process. They will merely place an order and await the delivery of the product. Issues such as what resources are to be used, how they need to be laid out, how to link the successive stages of the conversion process, and what kind of planning and coordination elements should be used are all made with this basic understanding. In contrast, in most service systems, customer participation in the conversion process is inevitable. Therefore, it poses a different challenge altogether and requires the designer to integrate the customer as an integral element in the design process.

Suppose we were to set up a restaurant in the city. Assume that we have been able to secure a 10,000 square feet independent building with some spacious land around it. When we think of a good restaurant, several things come to our mind with respect to the design of the system. Some of these include;

- A well-laid out dining space with stylish decoration of the surroundings and a good ambience,
- The nature and extent of offerings in the menu available for the customer, and
- The judicious use of technology and human elements so that the system is responsive.

From a service design perspective, achieving these outcomes essentially requires us to answer some questions regarding the design of the restaurant. There are several issues that we need to address in this process. Let us list some of them:

- Are there alternatives available for us to position the service? What factors influence service positioning and what are the implications of this on the overall service delivery design?
- What is the nature and level of interaction that we must design between the service provider and the customer? What are the implications of this?
- What is the overall level of technology that we must use? How and where should we deploy the technology?
- What are the elements of the front office and the back office of this service delivery system? How do we identify these elements?
- How should we design the dining area and the kitchen area? What are the factors that will influence the choice of the design?
- How should we lay out the service delivery system? Which are the areas that need greater attention with respect to look and feel?
- What should be the capacity of the dining area and the kitchen area? How can we estimate this, given a certain uncertainty in the arrival pattern and the demand for restaurant services?
- How should we measure and improve the quality of the restaurant?

This list is merely suggestive. It indicates the nature of decisions that are taken in the process to design a service system. One can develop similar sets of questions with respect to the design of other service systems such as a hospital, an automobile garage, an after-sales service outlet, a management consulting firm, or a travel agency.

Role of a Customer in Service System:

Customer contact signifies the extent to which the customer participates in the preparation and consumption of a service. It also indicates the level of exposure that the customer has to the various facets of the service system while receiving the service. Let us consider an automobile garage with two different options with which the service delivery mechanism could be designed.

In Design A, the customer is received at the front portion of the garage in a neatly laid out office. The customer assistant interacts with the customer, notes their complaints and the issues to be addressed while servicing the car, records them in the work sheet, and takes their approval. The customer assistant requests them to come back at a particular time to pick up the car after servicing. When the customer comes to pick up the vehicle, they meet the service assistant at the same office, make the payment, and drive the car away after completing the formalities.

In Design B, while the elements of the service are the same, the manner in which it is laid out and the extent to which the customer is exposed to various aspects of service delivery is different. For example, in Design B, the customer is allowed to visit the garage and is allowed to interact with the repair person and to seek his evaluation of the condition of the car. The customer will also have an opportunity to "see' the manner in which the car is being serviced.

In these examples, customer contact is varying. In Design B, the degree of customer contact is high as the customer has greater opportunities to participate in the service delivery process and discover several moments of truth.

A similar situation exists in the banking sector where a customer can use either an ATM or a branch office to withdraw or deposit cash/cheques. There are several situations in service systems where the process design enables the customer to either make use of self-service with helplines and menus and technology choices, or get a service agent to co-create the service along with the customer.

The degree of customer contact is a design choice that a service organisation has. Different choices would result in different impacts on the design and operation of the service delivery system. At the two extremes of the degree of customer contact, we find certain unique characteristics of the service system. When the degree of customer contact is very low, the system could be highly mechanised and firms can pursue efficiency goals very well.

On the other hand, when the degree of customer contact is high, it is difficult to pursue efficiency goals. Satisfying the customer requires clear trade-offs between the efficiency and the effectiveness of service delivery. Based on the degree of customer contact, one can visualise three types of designs for service processes:

- Low degree of customer contact: quasi-manufacturing.
- Medium degree of customer contact: mixed service.
- High degree of customer contact: pure service.

Therefore, customer contact is an important decision variable in the service process design problem. It affects several aspects of a service system. We shall take a look at some of these aspects.

> **Efficiency of operations:** When service systems are designed with a high degree of customer contact, pursuing efficiency goals becomes difficult or futile. In a high customer contact system, customers are likely to participate to a greater extent, along with the service personnel in co-creating the service. Therefore, convenience and quick-response requirements need to be met. These will affect organising the entire operations from a pure efficiency perspective.
>
> Therefore, we can conclude that in service systems designed with a high degree of customer contact, effectiveness goals are more important to pursue. The effectiveness of a service delivery is a function of how well, in the mind of the customer, the service was delivered. Low customer contact may allow a service organisation to pursue internally focused measures such as low cost and efficiency. Whereas, a high customer contact may require that the service organisation pursues externally focused measures pertaining to customer satisfaction.
>
> **Capacity choices:** From this discussion, we can easily understand that a service system designed with high customer contact may need to have a capacity in excess of average requirements. The organisation will be better off with moderate levels of utilisation.
>
> **Location of facilities:** Service organisations designed with a high degree of customer contact must look into the issue of location of facilities very carefully. Since customer participation in the service creation becomes inevitable in high customer contact situations, locating the service delivery system in a convenient place is very important.

➤ **Operational control:** The nature and level of operational control that must be put in place also depends on the level of customer contact. The variability of the service is likely to be more in a high customer contact system as each customer will bring his/her own peculiarity. Training and skill development of the service personnel and ensuring a high quality of service are some of the crucial aspects of a high customer contact service delivery system.

SERVICE BLUEPRINTING

In a manufacturing organisation, layout planning enables the operations manager to easily locate the resources in a shop floor so that:

- Jobs travel smaller distances.
- Are not handled too frequently and unnecessarily.
- Spend less time in the system before it is completed.

In the case of a service system as well, these necessities are equally important. For example, if we visit the local branch of the Life Insurance Corporation (LIC) of India Limited to process a new policy, similar requirements need to be met. We should not be travelling up and down across various departments to complete the task. We may not also like our requirements to be handled multiple times by multiple workforces. For instance, when we make a telephonic contact with a service provider, we find that the call is often transferred to other departments and each time we have to narrate the whole story all over again. This reflects a bad process and system design.

However, the major point of departure is with respect to the role of the customer. The customer often "co-creates" the service along with the service provider, other challenges crop up and need to be addressed over and above the issues mentioned so far.

Some of these are as follows:

➤ In a service system, the customer directly interacts with the service provider. Therefore, appropriate structural mechanisms must be in place to make the process simple, easy to use, and comfortable for the customer.

➤ The form of the place where the service is provided in itself influences the impressions and the service quality aspects. Hence, paying careful attention to the aesthetics and ambience of the system is very important while doing layout planning.

➤ Organisations have alternative choices with respect to customer contact and service complexity. These choices reflect in the service positioning. Certain aspects of the service need not be uncovered to the customer; therefore, layout planning for such elements of the service delivery could be very different from those in which there is direct customer contact. An example of this is the restaurant. In a restaurant, the layout for the kitchen and the stores is vastly different from that of the dining area.

Finally, the starting point in the layout design of a service system is to plot various activities affecting the service delivery process and identifying exactly how each step of the service delivery process will make an impact with respect to the service positioning strategy. Once this is done, the steps that require direct involvement and interaction of the customers could be isolated for one kind of layout planning and the rest with no direct customer interaction could be considered for an alternative layout planning.

The tool used to do this is known as service blueprinting.

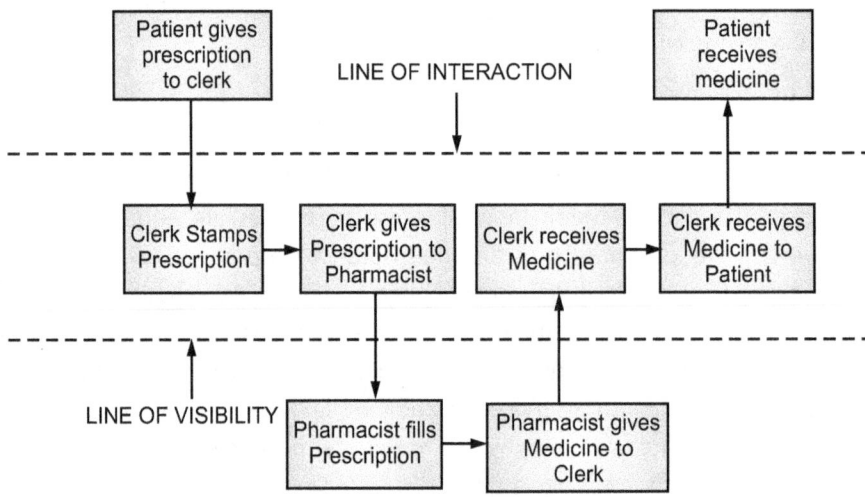

Fig. 2.6: Service Blueprinting

Service blueprinting is a method by which the service delivery process is broken down into individual parts through a step-by-step mapping of the process. Service blueprinting helps organisations to:

- Design
- Monitor
- Control and improve processes and the service delivery system.

While this is very similar to a process mapping done in manufacturing systems to analyse processes, we put on top a few more elements to make it relevant for service systems. We shall define these new aspects related, service blueprinting before using an example to understand this.

> **Line of interaction:** In a service layout planning exercise we need to draw the line of interaction. This line separates all the activities in which the customer has to have a direct interaction with the service provider as part of the service creation and delivery process.

- **Line of visibility:** This line includes all the structural, planning, and interactional elements of a service delivery process that fall within the eyesight of the customer. For example, in a restaurant, the kitchen is not in the line of visibility. However, the parking lots, the washroom, the eating space, the cash counter, the front lawns, and the food delivery counter are all in the line of visibility.
- **Front Office:** All aspects of a service delivery system that are in the line of visibility of a customer will be part of the front office. Essentially, the front office provides the customer with ample opportunities to discover his/her moments of truth about the service delivery process, the quality, the people, and a host of other issues.
- **Back office:** All aspects of a service delivery process that are behind (or beyond) the line of visibility constitute the back office. Customers normally do not have access to these aspects of the service delivery process as these are meant for internal interactions among the service delivery personnel. The back office may operate as a support arm for the front-line staff by providing them with data, information, planning tools, and processing support on several aspects of a service.

Let us try to understand these concepts using the example of a hospital. Suppose you want to visit a consultant in the Cardiac Department of a hospital. First, you call the cardiac department and ask for an appointment. You follow this up with a visit to the hospital at the appointed time. The receptionist first collects the consulting fee and extracts the file from the records room. If you are a first-time visitor, you also go through a registration process. You wait for your turn to meet the doctor. The doctor interacts with you and gets additional tests done, if required, before prescribing appropriate medicines. Finally, you will visit the pharmacy, buy the prescribed medicines and leave the hospital.

All structural elements in the line of visibility require a careful approach when it comes to layout planning. Cleanliness, comfort, convenience, proper lighting of the place, provision of adequate spaces, clear signage and unambiguous instructions are certain aspects of layout design. Also, the employees operating in the front office require good communication skills, the right attitude and temperament in dealing with the customers.

On the other hand, employees in the back office require greater planning and technical skills than interpersonal skills to match the efficiency in the operations generated by the other counterparts of the service delivery system.

Points to Remember

- A process based viewpoint facilitates a complete understanding of the various aspects of operations management.
- **A process viewpoint** essentially involves identifying the input, output, and the processing and feedback mechanisms in a system.

- Improper choice of capacity deployed and poor planning of the existing capacity will lead to loss of productivity.
- **A process** is the basic building block of operations. It is made up of a set of activities that need to be carried out by combining resources and time.
- The success of designing a process depends on the extent of detailing gathered by the Operations Manager.
- A pictorial representation of all this information should be developed using a process flow-charting methods.
- **Process flow-charting** employs a set of standard symbols and graphical tools to represent all the information about the process.
- **A process flow chart helps an operations manager as:**
    - It provides a pictorial and compact representation of the process.
    - It ensures faster and better understanding of the various aspects of the process.
    - By superimposing additional information such as the time taken for each stage of the process, certain useful measures can be computed.
    - For example, the management may be able to estimate the time required to complete the process.
    - Using this information, the management can also identify the bottlenecks in the process and the productive capacity of the process.
    - The management can also assess the amount of resources that need to be deployed at each stage in order to meet the projected requirements.
- The designing of manufacturing processes essentially consists of certain choices we make with respect to the flow of parts in a manufacturing system.
- If the manufacturing system is designed for a wide range of products, it demands a certain type of process design, as opposed to one that mass-produces just one or two variations of a product.
- **Volume** indicates the quantity of products produced in a manufacturing system.
- **Variety** refers to the number of sub categories of products and variants of each product produced in a manufacturing system
- Irrespective of the nature of activities involved, all manufacturing systems require some input material where the processes start. The material undergoes a conversion process from the raw material phase to the finished goods phase. Flow indicates the nature and intensity of this phenomenon.

- In general, volume and variety will have an inverse relationship. When the volume of production is very high, the firm is likely to be engaged in manufacturing fewer varieties of products.
- Process characteristics are largely determined by the flow of products in a manufacturing system.
- A continuous flow system is characterised by a streamlined flow of products in the operating system. The production process is sequential and the required resources are organised in stages. Continuous flow is largely a result of technological constraints and a high volume of production.
- **Job Production:** Job production is used to create one-off orders or 'jobs' especially made for the purpose.
- **Batch Production:** As the name suggests, products are produced in small or large batches. This process is useful to a firm that makes a number of different variations of basically similar products.
- **Flow production:** This is a production line method, where the product is continuously produced, flowing from one stage of production to the next.
- Product and process designs make up an integral part of the conversion process.
- A product layout simplifies production planning and control problems.
- The advantages of process layouts include greater flexibility and optimum utilisation of resources.
- Designing operations systems involves making choices for the location, technology, capacity, and layout of the system. These decisions directly influence other aspects of the operations, such as the people and skills to be deployed and the planning methodology to be put in place.

Questions for Discussion

1. Enumerate key aspects of process characteristics in operations. How they influence the process of an organisation?
2. What is the relationship between Volume, Variety and Flow with respect to a process design?
3. Elaborate the difference between Continuous Flow System and Intermittent Flow system.

4. Explain salient features of Intermittent Manufacturing.

5. What are key aspects of service process design? How are they different from manufacturing process design?

6. What is the role of customer contact in service system design?

7. What you understand by service blue printing? Explain capacity planning issues in service sector. How you will measure service quality?

8. Explain key aspects of process characteristics in operations.

9. Explain the dependency between Volume, Variety and Flow.

10. Explain difference between Product Layout and Process Layout.

11. What factors are to be considered while designing plant layout for a plant manufacturing number of consumer products under same roof?

12. Select suitable layout for each of following situations and justify your selection:

    (a) Ball Bearing manufacturing plan

    (b) Manufacturing of Bakharwadi at Chitale's

    (c) Repairs and overhaul of S.T. buses

    (d) Fabricator of solar water heaters

    (e) Manufacturer of large Windmills

    (f) Motor cycle manufacturer with production of one million per month.

Questions from Previous Examinations

1. What is the Basis of Selecting a Production System such as Batch production, Mass Production or Flexible Manufacturing System. Explain all factors considered ?
   [April 2006]

2. Explain various types of Manufacturing Methods, their basis of Selection and Characteristics. **[April 2007]**

3. What are the different Types of Layout ? How should an Organisation decide on which Layout to Choose ? **[April 2009]**

4. Discuss the Characteristics of Batch Production. **[April 2010]**

5. Give Examples and Characteristics of Various Methods of Manufacturing.

    [December 2010]

6. Explain the salient features of Intermittent Production with respect to in Process inventory, Materials handling, Layout of manufacturing facilities. **[April 2012]**

7. Discuss with example the Various Manufacturing Systems. State the Distinguishing Features of any two of them. **[December 2011]**

Chapter **3**...

Production Planning and Control (PPC)

Contents ...

3.1 Production Planning and Control (PPC)
    3.1.1 Objectives of the Production Planning and Control
    3.1.2 Functions of Production Planning and Control

3.2 Demand Forecasting
    3.2.1 Forecasting as a Planning Tool
    3.2.2 Forecasting Time Horizon
    3.2.2 (a) Short-term Forecasting
    3.2.2 (b) Medium-term Forecasting
    3.2.2 (c) Long-term Forecasting
    3.2.3 Sources of Data for Forecasting
    3.2.4 Accuracy of Forecast

3.3 Production Planning
    3.3.1 Aggregate production Planning
    3.3.2 Need for Aggregate Production Planning (APP)
    3.3.3 Alternatives for Managing Demand and Supply
    3.3.4 Master Production Schedule
    3.3.5 Capacity Planning
    3.3.6 Overview of MRP, CRP, DRP, MRP II

3.4 Production Control
    3.4.1 Scheduling
    3.4.2 Loading
    3.4.3 Scheduling for Job Shops and Floor Shops
    3.4.4 Gantt Charts

- Points to Remember
- Questions for Discussion
- Questions from Previous Examinations

Learning Objectives:
> To study Production Planning and Control (PPC) and understand its applicability in the manufacturing units
> To understand the techniques and flow of demand forecasting
> To define the scope and importance of Production Planning and study its tools and techniques
> To define the scope and importance of Production Control and study its tools and techniques

Introduction

In this chapter, we shall study the techniques of planning and control in accordance with the forecasting tools, and planning and control mechanisms executed by the organisation in optimising the efficiency of the manufacturing unit. As we saw earlier, process plays a very significant role in deciding the altitude of success of a unit. Similarly, the planning and controlling techniques work out the minimisation of deviations from the planned activities.

We will be studying ahead various important concepts such as Production Planning and Control, Demand Forecasting and the methods of Planning and Control which feed the optimisation of the output of an organisation.

3.1 Production Planning and Control (PPC)

As discussed in the previous chapter, once the decision has been taken regarding the product design and production processes and system, the next task is to take steps for production planning and control, as this function is essentially required for efficient and economical production system.

> *"The highest efficiency in production is obtained by manufacturing the required quantity of a product, of the required quality, at the required time by the best and cheapest method".*

PPC is a tool which is used to coordinate all manufacturing activities in a production system.

Production planning and control fundamentally consists of planning the production in a manufacturing organisation before actual production activities start and exercising control actions to ensure that the planned production is achieved in terms of quantity, quality, repayment schedule, delivery schedule and cost of production.

The various activities involved in production planning are:

- Designing the layout of physical facilities, material and material handling system.
- Determining the sequence of operations and the nature of the operations to be performed along with the requirements, and
- Specifying certain production quality and quality levels.

Objective of production planning is to provide a physical system together with a set of operationing guidelines for effective conversion of raw materials, human skills and other inputs into finished goods. Production Planning is a managerial function which is mainly concerned with the following important issues:

- What production facilities are required for our process?
- How these production facilities should be laid down in the area available for production? and

- How they should be utilised in order to produce the desired products at the desired cost and efficiency of production.

Broadly speaking, production planning is concerned with two main aspects:
- Routing or planning work tasks.
- Layout or three-dimensional relationship between the resources.

Production planning is dynamic in nature and always remains in fluid state as plans may have to be changed according to the changes in circumstances. Production control on the other hand is a mechanism to monitor the execution of the plans. It has several important functions:

- Making sure that production operations have been started at planned places and scheduled times.
- Observing the progress of the operations and recording it properly.
- Analysing the recorded data with our plans and measuring the deviations.
- Taking immediate corrective actions to minimise the negative impact of deviations from the plans.
- Feeding back the recorded information to the planning section in order to improve the future plans.

Production planning is an activity that is performed before the actual production process takes place. It involves determining the schedule of production, sequence of operations, economic batch quantities, and also the dispatching priorities for sequencing of jobs.

Production control is mainly involved in implementing production schedules and is the corollary to short-term production planning or scheduling. Production control includes initiating production, dispatching items, progressing and then finally reporting back to the production planning. In general terms, production planning means planning of the work to be done later and production control refers to working out or the implementation of the plan.

3.1.1 Objectives of the Production Planning and Control

1. To deliver superior quality goods in required quantities to the customer within the planned delivery schedule to achieve maximum customer satisfaction and minimise the costs.
2. To ensure optimum utilisation of all resources.
3. To minimise the product through-put time or production / manufacturing cycle time.
4. To maintain optimum inventory levels for smooth operations.
5. To maintain flexibility in manufacturing operations.

6. To co-ordinate between labour and machines and various supporting departments.
7. To plan for plant capacities for future requirements.
8. To remove bottle necks at all stages of production and to solve problems related to production.
9. To ensure effective cost reduction and cost control.

3.1.2 Functions of Production Planning and Control

The functions of Production Planning and Control have been discussed ahead:

1. **Materials:**
   Raw materials, finished products and bought-out components should be made available in required quantities and at the required time to ensure the correct beginning and end for each operation resulting in uninterrupted production. This function includes the specification of materials (quality and quantity), delivery dates, variety reduction (standardisations), procurement and make (or) buy decisions.

2. **Methods:**
   This function is concerned with the analysis of alternatives and selection of the best method with due consideration to the constraints imposed. Developing specification and determination of sequence of operations for the processes are important aspects of production planning and control.

3. **Machine and equipment:**
   This function is related with the detailed analysis of available production facilities, equipment down time, maintenance policy, procedure and schedule.

4. **Manpower:**
   Another function is to maintain the availability of appropriate manpower on appropriate machines at the right time.

5. **Process planning (Routing):**
   It is concerned with selection of path route, which the raw materials should follow to get transferred into the finished products.
   - Fixation of path of travel, giving due consideration to layout.
   - Breaking down of operations to define each operation in detail.
   - Deciding set up time and process time for each operation.

6. **Estimating:**
   Once the overall method and sequence of operations are fixed and process sheet for each operation is available, then the operation times are estimated. This function is carried out using extensive analysis of operations along with methods of routing and a standard time for operation is estimated using work measurement techniques.

7. **Loading and scheduling:**
Scheduling is concerned with preparation of machine loads and fixation of starting and completion date for each of the operations. Machines have to be loaded according to their capability of performing the given task and their capacity.
   - Loading the machines as per their capability and capacity.
   - Determining the starting and completion time for each operation.
   - To coordinate with sales department regarding delivery schedules.

8. **Dispatching:**
This is the execution phase of planning. It is the process of setting production activities in option through release of orders and instructions. It authorises the start of production activities by releasing materials, components, tools, fixtures and instruction sheets to the operators.
   - To assign definite work to particular machines, work centers and men.
   - To issue required material from stores; and also to issue jigs and fixtures and make them available at the correct point of use.
   - Release necessary work orders, time tickets, etc., to authorise timely start of operations.
   - To record start and finish time of each job on each machine (or) by each man.

9. **Expediting:**
This is the control tool that keeps a close observation on the progress of the work. It is a logical step after dispatching which is called follow-up (or) progress. It coordinates extensively to execute the production plan. Professing function can be divided into three parts, i.e. follow-up of materials, follow-up of work-in progress and follow-up of assembly.
   - Identification of bottlenecks and delays and interruptions because of which the production schedule may be disrupted.
   - To devise action plans (remedies) for rectifying the errors.
   - To ensure that production rates are in the line with schedule.

10. **Inspection:**
It is a major control tool. Though the aspects of quality control are elements of a separate function, it is important to production planning and control, both for the execution of the current plans and its scope for future planning. This forms a basis for becoming aware of the limitations with respect to method, processes etc.

11. **Evaluation:**
This stage is crucial to the improvement of productive efficiency. A thorough analysis of all the factors influencing the production planning and control helps to identify the weak spots and the corrective actions with respect to pre-planning and planning will be affected by a feedback. The success of this step depends on the communication, data and information gathering and analysis.

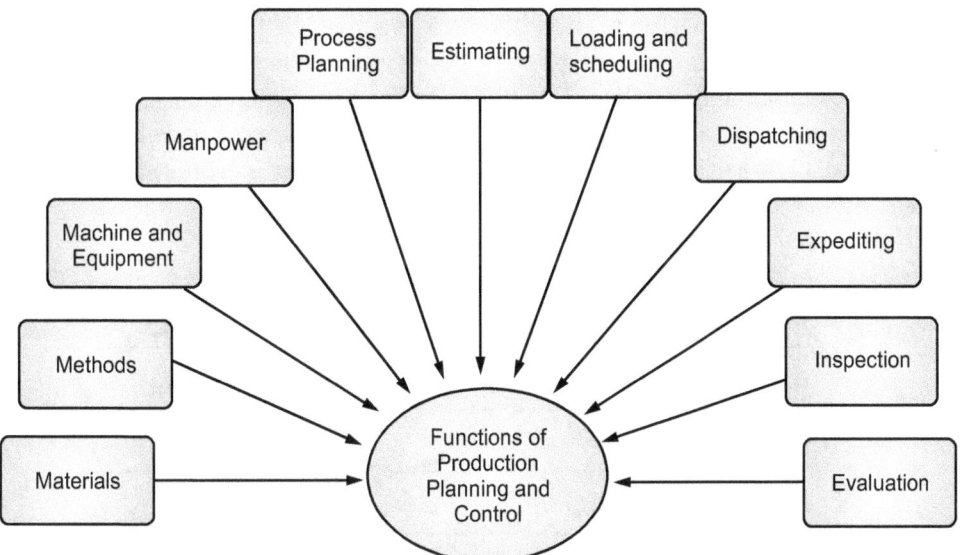

Fig 3.1 Functions of Production Planning and Control

3.2 Demand Forecasting

Forecasting is the process of making statements about events whose actual outcomes (typically) have not yet been observed.

Demand forecasting seeks to investigate and measure the forces that determine sales for existing and new products. Generally companies plan their business – production or sales in anticipation of future demand. Hence forecasting future demands becomes important. The art of successful business lies in avoiding or minimising the risks involved as far as possible and faces the uncertainties in a most befitting manner. Demand forecasting and estimation gives businesses valuable information about the markets in which they operate and the markets they plan to pursue. Forecasting and estimation are interchangeable terms that basically mean predicting what will happen in the future. If businesses do not use demand forecasting and estimation, they risk entering markets that have no need for the business's product.

The purpose of demand forecasting and estimation is to find a business's potential demand, so managers can make accurate decisions about pricing, business growth and market potential. Managers base pricing on demand trends in the market. For example, if the market demands for pizza is high in a city but there are few competitors, managers know they can price pizzas higher as compared to if the demand was lower. Established businesses use demand forecasting and estimation if they consider entering a new market. If the demand for their product is currently low, but will increase in the future, they will wait to enter the market. Managers and business owners use multiple techniques for demand forecasting and estimation. Using historical data is one method to determine the potential demand for a product or service. For example, businesses with high-end merchandise might examine census information to determine the average income of an area. Larger businesses might use test markets to estimate demand. Test markets are micromarkets in small cities that are similar to larger markets. If the demand for a product is high in the test market, managers assume that the product will perform well in the larger market.

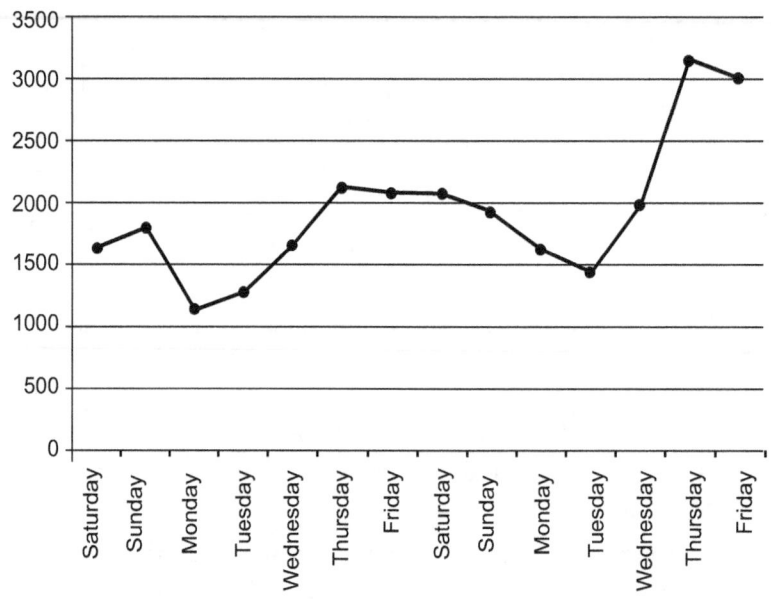

Fig. 3.2: Sample Demand Forecasting Graph

Demand forecasting and estimation is critical for inventory management. Businesses buy inventory based upon demand forecasts. For example, grocery stores increase their stock of certain items during hurricane season because they know from past data that demand increases. If businesses do not use accurate demand forecasting and estimation methods, they risk purchasing too much or too little inventory. Businesses with too much inventory might lose some of it to time and expiration dates. Businesses with too little inventory will upset customers and miss revenue opportunities. Demand forecasting and estimation methods are typically accurate for short-term business planning. Estimating demand for the long-term is difficult because there are many unforeseen factors that influence demand over time. For example, demand estimation might not take into account an economic recession or other financial problems. Natural disasters might also affect the demand for a business's product. To forecast long-term demand, managers must account for the social, political and economic history of their markets.

3.2.1 Forecasting as a Planning Tool

Before we understand how forecasting can be used as a planning tool, let us first understand the difference between planning, budgeting and forecasting. Though these terms seem to be similar and interchangeably usable, there is a considerable difference between them. This difference can be mapped as follows:

- Planning is usually the first step in setting up a small business, and continues to be used as things progress. Planning could be something simple like building your daily agenda, or long-range enough to envision where you want to see your business in five to 10 years. Some planning is done by the seat of the pants, with little more raw data than your vision for the business. But as more information is available, the planning focus sharpens. Once the business idea takes shape, you might put together a more formal business plan to outline who your customers are, where you plan to make your money and how you intend to attract new customers.

- Businesses set up how they will spend money with a budget. Budgets determine how existing financial resources are allocated. Budgets are usually set by how previous money was spent and expected income. The budgets often dictate how much is spent toward payroll, supplies and advertising expenses. Budgets tend to be closer to real-life action. While a plan or forecast can be wrong, an error-ridden budget invites financial disaster. Most companies set their budgets at the beginning of a calendar or fiscal year, and many leave some room for adjustment as revenues increase or decrease.

- Once you get an idea of how much money you're making through your business, you can start long-term forecasting to determine what you might be able to do in the long term. A forecast is based on past and current business numbers. A forecast might be inaccurate, so it would be a mistake to base a budget on that. Far from being an exercise in futility, though, forecasting acts to serve as a basis for further planning.

Budgeting, planning and forecasting are all useful tools when you run a business. It takes a plan to get things off the ground. The plan continues to serve through the life of the business. Budgeting works close to the operating side and determines how things will run in the present and immediate future. Forecasting, while every bit was uncertain as the future, can help clarify things regarding business far in advance.

Managerial decision making is often complicated due to an element of uncertainty in the variables affecting the decision-making process. For example, when the decision to build a new production facility is made, the demand for its products is not known with precision. Similarly, when a hospital chooses to add one more specialty healthcare wing, it needs to make some assumptions about the demand for the facility. Since these decisions often involve considerable cash flow and time in creating new facilities, accurate estimates of the future events for which the decisions have been made are crucial. Forecasting is a very important branch of operations management that addresses these issues and provides the manager with a set of tools and techniques for the estimation process.

For example, a tea shop operates in the vicinity of a commercial centre. As a large number of customers visit the commercial centre, one could expect a good demand for tea and snacks. Let us suppose that the owner of the tea shop estimates the daily demand for tea to be 3,000 cups. However, this information is not sufficient for the owner to service the demand. The timing of the demand is very crucial. For example, if 40 per cent of the estimated demand happens in just two blocks of two hours each in the morning and the evening, then the nature of planning and even operational practices during these peak hours could be very different. Manufacturing and service systems experience peak demand during certain times and average or even low demand during other times. Hence, estimating the timing of the demand is as important as estimating its magnitude.

The timing of the occurrence of events is not only important in short-term planning, as described; it is equally important in several other situations. Let us consider another example. Suppose a manufacturer of household appliances decides to add one more product line—microwave ovens—to its existing product portfolio. The decision to add microwave ovens to the product line requires a good understanding of the nature of demand for the range of microwave ovens proposed to be manufactured. Depending on both the timing and the magnitude of the demand, the manufacturer will schedule the building of new plants, planning of the product launch, and the creation of the necessary infrastructure for the marketing and distribution of the microwave ovens.

Forecasting is an important tool in public policy decisions as well. For example, the Government of India needs to have a reasonable estimate of the population growth over the next 10-20 years in order to formulate long-term plans for creating infrastructure for transportation and the development of cities and towns. Based on the estimates of population growth, the government may formulate detailed plans to channel investment into certain sectors of industry. Another example is the meteorological department's annual forecasting exercise to predict the monsoons.

In all these examples, we see that forecasting plays a vital role. Specifically, one can identify the following key functions of forecasting:

➢ An estimation tool.
➢ A way of addressing the complex and uncertain environment surrounding business decision making.
➢ A tool for predicting events related to operations planning and control.
➢ A vital prerequisite for the planning process in organisations.

3.2.2 Forecasting Time Horizon

The importance of forecasting is easily understood by our previous discussion. However, the type of data used, the nature of analysis done, and the tools and techniques employed will vary from time to time. Therefore, it is useful to understand what causes these variations and how one can sub-classify and group such situations. Amongst other parameters, the time horizon for forecasting provides a sound basis for classification. Forecasting based on time horizon can be mainly classified in three categories:

1) Short Term Forecasting
2) Medium Term Forecasting
3) Long Term Forecasting

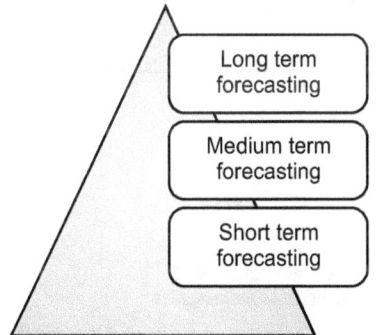

Fig. 3.3: Forecasting on Time Horizon

3.2.2 (a) Short-term Forecasting

Typically, short-term forecasting is employed to tune an existing plan on the basis of the latest available information. Forecasting acts as a tool for the tactical decisions that an organisation makes. For example, based on the sales in the last quarter, an organisation could develop better estimates of the demand in the next quarter and use that information for adjusting various quarterly plans. The errors in forecasting that are sought to be corrected by an alternative estimate are more related to random events than any long-term cyclical patterns or medium-term seasonal patterns. The forecasting data is used in a disaggregated fashion. For example, the sales data will be analysed by the region and the product variety for possible short-term impact in a particular region or for a variant of a product. Specific corrective measures could be taken after analysis of the response from the market. The techniques used in this case are simple extrapolation of the immediate past data and mechanisms for the integration of new data and period-by-period adjustments.

Table 3.1: Forecasting time horizon - some implications

Particulars	Short-term Forecasts	Medium-term Forecasts	Long-term Forecasts
Normal duration	1 to 90 days	1 year to 5 years	5 years to 10 years
Nature of decision	Purely tactical	Tactical and strategic	Purely strategic
Important considerations	Random (short-term) effects	Seasonal and cyclical effects	Long-term trends and business cycles
Nature of data Required	Mostly quantitative	Subjective and quantitative	Largely subjective
Degree of uncertainty	Low	Significant	High
Some examples	• Revising quarterly production plans • Rescheduling supply of raw material	• Annual production planning • Capacity augmentation	• New product introduction • Facilities location decisions • New business development

3.2.2 (b) Medium-term Forecasting

An organisation uses forecasting as an inception to the annual business planning exercises. This typically constitutes medium-term forecasting. In medium-term forecasting, the planning horizon is usually one year to five years. During this period, some accumulation of data is done. For example, if an organisation offers 15 variations of a product, the demand for the product is estimated at a macro level. Based on this information, capacity and material plans are be made. Since the forecasting is done for a slightly longer time, cyclical and seasonal patterns will make a significant impact and need to be incorporated in the analysis. The decisions taken using the forecasting information vary from purely tactical decisions such as annual production planning to somewhat strategic ones such as expansion of capacity in specific areas of business. Use of analytical methods, some subjective judgment and regression-based methodologies are often employed in medium-term forecasting.

3.2.2 (c) Long-term Forecasting

Long-term forecasts involve purely strategic decisions for a time period of about five years to ten years, so the forecasting processes need to cater to these requirements. For instance, an organisation may be projecting the future technology trends in their business and using it as the basis for developing new products, production technology, and human and other resources. Strategic decisions substantially draw particular knowledge from the expertise of senior management personnel in an organisation involved in the decision making. Furthermore, the level of uncertainty in the process tends to be high. Therefore, the forecasting approach should be able to use this data and develop reliable estimates. Some amount of detailed modeling based on some macro-level assumptions is often required for the success of this method.

3.2.3 Sources of Data for Forecasting

Forecasting is often as good as the quantity and quality of data that is available with an organisation performing a forecasting exercise. This is particularly true of forecasting exercises used for the purpose of planning. Therefore, it is important to know the type of data required and the normal sources through which such data could be collected.

1. **Sales Personnel Estimates:**

For every organisation, one of the most valuable sources of data is the sales department that operates in the field. Since the sales force spans the entire geographical area of operations, they have access to data on the actual consumption and the changing patterns in consumption in the market. They may also have information on the performance of competitor brands and the overall patterns in market share and market growth. An organisation will have to set up information-tracking mechanisms where the sales force can make periodic entries of actual consumption in the immediate past and also help us with the projected trends. Using this data, organisations can make an end-use analysis to project emerging scenarios in market demand and one's own share of the total demand. Moreover, the data obtained from the sales force is very valuable in short-term forecasting and medium term forecasting corrections in production and sales planning.

2. **Point of Sales (POS) Data Systems:**

Advances in information technology have enabled organisations to capture data at the point of sale using POS systems. Consider, for example, that you walk into a supermarket and buy a 500-gram Surf Excel pack. At the check-out counter, when the salesperson swipes the pack through a POS system, the data is captured and transmitted to the relevant database for the company for analysis. Using this technology, as a customer buys a unit of a product at a retail counter, the information is captured and instantaneously transferred to a common database. By developing systems to periodically analyse these databases, organisations can dramatically improve their planning and inventory management systems. These translate into efficient consumer response and better supply chain management. We can find such systems in use in Indian retail chains such as Big Bazaar, More, and Reliance Mart.

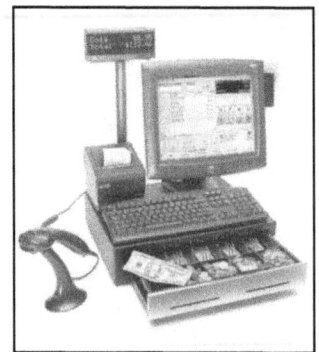

3. **Forecasts from Supply Chain Partners:**

Obtaining POS data is often not easy. Distributors and retailers (also known as supply chain partners) hesitate to share information. They often perceive a threat arising out of loss of their power. Hence, organisations often have to rely on their supply chain partners to obtain data on actual sales during a period. Moreover, supply chain partners provide vital information on market trends, competitor performance, and overall market sentiments and projections. These estimates are crucial for accurate forecasting of future demand, particularly during annual planning processes.

4. **Trade/Industry Association Journals:**

There are some useful sources of data for long-term forecasts. The most important among these are trade/industry association journals. These journals provide syndicated and researched data on the sector in which the organisation is operating. Such journals serve as antennae to catch the buzz on future developments and long-term directions for the industry. In addition to these, several market research firms and management consultancy companies also provide crucial sector-wise data of the market. This data is useful for forecasting purposes.

5. **B2B Portals/Marketplaces:**

B2B portals are the Business to Business portals available online. This is another useful source of data in the era of the World Wide Web is the existence of industry portals and B2B marketplaces. These are the digital variations of trade and industry association journals. B2B, marketplaces and powerful search engines on the Web provide a vital source of data for the purpose of long-term forecasting.

6. Economic Surveys and Indicators:

Studies conducted by research organisations on macroeconomic trends are good indicators of emerging trends in the consumption patterns of several classes of goods and services. Consider an organisation interested in finding out the demand for high-definition TV& (HDTVs) over the next five years. Clearly, the demand for HDTVs is influenced by the income-level distribution in the population, the prevailing taxation policies, the level of disposable income, the growth of related technology, literacy levels, and the rate of urbanisation. Economic research agencies such as the Central Statistical Organisation (CSO) and the Centre for Monitoring Indian Economy (CMIE) provide useful data to model these situations and estimate the emerging demand for such products.

7. Subjective Knowledge:

Several long-term forecasts enable strategic decision making. Since strategic decision making involves the use of considerable amounts of qualitative information, senior managers and subject experts are vital sources of such data. A forecasting system should be able to develop mechanisms to systematically collect and codify such data and use them for fruitful use in situations involving long-term strategic decisions.

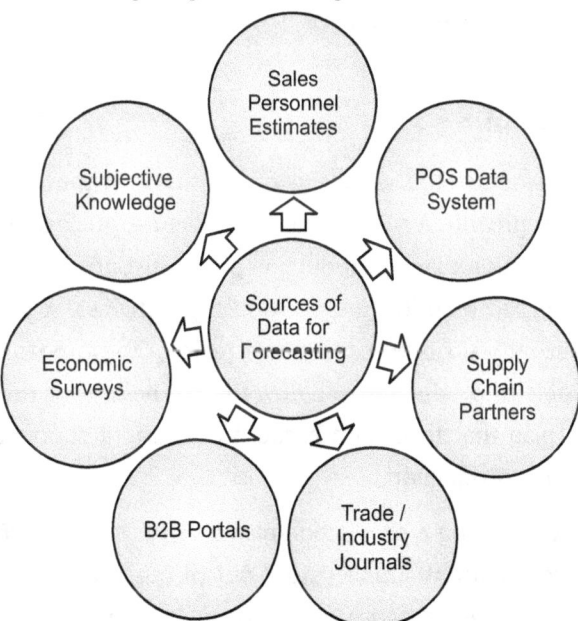

Fig 3.4: Sources of Data for Forecasting

Once the forecasting system designer has identified the sources of data appropriate for his/her requirements, the focus shifts to building the forecasting logic. In order to do this, the forecasting designer has to make use of several models available for developing a forecasting system. These models vary in terms of the nature of data employed, the manner in which the future estimates are made, and the level of mathematical treatment the data is subjected to.

3.2.4 Accuracy of Forecast

Once the researcher has calculated the forecast with a base of the assumptions and data sources as discussed earlier, the next important step is to judge the accuracy of such forecasts. There are various quantitative methods for calculating the accuracy of such forecasts. By understanding and interpreting the forecasts and the developments in the market demand, the researcher calculates the accuracy of the forecasts which have been made and reports the same to the higher level management for undertaking any further decisions required to be taken in that respect.

Once these calculations and interpretations are obtained, the higher level management checks the deviations and takes the necessary decisions regarding the corrective plans to reduce such deviations and improve the efficiency and effectiveness of such forecasts.

Capacity Planning:

(Discussed in detail later in this chapter)

3.3 Production Planning

Business plans are essential to the success of a business. Without them, businesses have no direction or plans for growth. A plan details the structure, goals and nature of a business and incorporates a production plan. A production plan is just one part of an overall business plan, and it serves as a road map for future production activities. A production plan gets a small business idea one step closer to becoming a reality. The purpose of a production plan is to lay out the schedule of production and how the business plans maintain that schedule. It is a medium-range plan that takes into account the current supply and demand factors involved in the company's production.

An important part of writing a production plan involves explicitly stating where you will purchase supplies. If your current supplier goes out of business, you need to know where you can buy alternate supplies so that production is not interrupted and you can maintain your production schedule. A production plan also details the production process for a business owner. It describes the production methods and techniques to be used that maximise the use of resources, such as supplies and time. For example, a production plan for a jewellery making business might state that the pieces will be completed one at a time by the owner within an hour instead of in an assembly-line fashion with two or three helpers to help.

3.3.1 Aggregate Production Planning

Aggregate Production Planning is a planning exercise done for operations using data at an aggregate level. Aggregate production planning serves the critical role of transforming the business plans and strategic intent to operational decisions. Using an aggregate production planning (APP) exercise, firms determine the quantity and timing of resources to be sourced to ensure continuous flow of goods and services to the customers. Usually, these decisions involve:

- The amount of resources to be committed,
- The rate at which goods and services need to be produced during a period, and
- The inventory to be carried forward from one period to the next.

To brief, under Aggregate Production Planning, three critical decisions are made:

- The rate of production,
- The amount of inventory to carry, and
- The amount of resource (in terms of working hours) to be committed on a period-by-period basis.

The entire planning exercise is done on the basis of some aggregate unit. There is no single basis on which the demand data is aggregated. The only requirement is the need to establish uniformities between variations. For example, suppose that one standard model of a bicycle takes 30 machine-hours to manufacture, a deluxe model takes 60 machine-hours, and a sports model takes 90 machine-hours. It is obvious that manufacturing one deluxe model is equivalent to manufacturing two standard models and manufacturing one sports model is equivalent to manufacturing three standard models. Then a monthly demand of 1,000 bicycles of the basic model, 500 of the deluxe model, and 250 of the sports model can be aggregated as 2,750 basic models on the basis of machine-hours.

Typically, the aggregated unit turns out to be a measure of the capacity of the company. For example,

- A steel processing mill may make several variations of steel but may prefer to do the APP on the basis of number of heats that can be extracted from a furnace.
- A textile manufacturer may manufacture several varieties of cloth but may plan on the basis of metres of cloth production.

Hence, APP can be viewed as a capacity planning exercise over the medium term of 9-12 months.

3.3.2 Need for Aggregate Production Planning (APP)

Aggregate Production Planning is mainly required for the following purposes:

1. **Demand fluctuations:**

Organisations hardly experience steady or even demand. As we saw in the previous chapter, several sectors of the manufacturing and service industry experience a significant upswing in demand during certain periods. The demand for garments in India is high between August and October due to the festive season. Former planning is required to meet these swells in demand.

2. **Capacity fluctuations:**

While demand fluctuations occur on account of seasonality, there are fluctuations in capacity too. The capacity available in the month of February will be lower than that in the month of May on account of fewer calendar days. Moreover, scheduled and unscheduled plant shutdowns have a significant impact on capacity availability.

3. **Difficulty level in altering production rates:**

Production systems are complex. Varying the rate of production from one level to another requires some amount of prior planning and coordination with related systems on the supplier and distributor margins. Thus, an organisation manufacturing diesel engines at the rate of 4,000 engines per day cannot individually change it to 5,000 engines. It needs to ensure that the required material, capacity, and other resources are available for the incremental plan. Similarly, it needs to ensure that the distributors have the required capacity to handle the additional load on them.

4. **Benefits of multi-period planning:**

It is known that planning just for a particular period with no consideration of potential events in the near future amounts to a knee-jerk reaction than an attempt to reach optimal and cost-saving decisions. For example, while planning the production for a month, an organisation is better off by taking into consideration the likely scenario in the next few months. If the estimates indicate a rising demand in the next few months, it is better to produce at a slightly higher, although uniform speed and accumulate inventory to handle the additional demand in the future than to react every month. Such month-by-month reactions to the market are not only expensive but also not feasible for the reasons discussed earlier.

Hence, for several reasons, supply and demand may not match exactly on a period-by-period basis in an organisation. For instance, during the festive season, a manufacturer of appliances, such as refrigerators, may experience higher demand than average since many employees might have received bonuses, special festival allowances, and advances. If the manufacturer has sufficient capacity to meet this demand, then the flow is maintained. On the other hand, if the capacity is less, then the organisation has to either forego the unfulfilled demand or try to influence the demand or the supply. Therefore, aggregate production planning is done in an organisation to match the demand with the supply on a period-by-period basis in a cost-effective manner.

3.3.3 Alternatives for Managing Demand and Supply

It is often the practice in organisations to manage demand using some strategies. These strategies basically aim at shifting the demand from one period to another without losing them for want of capacity. Normally, capacity is far in excess of demand during non-peak hours and vice versa during peak hours. Therefore, any attempt to even out the demand by shifting the demand from peak hours to non-peak hours is a necessary step. The aggregate production planning exercise provides a few alternatives to achieve this goal. These alternatives are as follows;

1. **Reservation of Capacity:**

One method used to manage demand is to moderate and shift the excess demand out of a busy period to any future period without completely losing it. Consider, for instance, a multispeciality healthcare unit where patients go for consultation. If there is no reservation of capacity (in this case, the doctor's time for consultation), some patients may go unattended and the hospital might lose the opportunity of servicing the demand. Therefore, an appointment system helps to capture the demand by scheduling the service on another day when there is sufficient capacity. Capacity reservation is a very popular method in services based organisations.

2. **Influencing Demand:**

Another method to manage demand is to influence the demand during a particular period through some tools and encourage customers to willingly shift the demand to other periods when there is comparatively lower demand. This is done by special tariffs, differential discount structures, and limited period product promotions. Consider the differential tariffs promoted by telecommunication companies in the country. The demand for bandwidth tends to be low during late night and early morning (10 p.m. to 9 a.m.). Therefore, to induce customers to use the bandwidth during this time, special rates in the name of happy hours are applied. There are several similar examples, which induce customers to shift the demand from peak to non-peak periods. This includes special off-season discounts for several seasonal products such as the end of season sales in the shopping malls. It is clear that strategies for influencing demand stem largely from a variety of initiatives in the marketing function in an organisation. Therefore, close coordination and planning by production planning and marketing functions is important to implement these set of strategies.

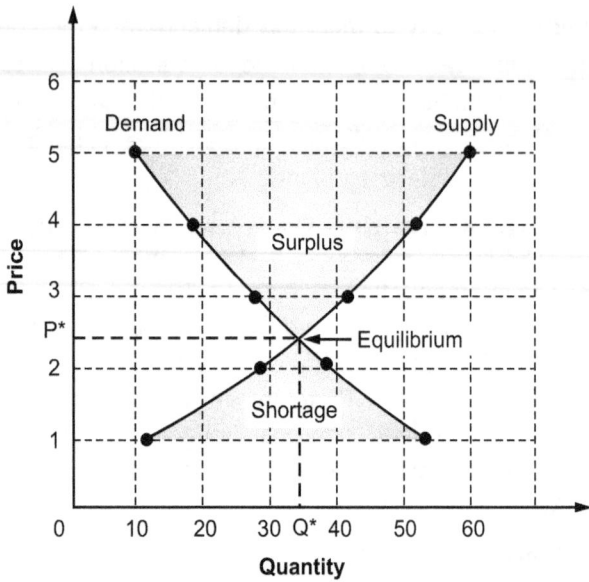

Fig 3.5: Supply and Demand

Organisations have several options to modify supply to meet the demand during a period. Supply can be modified through any one of these alternatives:

- Inventory-based alternatives,
- Capacity adjustment alternatives,
- Capacity augmentation alternatives.

In the case of inventory-related strategies, changes are made in the inventory levels to match the demand with supply whereas in the case of capacity related strategies, changes in capacity availability root corresponding changes in the supply.

Inventory-based Alternatives:

Matching the demand with supply could be done in four ways using inventory.

- By building inventory during periods of lean demand and utilise them during periods of comparatively higher demand. For instance, consider a textile manufacturer such as Arvind Mills. Suppose the forecast demand for denim during the months of April-June is 35,000 metres per month and during July-September is 55,000 meters per month. Let us also assume that the production capacity is 45,000 metres per month. Then, the firm could maintain the production at a level of 45,000 metres during April-September and carry inventory from the first three months to meet the demand during the next three months. Similarly, in a fast-food restaurant, a pre-processed inventory of certain food items is built in the preceding period in order to handle the high demand during peak periods.

> Another option is to back order the current period's demand in a future period. Back ordering is a method of pushing an order to a future period on account of insufficient inventory or capacity to supply during the current period. For example, in a watch manufacturing firm, if the demand for watches during the month of October is 40,000 and if the firm has capacity to manufacture only 30,000 watches and has on-hand inventory of 5,000 watches, then the balance 5,000 watches is scheduled in the month of November, although the demand is for the month of October.

Table 3.2 Different Strategies

Strategies	Description of the Strategies	Costs
Managing Demand	Reservation of capacity	Planning and scheduling costs
	Influencing demand	Marketing-oriented costs
Managing supply	**Inventory based alternatives**	
	(a) Build inventory	• Inventory-holding costs
	(b) Backlog/backorder/shortage	• Shortage/loss of goodwill costs
	Capacity adjustment alternatives	
	(a) Overtime/undertime	• OT premium, lost productivity
	(b) Variable number of shifts	• Shift-change costs
	(c) Hire/lay-off workers	• Training/hiring costs, morale issues
	Capacity augmentation alternatives	
	(a) Subcontract/outsource	• Transaction costs of subcontract
	(b) De-bottleneck	• Annualised de-bottlenecking cost
	(c) Add new capacity	• Annualised cost of new capacity

3.3.4 Master Production Schedule

Master Production Schedule (MPS) represents the critical linking between planning and execution of operations. It is a crucial stage in the production planning process in any organisation after aggregate production planning is done. Aggregate production planning is a rough-cut capacity planning exercise on the basis of forecasted quantities of products. MPS makes use of actual customer orders for the purpose of capacity planning and resource allocation to specific customer orders. As aggregate production planning ensures that adequate capacity is available on a period-by-period basis, organisations need to relate the capacity needs of specific varieties of products and services which they offer against the overall capacity available with them. MPS is the process where dis-aggregation of variations is done. Using this information, additional planning is carried out to assign the required capacity to each variety. At this stage, planning is done for the material required for production during each successive step. Master production scheduling is required for a variety of reasons:

- At the stage of aggregate production planning, the forecasted demand is normally taken for the purpose of estimating the capacity required. However, when actual orders are received, the information sourced from MPS delivers a better input and additional opportunity for the planning exercise.

- APP exercise is to ensure availability of capacity in broader terms. However, as we approach the planning horizon, it is important to relate material and capacity availability to specific varieties of products and services which an organisation plans to produce during a planning horizon. Thus, MPS uses actual and the latest available information while reconsidering the planning problem and ensure specific material and capacity availability in a particular time period.

- As customer orders get revised or cancelled, the information has a bearing on capacity availability. Therefore, as orders flow in, the marketing department may want to know if there is scope for accepting newer order inquiries. The marketing department may also want to know if delivery commitments can be made to customers while accepting orders. The MPS module serves this important purpose of computing capacity available to commit. Based on the disaggregation, capacity planning and materials planning are performed to ensure their adequate availability. If there is some infeasibility in either capacity or material availability, the plans are altered to arrive at feasible production plans. Therefore, MPS determines what needs to be ultimately produced, not what is demanded.

There are two stages involved in MPS. The first step is to update the projected demand based on earlier forecast and current market information. The second step involves disaggregation of product information and linking it to precise material and capacity requirements. After the disaggregation process, it is possible to accurately estimate the amount of material and capacity required for planned units of production of each variety. If either capacity or material is not available, that information is made use of in MPS and plans are re-worked. This is an iterative process and the actual production plan is finally arrived at. The two steps are explained ahead.

Step 1: Integrating current market information into the production plan:

Master Production Schedule is normally done several times during the planning horizon. Therefore, at each instance it is possible that additional information would be available for the planner. Let us assume that the Aggregate Production Planning exercise was done in October for the next financial year which begins in April. At that time the demand for June, July and August would have been based on some forecasting. If the MPS exercise was carried out in the month of April it is possible that some customers would have already placed firm orders. Hence, while planning is done at that time it is important that firm orders are also taken into consideration. If the forecast quantities are higher than the firm orders it is a normal practice to work on the basis of forecasted quantities. On the other hand if the firm orders are more than the forecast quantities, then it is desirable to integrate this information for the purpose of planning. Moreover, between one Master Production Schedule exercise and the other order cancellations, order amendments and new orders are received. Therefore, the MPS exercise must include all this information at the time of planning itself.

Step 2: Disaggregation of product information

At the time of Aggregate Production Planning an aggregate unit was chosen and different varieties of a product or service were converted to a "corresponding" product/service. Thus, it is imperative that the process be reversed at the time of detailed planning. The Master Production Scheduling exercise performs this process known as disaggregation.

Aggregate production planning and master production scheduling are the first two steps in every production planning and control activity in an organisation. These form the critical inputs for further planning and control of operations.

Operations management requires planning and control at various levels and time horizons. Configuration of a manufacturing system at the right location and choice of appropriate process and product designs are issues associated with the long term. On the other hand, aggregate planning and material and capacity requirements planning are issues associated with the medium term. In the same manner, there are multiple issues that we need to address in short-term planning. In the short term, there is more emphasis on operational control than on planning. This, however, does not imply that there is no planning involved. In fact, planning does half the job of control.

"Short term" denotes a time horizon close to real time. Usually, in a majority of manufacturing and service organisations, short term would imply a horizon ranging from a day to at most a week or two. In some special cases, "short term" may mean a few hours or a shift, as in the case of a power transmission firm or an event management firm. One question that comes to our mind is: When we have exercised so much care in the previous stages of planning, why do we still need to continue with the planning exercise? Before we proceed with the concepts and techniques of operations scheduling, it is best to clarify this issue. Planning for the short term becomes inevitable for three important reasons:

- As we approach execution, some additional information becomes available to an organisation. Use of this new information makes the plans far more tough and representative of reality. For instance, some customer orders could be cancelled. Some new orders could be booked, and the terms of the existing orders could be revised. Clearly, considering this information makes operations more accurate than choosing to simply ignore them.
- The occurrence of unexpected events is inevitable in business. These include the sudden breakdown of a machine, absenteeism of skilled labour, delays in the supply of key raw material, and a sudden revision of job priorities. It is not possible to include these details accurately while planning for the medium term as they are unknown. Broad assumptions and approximations are made about these at that time of planning. Therefore, we need to revise these assumptions and fine-tune our planning and decision-making practice.
- In the short term, we need to focus on micro-resources, a single machine, a set of workers, and such other singular aspects. Such a focus is neither possible nor warranted in medium or long-term planning. In the short term, several questions need to be answered.

Operations scheduling has a direct linkage with MRP systems in an organisation. The function of an MRP exercise is to generate feasible production orders and procurement notices. Production orders are nothing but specific sets of instructions to utilise a set of resources for the manufacturing and assembling of the components under question during a particular time period. The shop planners also need to prioritise all such jobs in the shop with respect to each machine they visit, and ensure completion of the job without delay. This indicates that the output of an MRP exercise becomes the input for job scheduling.

3.3.5 Capacity Planning

Capacity planning is an activity which is undertaken to identify the amount of production required to satisfy the demand for the goods and services produced by a business at a period of time. The idea is to balance the purchase of resources, the maintenance of production facilities, the hiring of labour and the final output so that consumers have a steady supply of the goods they demand. At the same time, capacity planning also seeks to increase profits by eliminating unnecessary waste, including the overproduction of any good or service. The actual process of capacity planning will vary significantly from one industry to other. While there are factors unique to each industry which help in shaping the approach of effective planning, there are a few basic elements which tend to relate in any situation. Many of these are concerned with adjusting the amount of production based on anticipated demand for the products, both now and in upcoming production periods. A simple formula for capacity planning in manufacturing situations involves identifying the number of machines used in the production process, along with the labour needed to operate these machines.

Capacity planning is the process of defining the production capacity needed by an organisation to meet changing demands for its products. In the context of capacity planning, "design capacity" is the maximum amount of load that an organisation is capable of effecting in a given period, "effective capacity" is the maximum amount of work that an organisation is capable of completing in a given period due to constraints such as quality problems, delays, material handling, etc. A discrepancy between the capacity of an organisation and the demands of its customers results in inefficiency, either in under-utilised resources or unfulfilled customers. The goal of capacity planning is to minimise this discrepancy. Capacity can be increased by hosting new techniques, equipment and materials, increasing the number of workers or machines, increasing the number of shifts, or acquiring additional production facilities.

3.3.6 Overview of MRP, CRP, DRP, MRP II

1. Material Requirements Planning (MRP):

Material Requirements Planning (MRP) is a software-based production planning and inventory control system used to manage manufacturing processes. Although it is not common nowadays, it is possible to conduct MRP by hand as well. Material Requirements Planning (MRP) is a material planning methodology developed in the 1970's making use of computer technology. The main features of MRP are the creation of material requirements by way of exploding the bills of material, and time-phasing of requirements using posted average lead times. MRP II was developed as the second generation of MRP and it features the closed loop system: production planning drives the master schedule which drives the material plan which works as an input to the capacity plan. An MRP system is intended to simultaneously meet three objectives:

- Ensure materials are available for production and products are available for delivery to customers.
- Maintain the lowest possible level of inventory.
- Plan manufacturing activities, delivery schedules and purchasing activities.

Material requirements planning systems add a level of automation to inventory control. When the minimum and maximum stock levels are set on a simple inventory tracker, the MRP process starts. MRP software takes a bill of goods for the product and explodes it into components and sub-assemblies, adds time factors for both ordering processes and manufacturing cycles, and allows a small-business owner to manage ordering of raw materials.

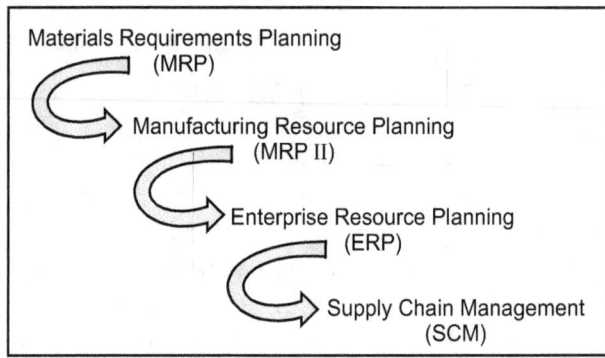

Fig 3.6: Materials Requirement Planning (MRP)

2. **Manufacturing Resource Planning II (MRP II):**

Manufacturing Resource Planning (MRP II) has been evolved from early Materials Requirement Planning (MRP) systems by including the integration of additional data, such as employee and financial needs. Material requirements planning (MRP) and manufacturing resource planning (MRP II) are predecessors of enterprise resource planning (ERP), a business information integration system. Both MRP and MRPII are still widely used, independently and as modules of more comprehensive ERP systems, but the original vision of integrated information systems as we know them today began with the development of MRP and MRP II in manufacturing.

Characteristic basic modules in an MRP II system are:

- Master production schedule (MPS)
- Item master data (technical data)
- Bill of materials (BOM) (technical data)

- Production resources data (manufacturing technical data)
- Inventories and orders (inventory control)
- Purchasing management
- Material requirements planning (MRP)
- Shop floor control (SFC)
- Capacity planning or capacity requirements planning (CRP)
- Standard costing (cost control)
- Cost reporting / management (cost control).
- Some of the related systems are:
  - *General ledger*
  - *Accounts payable (purchase ledger)*
  - *Accounts receivable (sales ledger)*
  - *Sales order management*
  - *Distribution requirements planning (DRP)*
  - *Automated warehouse management*
  - *Project management*
  - *Technical records*
  - *Estimating*
  - *Computer-aided design/computer-aided manufacturing (CAD/CAM)*
  - *CAPP.*

The MRP II system integrates these modules together so that they use common data and freely exchange information, in a model of how a manufacturing enterprise should and can operate. The MRP II approach is therefore very different from the "point solution" approach, where individual systems are deployed to help a company plan, control or manage a specific activity. MRP II is by definition fully integrated or at least fully interfaced. MRP II systems have been implemented in most manufacturing industries.

The vision for MRP and MRPII was to centralise and integrate business information in a way that would facilitate decision making for production line managers and increase the efficiency of the production line overall. While MRP allows for the coordination of raw materials purchasing, MRPII facilitates the development of a detailed production schedule that accounts for machine and labour capacity, scheduling the production runs according to the arrival of materials.

An MRPII output is a final labour and machine schedule. Data about the cost of production, including machine time, labour time and materials used, as well as final production numbers, is provided from the MRPII system to accounting and finance. In order to calculate the raw materials needed to produce products and to schedule the purchase of those materials along with the machine and labour time needed, production managers recognised that they would need to use computer and software technology to manage the information.

3. Capacity Requirement Planning (CRP):

Capacity Requirements Planning (CRP) is the process of determining what personnel and equipment capacities (times) are needed to meet the production objectives embodied in the master schedule and the material requirements plan. MRP focuses upon the priorities of materials, whereas CRP focuses primarily upon time. Although both MRP and CRP can be done manually and in isolation, they are typically integrated within a computerised system, and CRP (as well as production activity control) functions are often assumed to be included within the concept of "an MRP system." Computerised MRP systems can effectively manage the flow of thousands of components throughout a manufacturing facility. Capacity is a measure of the productive capability of a facility per unit of time. In terms of the relevant time horizon, capacity management decisions are concerned with the following:

- Long range-resource planning of capital facilities, equipment, and human resources.
- Medium range-requirements planning of labour and equipment to meet MPS needs.
- Short range-control of the flow (input-output) and sequencing of operations.

Capacity requirements planning (CRP) applies primarily to medium-range activities. The CRP system receives planned and released orders from the material-requirements planning system and attempts to develop loads for the firm's work centers that are in good balance with the work-center capacities. Like MRP, CRP is an iterative process that involves planning, revision of capacity (or revision of the master schedule), and replanning until a reasonably good load profile is developed. Planned-order releases (in the MRP system) are converted to standard hours of load on key work centers in the CRP system.

4. Distributions Requirements Planning (DRP):

"Distributions Requirements Planning" is a method which is used by supply chain entities to plan orders in the whole supply chain considering the inventories to be kept along with buffer or safety stock, placing the orders with the manufacturer to replenish inventories to meet customer orders, etc. It is similar to materials requirements planning (MRP) except that MRP is used in manufacturing companies and DRP is used in logistics companies. DRP tries to efficiently carry out the whole process of completing customer orders by minimising shortages and reducing the overall costs comprising of ordering, transporting and inventory holding costs.

DRP is a process for determining inventory requirements in a multiple plant/warehouse environment. It may be used for both distribution and manufacturing. In manufacturing, DRP will work directly with MRP. DRP may also be defined as Distribution Resource Planning which also includes determining labour, equipment, and warehouse space requirements.

3.4 Production Control

Control implies ensuring that the actual performance of the organisation meets the predetermined or planned standards. Further, "production control" refers to a set of steps for verifying whether production operations occur in conformity with the production plans adopted by the organisation. It guides and directs the flow of production so that the goods of desired quality are manufactured at the right time and in an optimised economic mode. It may be noted that "production control" is frequently used synonymously with "production planning and control" with planning being implied.

Spriegel and **Lansburgh** defined production control as *"the process of planning production in advance of operations, establishing the exact route of each individual item, part or assembly, setting, starting and finishing dates for each important item, assembly, and the finished products and releasing the necessary orders as well as initiating the required follow-up to effective the smooth functioning of the enterprise."*

James Lundy says; *"Basically, the production control function involves the co-ordination and integration of the factors of production for optimum efficiency. The principal objective of production control is to facilitate the task of manufacturing and see that everything is being done strictly in accordance with the plan. It co-ordinates and integrates the factors of production for optimism and directs and checks the course and progress of work."*

The difference between Production Planning and Production Control can be emphasised as follows;

Production Planning is understood as;

- It deals with planning the work.
- Planning is forward thinking.
- Planning involves collection of data on materials, machines, tools and equipment, drawings, layouts etc.
- Planning is basically a centralised activity controlled by the top management.
- Planning is basically a thinking process so it involves lot of paper work, preparing necessary forms etc.
- Planning needs feedback so as to know whether the actual performance is taking place according to the plan or not.
- The main functions of production planning include estimative output to be produced, routing or determine sequence of operations, scheduling and loading. Thus it may be observed that production planning and control are not only complementary to each other but they are so interrelated that they are often considered as being one function.

Whereas Production Control implies;
- It deals with implementing the plan.
- Control involves utilisation of data, reporting about output, efficiency of labour and machines, inventory control, quality control, etc.
- Control involves actual use of these forms for reporting about production activities to the higher authorities.
- Control aims at keeping control over actual properness to take place as per plan. If any deviation is observed then corrective action is taken
- Control involves looking backwards and taking steps to maintain time schedule.
- Control is a decentralised activity that takes place in shop floors.
- Production control includes the functions of dispatching expediting follow up, progressing.

3.4.1 Scheduling

Scheduling is defined as;
- Prescribing of when and where each operation necessary to produce a product is to be performed
- Fixing up starting and finishing times of each operation comprising a procedure.

Scheduling is an important tool for manufacturing and operations management. It has a major impact on the productivity of a manufacturing process. In manufacturing, the purpose of scheduling is to minimise the production time and costs, with the help of a powerful production facility which answers the questions such as; when to make, with which and how much staff, and with which equipment. Production scheduling aims to maximise the efficiency of the operations while reducing the costs. Production scheduling tools greatly leave behind older manual scheduling methods.

Companies use backward and forward scheduling to allocate plant and machinery resources, plan human resources, plan production processes and purchase materials. Forward scheduling is planning the tasks from when the date resources become available to determining the shipping date or the due date whereas backward scheduling is planning the tasks from the due date or required-by date to determine the start date and/or any changes in capacity required.

Operations scheduling involves the decision to allocate available resources over relatively shorter period of time using aggregate planning. On an operational level, scheduling relates to the use of equipment and facilities, the scheduling of human activities and the receipt of materials. Operations scheduling is important for both - manufacturing and service based organisations in order to meet customer requirements on time and improve their operational efficiency. Successful operations scheduling involves going within the budget, completing the jobs on time and ensuring high performance of the product or the service which is being provided.

Aggregate planning is considered to be a medium term issue, while operations scheduling is considered more of a short term issue. Hence, scheduling is the final step in a firm's transformation process before the actual products or services are provided through the operations. Scheduling decisions deal with adjustments among conflicting goals for efficient utilisation of labour and equipment, inventory levels and the quality of customer service. The fast pace of the information age has increased the need for effective operations scheduling to meet customer expectations with a consideration of emergency transactions. Several scheduling software packages are available for automated scheduling or assistance in scheduling evaluation and generation. Even though automated scheduling is very useful, especially for scheduling simple monotonous operations, more complex or advanced scheduling requires human judgment and experience to manage and schedule unexpected operational events and tasks.

An operation can be scheduled in several different ways and the scheduling method varies with the type of operation. Factors which directly influence the type of scheduling method to be used include the types of operations or jobs to be processed and the resources required to do so, the availability of these resources, the times involved with setting up and completing the operation, downtime and planned maintenance, as well as the amount of shifts or time available for the necessary scheduling. An operations manager needs to take such variables into consideration to determine the best type of scheduling tool for the firm's operations scheduling needs.

Operations scheduling has a direct linkage with MRP systems in an organisation. Function of an MRP exercise is to generate feasible production orders and procurement notices. Production orders are nothing but specific sets of instructions to utilise a set of resources for the manufacturing of the components under question during a particular period of time.

For example; there is a sub-assembly X. If the MRP schedule indicates that during January a designated shop, S1, should manufacture 2000 units of X, then it is clear that during January, the planner needs to ensure that the job is assigned to Shop S1 and provide capacity for manufacturing 2000 units of X. During the same week, there could be several jobs assigned to Shop S1. Therefore, the shop planners also need to prioritise all such jobs in the shop with respect to each machine they visit, and ensure completion of the job without delay. This example indicates that the output of an MRP exercise becomes the input for job scheduling.

3.4.2 Loading

Once scheduling is done, the next important factor to be studied under operations management is 'Loading'.

Loading can be defined as the study of the relationship between the load and the capacity of work centres or production / service facilities.

The main difference between loading and scheduling is the intention. When engaged in planning the order and sequence of work, with a view to completing it by a given due date, the operation being done is termed as "scheduling". Whereas when thinking to compare load and capacity with a view, for example, to fix if there is sufficient capacity for a given production plan or programme if there is some spare capacity, which can be used for other work, it is described as loading.

The primary aim of loading is hence;

- To keep the operator idle time minimum.
- To keep machine idle time minimum.
- To keep material waiting time minimum.
- To assist in balancing plant and labour force.

When there are several similar machines available with the company, the first step in scheduling is to assign the jobs and the organisational resources. While loading takes care of the idle times spotted after the scheduling function. It is not an easy task to arrive at the optimum schedule for a manufacturing unit. Numerous combinations are possible for scheduling the jobs in a shop.

3.4.3 Scheduling for Job Shops and Floor Shops

When there are multiple replicas of the same machine type, the first step in scheduling is to assign the jobs to these resources. As we have seen earlier, this is achieved through scheduling and a backup of loading. Let us study a simple illustration to backup this thought. Suppose three milling machines are available on a shop floor and each of them provides a weekly capacity of 45 hours (Assuming that each day, 7.5 hours are operational and the factory works for 6 days in a week). During the coming week, let us say 30 jobs need processing in the machine and a total of 110 hours of machine capacity is required. While the required capacity is available, it still requires some planning so that the jobs are assigned to these machines such that none of the machines are either overloaded or under-loaded. This is achieved by using loading. For this purpose, one can use the assignment method, a variation of the linear programming model.

The assignment method in this regard is useful only when one job is assigned to one machine and there are as many machines available for assignment as there are jobs.

- If there are fewer jobs than machines, one can still use the assignment method by adding some fictitious jobs and solving the standard assignment problem.
- On the other hand, if there are fewer machines than jobs, other methods are available for loading jobs on machines. In this case, several jobs are assigned to each machine as long as sufficient capacity is available for processing and other constraints are taken care of.

It is not an easy task to arrive at an optimum schedule for a manufacturing shop. Numerous combinations are possible for scheduling jobs in a shop. In a flow shop, the number of combinations grows non-linearly. Therefore, it will not only be difficult but also pointless to resort to complete listing of these alternatives. However, we have noted earlier that a grouping of the shop configuration, the scheduling rule, and the performance measure could lend itself to identifying the optimum combination without much computational effort.

Shop configuration denotes the manner in which the machines are organised on the shop floor and the flow pattern of these jobs by utilising these machines. There are two alternative options available for configuring these machines in the manufacturing system. These options are;

1. Flow Shop, and
2. Job Shop.

1. Flow Shop:

Since these options differ in terms of the deployment of resources, the scheduling methodology also differs. Flow shop is the simplest configuration as the resources are organised one after the other in the order the jobs are processed. In a flow shop, the jobs start processing at Machine 1, and as per the processing flow, they flow through the further machines – Machine 2, Machine 3, etc. Since in a flow shop, all jobs follow the same order of visiting the machines. The scheduling function is essentially reduced. Once the jobs are scheduled in front of the first machine, they follow the same order through the rest of the machines.

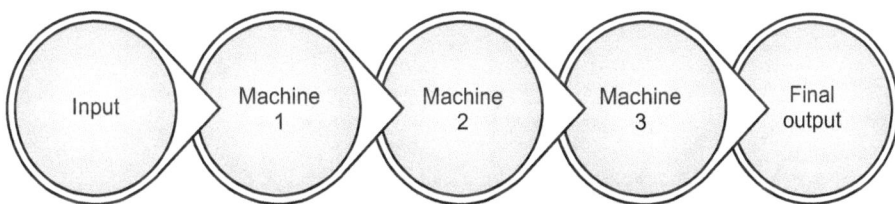

Fig 3.7: Format of a Flow Shop

Fig. 3.8: Flow Shop (Car Manufacturing)

2. Job Shop:

The second option is a job shop. In a job shop, machines are not organised in any processing order. Rather, similar types of resources are grouped together. Each job goes through a different and unique order where it visits the machines for the processing activities. Moreover, there is no requirement for all the jobs to visit the first machine for starting the manufacturing process. As each job has its own distinct route, the set of jobs visiting each machine is determined separately. As a result of this each job has to be dedicated a distinct scheduling pattern, which makes scheduling a very challenging task for job shops.

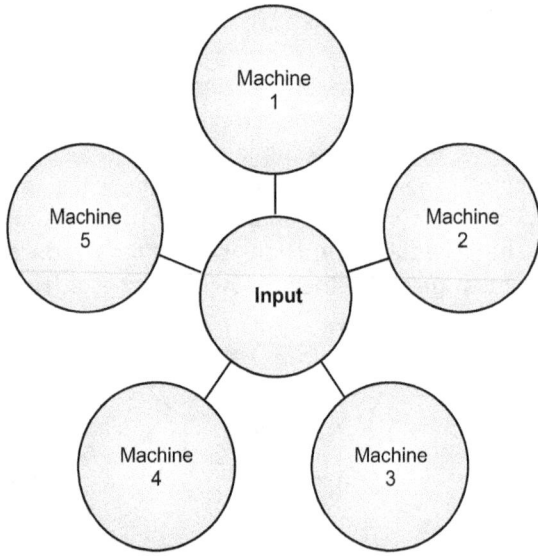

Fig 3.9: Format of a Job Shop

Fig 3.10: Job Shop (Clothes Manufacturing)

3.4.4 Gantt Charts

A Gantt chart, commonly used in project management, is one of the most popular and useful ways of showing activities (tasks or events) displayed against time. On the left of the chart is a list of the activities and along the top is a suitable time scale. Each activity is represented by a bar; the position and length of the bar reflects the start date, duration and end date of the activity. This allows you to see at a glance:

- What the various activities are?
- When each activity begins and ends?
- How long each activity is scheduled to last?
- Where activities overlap with other activities, and by how much?
- The start and end date of the whole project?

This method, which was introduced in 1917, and is the oldest and the most extensively used method for production planning, scheduling and control. The Gantt chart shows the relationship between different activities over a specified time span. Time frame, expressed either in terms of hours, days, weeks or months is shown on the horizontal or X-axis and activities are plotted against the Y-axis.

The time frame or time scale would depend on the nature of operations and activities, which may be determined by the previous experience or an approximation based on which activities may be scheduled and monitored.

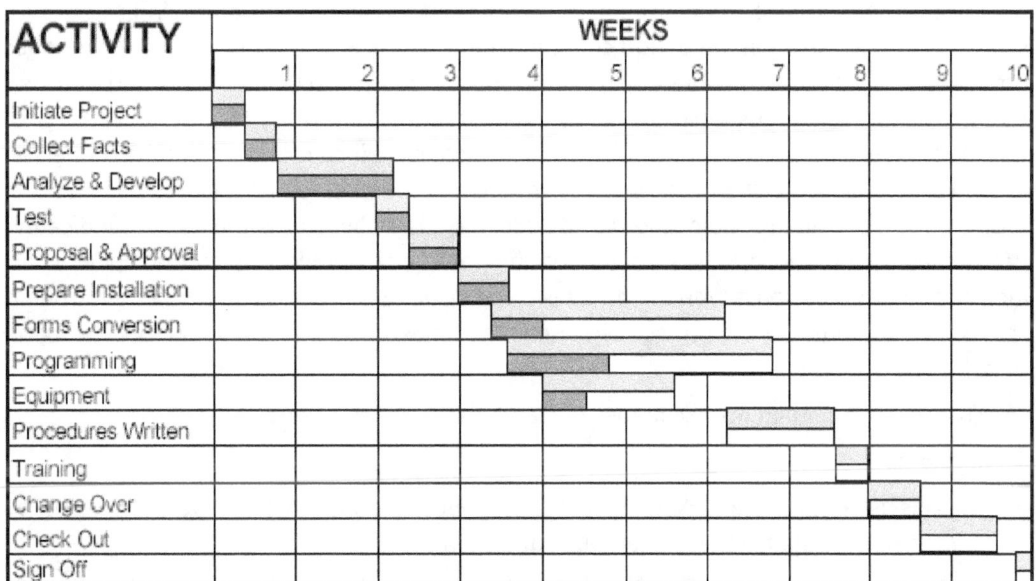

Fig 3.11: Sample Gantt Chart

The charts may be in the form of any of the following:

(a) Scheduling or progress charts, which show the sequence of job progress.

(b) Load charts which show the work assigned to a work group or allocated to machines.

(c) Record charts which track the actual time spent and delays, if any.

Gantt charts need to be updated at regular intervals, for instance, when a work is delayed at the start or when work continues beyond its time schedule or if the progress of work is not as per the actual plan. If unforeseen eventualities occur, corrective actions may have to be taken, and this will also need corresponding changes in Gantt charts.

A Gantt chart is a matrix which lists on the vertical axis all the tasks to be performed. Each row contains a single task identification which usually consists of a number and name. The horizontal axis is headed by columns indicating estimated task duration, skill level needed to perform the task and the name of the person assigned to the task, followed by one column for each period in the project's duration. Each period may be expressed in hours, days, weeks, months and other time units. In some cases it may be necessary to label the period columns as period 1, period 2 and so on.

The graphical portion of the Gantt chart consists of a horizontal bar for each task connecting the period start and period ending columns. A set of markers is usually used to indicate the estimated and the actual start and end. Each bar on a separate line and the name of each person assigned to the task is on a separate line. In many cases, when this type of project plan is used, a blank row is left between tasks.

When the project is under way, this row is used to indicate progress, indicated by a second bar which starts in the period column when the task is actually started and continues until the task is actually completed. Comparison between the estimated start and end and the actual start and end should indicate project status on a task-by-task basis. Variants of this method include a lower chart which shows personnel allocations on a person-by-person basis. For this section, the vertical axis contains the number of people assigned to the project, and the columns indicating task duration are left blank, as is the column indicating persons assigned. The graphics consist of the same bar notation as in the upper chart indicates that the person is working on a task. The value of this lower chart is evident when it shows the slack time for the project personnel, i.e., times when they are not actually working on any project.

The advantages and disadvantages of Gantt charts are as below:

Advantages:

1. This is a simple and very inexpensive method and can be developed even by supervisory staff with some amount of training.
2. These charts clearly show the decided time and work schedules for every job.

3. Monitoring and control are easier and can be done within a minimum time frame and at the lowest cost.
4. These charts can be changed and updated quickly at a lower cost.
5. There is no need to develop the customised Gantt chart boards as the standard chart boards are available in the market.

Disadvantages:

In spite of the above-mentioned advantages, there are certain disadvantages.

1. They do not show job interrelationships and interdependence
2. Cost implications cannot be shown
3. With these charts, it is not possible to depict other alternatives for project completion
4. The shape and form of Gantt charts can differ according to the nature of the requirement.

Hence the Gantt chart is a very effective and a cost efficient tool which is used for optimised scheduling and loading activities across the organisations of various sectors and segments.

Points to Remember

"The highest efficiency in production is obtained by manufacturing the required quantity of a product, of the required quality, at the required time by the best and cheapest method".

PPC is a tool which is used to coordinate all manufacturing activities in a production system. Production planning is concerned with two main aspects:

1. Routing or planning work tasks.
2. Layout or three-dimensional relationship between the resources.

Production planning is an activity that is performed before the actual production process takes place.

Production planning means planning of the work to be done later.

Production control refers to working out or the implementation of the plan.

Functions of Production Planning and Control

1. Materials
2. Methods
3. Machine and equipment
4. Manpower
5. Process planning (Routing)
6. Estimating

7. Loading and scheduling
8. Dispatching
9. Expediting
10. Inspection
12. Evaluation

Forecasting is the process of making statements about events whose actual outcomes (typically) have not yet been observed.

Demand forecasting seeks to investigate and measure the forces that determine sales for existing and new products. Generally companies plan their business – production or sales in anticipation of future demand. Hence forecasting future demands becomes important.

Functions of forecasting:
- An estimation tool.
- A way of addressing the complex and uncertain environment surrounding business decision making.
- A tool for predicting events related to operations planning and control.
- A vital prerequisite for the planning process in organisations.

Forecasting based on time horizon can be mainly classified in three categories:
1. Short Term Forecasting.
2. Medium Term Forecasting.
3. Long Term Forecasting.

Sources of Data for Forecasting
1. Sales Personnel Estimates.
2. Point of Sales (POS) Data Systems.
3. Forecasts from Supply Chain Partners.
4. Trade/Industry Association Journals.
5. B2B Portals/Marketplaces.
6. Econmica surveys and indicators.
7. Subjective Knowledge.

A plan details the structure, goals and nature of a business and incorporates a production plan. A production plan is just one part of an overall business plan, and it serves as a road map for future production activities. A production plan gets a small business idea one step closer to becoming a reality. The purpose of a production plan is to lay out the schedule of production and how the business plans maintain that schedule.

Aggregate Production Planning is a planning exercise done for operations using data at an aggregate level. Aggregate production planning serves the critical role of transforming the business plans and strategic intent to operational decisions.

Three critical decisions are made under Aggregate Production Planning:
- the rate of production,
- the amount of inventory to carry, and
- the amount of resource (in terms of working hours) to be committed on a period-by-period basis.

Need for Aggregate Production Planning (APP)
1. Demand Fluctuations.
2. Capacity Fluctuations.
3. Difficulty level in altering production rates.
4. Benefits of multi - period planning.

Alternatives for Managing Demand and Supply:
1. Reservations of capacity.
2. Influencing Demand.

Master Production Schedule (MPS) represents the critical linking between planning and execution of operations. It is a crucial stage in the production planning process in any organisation after aggregate production planning is done.

There are two stages involved in MPS:

Step 1: Integrating current market information into the production plan:

Step 2: Disaggregation of product information.

Capacity planning is an activity which is undertaken to identify the amount of production required to satisfy the demand for the goods and services produced by a business at a period of time. Capacity planning is the process of defining the production capacity needed by an organisation to meet changing demands for its products. In the context of capacity planning, "design capacity" is the maximum amount of load that an organisation is capable of effecting in a given period, "effective capacity" is the maximum amount of work that an organisation is capable of completing in a given period due to constraints such as quality problems, delays, material handling, etc.

MRP - Material Requirements Planning (MRP) is a software-based production planning and inventory control system used to manage manufacturing processes.

MRP II - has been evolved from early Materials Requirement Planning (MRP) systems by including the integration of additional data, such as employee and financial needs.

Capacity Requirements Planning (CRP) is the process of determining what personnel and equipment capacities (times) are needed to meet the production objectives embodied in the master schedule and the material requirements plan. Capacity-requirements planning (CRP) applies primarily to medium-range activities.

"Distributions Requirements Planning" is a method which is used by supply chain entities to plan orders in the whole supply chain considering the inventories to be kept along with buffer or safety stock, placing the orders with the manufacturer to replenish inventories to meet customer orders, etc. It is similar to materials requirements planning (MRP) except that MRP is used in manufacturing companies and DRP is used in logistics companies. DRP tries to efficiently carry out the whole process of completing customer orders by minimising shortages and reducing the overall costs comprising of ordering, transporting and inventory holding costs.

Production Control implies ensuring that the actual performance of the organisation meets the predetermined or planned standards. Further, "production control" refers to a set of steps for verifying whether production operations occur in conformity with the production plans adopted by the organisation. It guides and directs the flow of production so that the goods of desired quality are manufactured at the right time and in an optimised economic mode.

Scheduling is defined as:
- Prescribing of when and where each operation necessary to produce a product is to be performed,
- Fixing up starting and finishing times of each operation comprising a procedure.

Loading can be defined as the study of the relationship between the load and the capacity of work centres or production / service facilities.

The main difference between loading and scheduling is the intention.

The primary aim of loading is hence:
- To keep the operator idle time minimum,
- To keep machine idle time minimum,
- To keep material waiting time minimum,
- To assist in balancing plant and labour force.

A Gantt chart, commonly used in project management, is one of the most popular and useful ways of showing activities (tasks or events) displayed against time. On the left of the chart is a list of the activities and along the top is a suitable time scale. Each activity is represented by a bar; the position and length of the bar reflects the start date, duration and end date of the activity.

Questions for Discussion

1. Define Production Planning and Control.
2. List the objectives of PPC.
3. What are the phases of production planning and control?

4. List various functions of PPC.
5. Write a note on forecasting as a planning tool.
6. What is APP and write why there is a need for APP.
7. What is the importance of Production Planning and Control?
8. Discuss Forecasting Time Horizon.
9. Discuss MRP I and DRP I as planning tools of Logistics Management. Contrast between the two.
10. What is Demand Forecasting? Explain the three techniques of Demand Forecasting.
11. What are the advantages and disadvantages of the Gantt Chart?
12. Write Short notes on:
    (a) Gantt Chart
    (b) Loading
    (c) Scheduling
    (d) MRP
    (e) CRP
    (f) DRP
    (g) Job shop
    (h) Flow shop
    (i) Sources of data for forecasting
    (j) APP

Questions from Previous Examinations

1. "Production Planning and Control functions involves balancing between priority (Demand) and Capacity (Resources). Discuss the statement. **[April 2006]**
2. Explain the term Scheduling In Production Planning. **[December 2006]**
3. Narrate the Functions of Production Planning and Control. Explain their Objectives. **[April 2007]**
4. Discuss In brief Importance of Production Planning and Control in a Manufacturing Organisation. **[December 2009, April 2010]**
5. Define Production Planning and Control (PPC). Explain Objectives, Scope and Elements of PPC. **[April 2011]**
6. Write Short Notes :
   (A) Production Control. **[December 2010]**

Chapter 4...

Inventory Planning and Control

Contents ...

- 4.1 Inventory Planning and Control
    - 4.1.1 Inventory Planning
    - 4.1.2 Inventory Control
    - 4.1.3 Continuous and Intermittent Demand System
    - 4.1.4 Comparison of Continuous and Intermittent System
    - 4.1.5 Need of Inventory Management
    - 4.1.6 Types of Inventory
    - 4.1.7 Implications of Inventory Control Methods
- 4.2 Costs Associated with Inventory
- 4.3 Economic Order Quantity (EOQ)
    - 4.3.1 Assumptions Underlying the EOQ Model
    - 4.3.2 Preparation of the Model
    - 4.3.3 Proof of Optimal Buying
    - 4.3.4 Economic Order Quantity with Price Discounts
- 4.4 Inventory or Material Control
    - 4.4.1 Classification of Material or Inventory
    - 4.4.2 Inventory Turnover Ratios
    - 4.4.3 Fixed Order Quantity Model
- Points to Remember
- Questions for Discussion

Learning Objectives:
- To study Production Planning and Control (PPC) and understand its applicability in the manufacturing units
- To understand the techniques and flow of demand forecasting
- To define the scope and importance of Production Planning and study its tools and techniques
- To define the scope and importance of Production Control and study its tools and techniques

Introduction

In this chapter, we shall study the techniques of planning and control in accordance with the forecasting tools, and planning and control mechanisms executed by the organisation in optimising the efficiency of the manufacturing unit. As we saw earlier, process plays a very significant role in deciding the altitude of success of a unit. Similarly, the planning and controlling techniques work out the minimisation of deviations from the planned activities.

The control of inventories is one of the most complex, yet crucial of all business activities. It has wide organisational implications and is the focal point of many conflicting objectives - both long term and short term. It's planning and execution involves participation from all functional departments.

Inventory control is important to almost every type of business, whether product or service oriented. Inventory control touches almost every facet of organisations.

Concept of Inventory and Inventory Management:

The word inventory basically means the total of goods and services that businesses hold in stock. There are several categories or types of such inventory. The most basic is materials and components. This usually consists of the essential items needed to create or make a finished product, such as gears for a bicycle, microchips for a computer, or screens and tubes for a television set. The second type of inventory is called WIP, or work in progress inventory. This refers to items that are partially completed, but not the entire finished product. They are on their way towards becoming complete products but are not yet complete. The third and the most common form of inventory are called as finished goods. These are the final products that are ready to be purchased by customers and consumers. Finished goods can range from cakes to furniture to vehicles. Most people think of the finished goods as being part of an inventory stock, but the parts that create them are held accountable in inventory as well.

The term **'Inventory'** has a wider meaning than the term 'materials'. Inventory includes stock of raw material, work-in-progress, finished goods, components and supplies:

The **I.C.A.I** defines 'Inventory' as tangible property held:

(i) For sale in ordinary course of business or

(ii) In the process of production for such sale, or

(iii) In the form of maintenance or supplies to be consumed in the production process or rendering of services.

On the basis of the above definition, **Inventories** may be **Classified** as follows :

(i) **Productive Inventories** e.g. raw materials, spare parts, components, etc. which are used in the production process.

(ii) **Non-productive Inventories** e.g. office stores, machine spare parts, scrap, lubrication oil, etc.

(iii) **In-process Materials** i.e. semi-finished goods lying at different stages of production process.

(iv) **Finished Goods Inventories** i.e. products ready for sale.

(v) **Scrap, Obsolete Materials** are also sometimes considered as form of inventory.

Gordon B. Carson defines **Inventory Control** as, "*the process whereby the investment in materials and parts carried in stock is regulated within predetermined limits set in accordance with inventory policy established by the management*".

The word 'inventory' can refer to both the total amount of goods and the act of counting them. Many companies take an inventory of their supplies on a regular basis in order to avoid running out of popular items. Others take an inventory to insure the number of items ordered matches with the actual number of items counted physically. Shortages or overages after an inventory can indicate a problem with theft (called 'shrinkage' in retail circles) or inaccurate accounting practices. There are many different ways through which the companies handle their inventory. Overall it depends on what kind of business it is. For example, a food manufacturer who makes canned fruit may take into account every single piece of that can in its inventory. The materials used to make the can, the labels, the fruit, and the sugary filling could all be part of the overall analysis of inventory. Keeping track of inventory can be a complex process.

Inventory is a list of goods and materials stored for future use, mainly in the production process or those goods and materials themselves, held available in stock by a business. Thus, today's inventory is tomorrow's production. The raw materials, work-in-process goods and completely finished goods that are considered to be a portion of a business's assets which are ready or will be ready for sale. The turn-over of inventory represents one of the primary sources of revenue generation and subsequent earnings for the company/business. Therefore, inventories are materials or resources of any kind having some economic value, either awaiting conversion or use in future.

4.1 Inventory Planning and Control

4.1.1 Inventory Planning

Inventory planning is the method and procedures companies use to determine the amount of products they should have on hand for meeting consumer demand. This planning may involve several steps, depending on the company's inventory management system and business operations. Inventory is often the second largest expense that companies can have outside of payroll, making inventory management and planning an important business function.

- The first step of inventory planning is to estimate future sales. This estimation analysis can be conducted by reviewing historical sales records to ascertain various sales trends for company products. Businesses often add a buffer amount to their sales estimates. This buffer amount can ensure that companies do not run out of various products if higher sales occur than previously estimated. Companies may also conduct an economic market analysis to assess consumer demand, behaviour, and income. These economic factors can lead to higher consumer purchases and result in lower overall on-hand available inventory.
- The next step in inventory planning is to purchase the necessary products for business locations. This process includes selecting the products, displays, receiving or verification methods, and reorder system. Many companies attempt to order consumer goods that coincide with holidays or seasons. Companies can also order popular products that will sell quickly and generate higher revenues. This inventory planning process often includes an accounting budget. This budget ensures that companies do not overspend on products that will result in sluggish sales and higher warehousing or other business costs.
- Companies may also make plans for moving inventory quickly before new items must be purchased for upcoming seasons. These methods include promotional sales, markdowns, and clearance or liquidation sales. These processes ensure that companies do not get stuck with old inventory that becomes unsellable. Unsellable inventory is commonly called obsolescence in the business environment. Obsolete inventory may require companies to write off the products as a loss against operational income. Depending on the amount of inventory on-hand, this loss can represent significant reductions to the company's income.

An important consideration in inventory planning is keeping track of all physical products in the company's inventory. Companies use one of two accounting methods: perpetual or periodic.

- A perpetual inventory system maintains an accurate count after every purchase or sale of products.
- The periodic inventory system only updates inventory numbers at specific time periods during the accounting year. Most companies choose to update inventory on a monthly or quarterly basis, depending on their business operations.

4.1.2 Inventory Control

Inventory control is the process of managing an inventory so that the business derives the most overall benefit from the existence of the inventory. The strategy normally involves such functions as setting limits on the actual size of the inventory, while also taking care to maintain enough items on hand to allow the business to operate at maximum efficiency. When conducted responsibly, inventory control also helps businesses to manage their tax obligations more effectively, and thus add to the overall profitability of the operation.

While there are many different theories and processes that are employed with inventory control, many of them are based on the concept of usage. This is particularly true when the inventory in question is composed of raw materials or equipment that is important to the on-going operation of a production facility. The idea is to make sure there are always sufficient resources on hand to maintain the desirable level of production, but not so many resources that they suffer in storage for long periods of time.

In many nations, taxes are imposed on inventories of this type. By practicing responsible inventory control, businesses are able to keep inventories as low as possible to reduce the tax burden, but also never run short on what is needed to allow the business to fill orders from customers. This delicate balance is normally achieved by establishing order procedures that allow materials to be received shortly before they are needed for production, thus ensuring they do not spend much time in the stored inventory.

The same general approach to inventory control also applies to finished goods inventory. Here, the idea is to produce enough goods to meet customer demands and fill orders in a timely manner, but not create situations in which finished goods must be stored for long periods of time. By accurately projecting the usage of customers, it is possible to adjust production quotas so that orders are processed efficiently, without the need to maintain large inventories to fill those orders. This aspect of inventory control can also help aid in loss prevention efforts, since the less time that finished goods remain in storage, the less opportunity there is for those goods to be damaged in some manner.

Solid inventory control also allows a business to make the most efficient use of its resources. Lower inventories means less company resources tied up in the value of the inventories themselves. Along with the lower tax burden, the company with efficient inventory control procedures can dedicate more of its available finances to other essential operations, such as marketing campaigns, research and development, and the refinement of the manufacturing process.

4.1.3 Continuous and Intermittent Demand System

The term inventory refers to any idle resource which is stored for an anticipated future use. Manufacturing and Service Organisations have significantly invested in the inventory. Normally, investments in inventory have a direct bearing on the profitability of a firm. In manufacturing organisations, finished goods and spare parts typically belong to the category of independent demand items. While planning for a dependent demand item is done to meet customer requirements, in the case of dependent demand items, it is done in order to meet the customer requirements. Such requirements influence the demand for a commodity and hence, such demands can be broadly classified under two categories. These categories, based on the aspect of regularity of demand have been discussed ahead.

Continuous Demand System:

Continuous demand system is a practice of inventory management and inventory control which is executed by organisations where there is a regular and consistent demand for the manufactured finished products in the market. When the demand for the products is consistent in the market throughout the year, the company has to maintain the stock levels throughout the year in order to meet the demand from the market. Inefficiency on account of the company towards efficient inventory management costs the company its market share. Considering the tough competition in the dynamic markets these days, if a particular product is not available of any company, there are numerous other competitors who provide similar features and hence grab the market shares in the period of insufficient stock levels of a company.

Moreover, to maintain these stock levels throughout the year, it's not an aspect merely of finished goods. In order to maintain the regular flow, companies have to maintain this regular, continuous and consistent flow of inventories in raw materials, WIP and finished goods as well. Companies also have to consider the Shop Supplies and Consumables required by the machines and the shop floor in order to avoid emergency disruptions.

Continuous means something that operates constantly without any irregularities or frequent halts. In the continuous production system, goods are produced constantly as per demand forecast. Goods are produced on a large scale for stocking and selling. They are not produced on customer's orders. Here, the inputs and outputs are standardised along with the production process and sequence.

Examples: Hotel Industries, Fuel Stations

The characteristics of a continuous production system are listed as follows:
- The flow of production is continuous. It is not intermittent.
- The products are standardised.
- The products are produced on predetermined quality standards.
- The products are produced in anticipation of demand.
- Standardised routing sheets and schedules are prepared.

Intermittent Demand System:

In case of Intermittent Demand Systems, organisations work exactly opposite as compared to the structure of Continuous Demand Systems. As against Continuous Demand System, Intermittent demand systems enjoy very irregular flow of demand and hence anticipating the demand forecast becomes a substantially difficult task. Hence, mostly such demand systems work on the customisation of orders. The operations start after the customer orders are received. This helps in avoiding wastage and reducing the implied costs thereon.

Intermittent means something that starts (initiates) and stops (halts) at irregular (unfixed) intervals (time gaps).

In the intermittent production system, goods are produced based on customer's orders. These goods are produced on a small scale. The flow of production is intermittent (irregular). In other words, the flow of production is not continuous. In this system, large varieties of products are produced. These products are of different sizes. The design of these products goes on changing. It keeps changing according to the design and size of the product. Therefore, this system is very flexible.

Examples: Tailor, Goldsmith

The characteristics of an intermittent production system are listed as follows:
- The flow of production is not continuous. It is intermittent.
- Wide varieties of products are produced.
- The volume of production is small.
- General purpose machines are used. These machines can be used to produce different types of products.
- The sequence of operation goes on changing as per the design of the product.
- The quantity, size, shape, design, etc. of the product depends on the customer's orders.

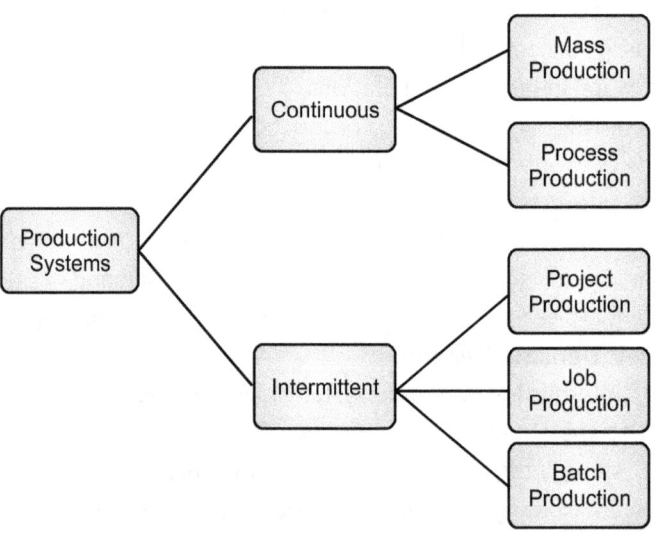

Fig 4.1: Continuous and Intermittent Demand System

4.1.4 Comparison of Continuous and Intermittent System

Continuous System and Intermittent System can be better understood by studying in a comparative manner. A comparative analysis of these two concepts suggests us the following:

1. **Nature of product**:
   - In intermittent production system, goods are produced based on customer orders and not for stocking.
   - In continuous production system, goods are produced based on demand forecast and for stocking.

2. **Flexibility of process**:
   - In intermittent production system, production process is flexible. The product design goes on changing.
   - In continuous production system, production process is not flexible. It is standardised. The same product is manufactured continuously.

3. **Scale of production**:
   - In intermittent production system, goods are produced on a small scale, so there are no economies of scale.
   - In continuous production system, goods are produced on a large scale, so there are economies of large-scale production.

4. **Per unit cost**:
   - In intermittent production system, cost per unit may be higher because production is done on a small-scale.
   - In continuous production system, cost per unit may be lower because production is done on large-scale.

5. **Range of products**:
   - In intermittent production system, wide ranges of products are manufactured.
   - In continuous production system, normally one particular type of product is manufactured.

6. **Instructions** :
   - In an intermittent production system, many detailed instructions must be provided depending upon the customer's specification.
   - In continuous production system, single set of instructions is sufficient for operation. Here, there is no need to repeat the instructions.

7. **Staff**:
   - Intermittent production system requires staff with high technical skills and abilities.
   - Continuous production system requires more managerial skills and less technical skills.

8. **Storage of final products:**
   - In an intermittent production system, there is no need to store and stock the final products, because items are produced as per customer's orders.
   - In a continuous production system, there is a need to store and stock the final products until they are demanded in the market.
9. **Location change:**
   - In an intermittent production system, change in location is easy.
   - In a continuous production system, change in location is difficult.
10. **Capital invested:**
    - In an Intermittent production system, capital invested is small.
    - In a continuous production system, capital invested is very huge.

4.1.5 Need of Inventory Management

Inventory is a necessary process that every organisation has to maintain for various purposes. Optimum inventory management is the goal of every inventory manager. Excess inventory or inventory shortage - both cause financial impact and they affect the business opportunities. Inventory holding is resorted to by organisations as hedge against various external and internal factors, as precaution, as opportunity, as a need and for speculative purposes.

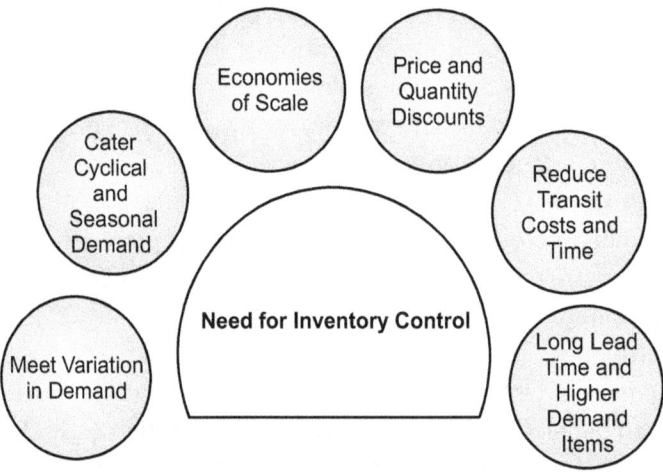

Fig 4.2: Need for Inventory Control

Most of the organisations have inventory warehouses attached to the production facilities where raw materials, consumables and packing materials are stored and follow the task of issue for production. The reasons for holding inventories can vary from organisations to organisations. The need for Inventory Management can be summarised as follows:

1. **Meet Variation in Production Demand:**
   The production plan changes with a response to the sales, estimates, orders and stocking patterns of a unit. Accordingly the demand for raw material supply for production varies with the product plan in terms of specific batch quantities. Holding inventories at a nearby warehouse helps issue the required quantity and item to production just in time.

2. **Cater to Cyclical and Seasonal Demand:**
   Market demand and supplies are seasonal depending upon various factors such as seasons; festivals etc. and past sales data help companies to anticipate a huge surge of demand in the market well in advance. Accordingly they stock up raw materials and hold inventories to be able to increase production and rush supplies to the market to meet the increased demand.

3. **Economies of Scale in Procurement:**
   Buying raw materials in larger lot and holding inventory is found to be cheaper for the company than buying frequent small lots. In such cases one buys in bulk and holds inventories at the plant warehouse.

4. **Earn advantage of Price Increase and Quantity Discounts:**
   If there is a price increase expected few months down the line due to changes in demand and supply in the national or international market, impact of taxes and budgets etc. the company's tend to buy raw materials in advance and hold stocks as a hedge against increased costs.

   Companies resort to buying in bulk and holding raw material inventories to take advantage of the quantity discounts offered by the supplier. In such cases the savings on account of the discount enjoyed would be substantially higher that of inventory carrying cost.

5. **Reduce Transit Cost and Transit Times:**
   In case of raw materials being imported from a foreign country or from a distant vendor within the country, one can save a lot in terms of transportation cost by buying in bulk and transporting as a container load or a full truck load. Part shipments can be costlier.

   In terms of transit time too, transit time for full container shipment or a full truck load is direct and faster unlike part shipment load where the freight forwarder waits for other loads to fill the container which can take several weeks.

   There could be a lot of factors resulting in shipping delays and transportation too, which can hamper the supply chain forcing companies to hold safety stock of raw material inventories.

6. **Long Lead and High demand items need to be held in Inventory:**
   Often the raw material supplies from vendors have long lead running into several months. Coupled with this if the particular item has a very high demand and relatively short supply one can expect disruption of supplies. In such cases it is safer to hold inventories and have control.

4.1.6 Types of Inventory

Inventory, as we have studied by now, is an extremely important function for an organisation. Such inventory will be maintained by the company based on various factors which influence the process. These factors may be the production pattern, demand pattern, availability of inventory, and many more such aspects. The ways of maintaining this inventory based on a few such aspects shall be studied ahead.

Fig. 4.3: Market in Non Peak Hours

Fig 4.4: Market in Peak Hours

1. **Seasonal:**

    Organisations maintain inventory to meet the fluctuations in demand arising out of seasonality. For instance, during the festive season (for example Diwali, Christmas or Eid), the demand for clothing may be high due to an increase in the disposable income of the customers. In order to meet this flow in demand, inventory is built up in the non-peak periods to minimise the burden which may arise in the market peak period.

    In short, the demand which may arise in the season is anticipated and is thus taken care of by adjusting the inventory levels during the non-peak periods.

2. **Decoupling:**

    Very rarely, one will be able to see a production facility where every machine in the process produces at exactly the same rate. In fact, one machine may process parts several times faster than the machines in front of or behind it. Yet, if one walks through the plant, it may seem that all machines are running smoothly at the same time. It also could be possible that one notices several machines are under repair or are undergoing some form of preventive maintenance.

    Even so, this does not seem to interrupt the flow of WIP through the system. The reason for this is the existence of an inventory of parts between machines, a decoupling inventory that serves as a shock absorber, cushioning the system against production irregularities. As such, it decouples or disengages the plant's dependence upon the requirements of the system.

    Manufacturing systems typically involve a series of production and assembly workstations. The raw material passes through these levels before it is transformed into finished goods. Each level behaves distinctively because of the different process times, downtimes and the availability of resources.

    Hence, the planning and control of such multi-level production process becomes very complex. A way to simplify the production planning and control problem is to separate the successive levels which use this inventory at some intermediate points. Each level will have an input buffer and an output buffer.

    The output buffer of the preceding level becomes the input buffer of the succeeding level. Inventory decisions in this case require analysis of the workstation capacities, availability of resources and the sub processes of the organisation.

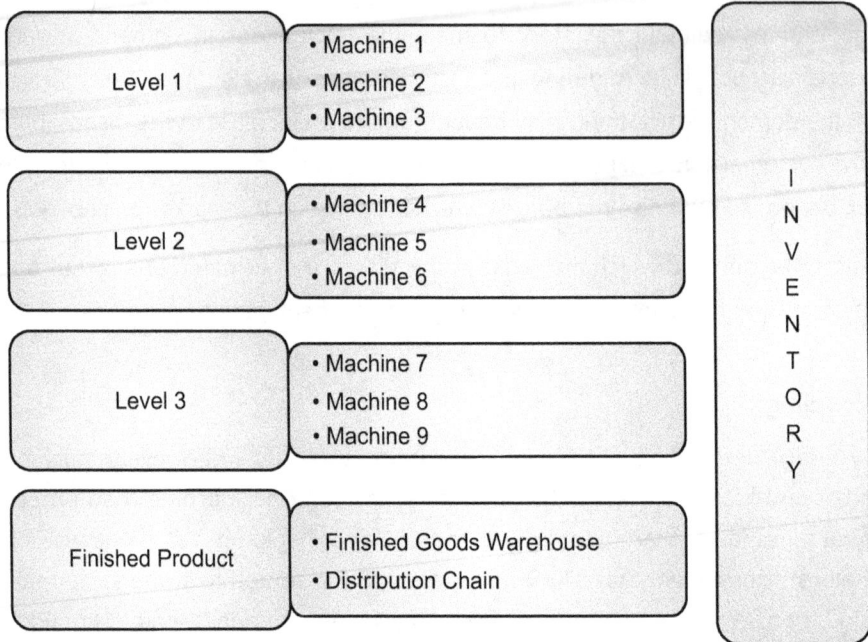

Fig. 4.5: Decoupling

If inventories are positioned between process stages, those inventories decouple the flow of materials being received at a work station from an up-stream process. This allows the two process stages to be scheduled somewhat independently of one another. This decoupling process allows for more effective and efficient scheduling of each process stage. While the ideal plant would like to achieve a continuous flow of material through the entire process train, this synchronisation is often difficult to achieve. Where synchronisation is not possible, it becomes advisable to decouple process stages.

3. **Cyclic Inventory:**

When the demand for some products is identified at regular intervals and in uniform quantities, they are termed to fall under the category of cyclic inventory. Unlike other patterns, where inventories are revised after they fall at a certain level, under Cyclic Inventory method, inventories are revised at predetermined regular intervals by identifying the demand pattern in the unit. For example, in a hospital 500 syringes are required in a day, and the hospital orders say 10000 syringes in an order. Then it will take 20 days on average for the stock to get over. Under Cyclic Inventory method, on or before the 20th day, the stock of syringes will again be refilled with an order of 10000 syringes. Hence, this pattern of inventory control works irrespective of the demand pattern and typical stock level calculations.

Economic Order Quantity (EOQ) is an attempt to balance inventory holding or carrying costs with the costs incurred from ordering or setting up machine. When large quantities are ordered or produced, inventory holding or carrying costs are increased, but ordering /set-up costs decreases. Conversely, when lot sizes decrease, inventory holding or carrying costs decrease, but the set-up or ordering cost increases since more orders are required to meet demand. When these two costs are equal, the total cost is minimised. Cycle inventory results from ordering in batches or lot sizes rather than ordering material strictly as needed. Therefore, they are also called as lot-size inventories.

4. **Pipeline Inventory:**

   Pipeline inventory, also understood as pipeline stock is used to refer such goods which have left the firm's warehouse but are still in company's distribution chain as they are yet to be bought by ultimate consumers. A distribution chain is the link which connects the manufacturers to the final customers. Hence, all such goods which have left the company's warehouse, but are still in stock with the wholesalers, retailers, agents or dealers but are not purchased by the final customers or consumers are considered as pipeline inventory. This concept looks similar to the work in progress inventory, where the product is still under production; whereas in pipeline inventory the finished good is still under the process of delivery.

   For example, the inventory with Flipkart which is still to be delivered but has left their warehouse is considered as Pipeline inventory.

5. **Safety Inventory or Safety Stock:**

   Safety stock (also known as buffer stock) is a term which is used to describe a level of extra stock that is maintained to mitigate the risk of stock outs (shortfall in material) due to uncertainties arising in the supply and demand. Adequate safety stock levels permit business operations to proceed according to their plans. Safety stock is held when there is uncertainty in the demand level or lead time for the product; it serves as an insurance against stock outs. With a new product, safety stock can be utilised as a strategic tool until the company can judge how accurate their forecast is after the first few years, especially when used with a material requirements planning worksheet. The less accurate their forecast, the more safety stock is required. With material requirements planning (MRP) worksheet a company can judge how much they will need to produce to meet their forecasted sales demand without relying on safety stock. However, a common strategy is to try and reduce the level of safety stock to help keep inventory costs low once the product demand becomes more predictable. This can be extremely important for companies with a smaller financial cushion or those trying to run on lean manufacturing, which is aimed towards eliminating waste throughout the production process. The amount of safety stock an organisation chooses to keep on hand can dramatically affect their business. Too much safety stock can result in high holding costs of inventory. In addition, products which are stored for too long a time can spoil, expire, or break during the warehousing process. Too little safety stock can result in lost sales and, thus, a higher rate of customer turnover. As a result, finding the right balance between too much and too little safety stock is essential.

4.1.7 Implications of Inventory Control Methods

The impacts of the implications of the Inventory Control Methods have been discussed ahead:

1. **Protects from fluctuations in demand:**
   Many a times, the demand forecast of a product is not accurate. There is always a small difference between the demand forecast and actual demand. However, sometimes, there is a big difference between the demand forecast and actual-demand. So, there are always chances of fluctuations in the demand of a material. These fluctuations can be adjusted if there are sufficient items in the stock of inventory. Therefore, proper inventory control protects the company from fluctuations in demand.

2. **Better services to customers:**
   If the company maintains a proper inventory of raw-materials, then it can complete its production in time. So, it can deliver the finished goods to the customers in time. Similarly, if the company has a proper inventory of finished goods, then it can satisfy the additional demand of the customers. So, inventory control helps the company to deliver goods at the right time as demanded by the customers. After making timely delivery, the company can concentrate on giving other services to the customers.

3. **Continuity of production operations:**
   Proper inventory control helps to maintain continuity of production operations. This is because it maintains a smooth flow of raw materials. So, there are no shortages of raw-materials required for production process.

4. **Reduces the risk of loss:**
   Proper inventory control helps to reduce the risk of loss due to obsolescence (outdated) or deterioration of items. This is because it checks all the items regularly. Furthermore, it sells all the slow-moving items, in time, at the market prices. It only maintains the right stock at all times. So, the chances of any item getting outdated are reduced.

5. **Minimises the administrative workload:**
   Proper inventory control helps to minimise the administrative work load of purchasing, inspection, warehousing, etc. This will reduce the manpower requirement and will minimise the labour cost too.

6. **Protects fluctuation in output:**
   Inventory control tries to reduce the gap between planned production and actual production. There are cases where the production schedule cannot be followed because of:
   - Sudden breakdown of machines,
   - Problems in supply of materials,
   - Sudden labour strikes,
   - Loss due to failure of power supply, etc.

   In such cases, the difference between planned production and actual production can be bridged by inventories held in stock.

7. **Effective use of working capital:**
   Proper inventory control helps to make effective use of working capital. Inventory control helps in maintaining the right amount of stocks of materials, components, etc. Over stocking is avoided. Therefore, the working capital will not be blocked in excess inventory.

8. **Check on loss of materials:**
   Inventory control helps to maintain a check on the loss of materials due to carelessness or pilferage (stealing). If there is no proper inventory control, then there are more chances of carelessness and pilferage by the employees, especially in the store-keeping department.

9. **Facilitates cost accounting activities:**
   Inventory control facilitates cost accounting activities. This is because, inventory control provides a means of allocating materials cost of products, departments or other operating accounts.

10. **Avoids duplication in ordering:**
    Inventory control avoids duplication in ordering of stock. This is done by maintaining a separate purchase department. This department will do all the purchasing for the full organisation. No other department is allowed to do purchasing. So there will not be any duplication in ordering of stock.

4.2 Costs Associated with Inventory

Inventory management is an attempt to maintain an adequate supply of goods while minimising inventory costs. How do we balance this supply with its costs? Investment in inventory costs money. The money which is locked up in inventories absorbs as a major part of the working capital of many organisations, which would have earned interest if kept in a bank. Thus this loss of opportunity also counts. There are some associated costs in carrying inventories. There are four types of costs that together constitute total inventory costs :

(i) Holding or carrying costs.   (ii) Set-up costs.
(iii) Purchasing costs.   (iv) Shortage Costs

(i) **Holding or carrying costs :** Inventory in excess of current demand frequently means that its holder must provide a place for its storage when not in use. This could range from a small storage area near the production line to a huge warehouse or distribution centre. A storage facility requires personnel to move the inventory when needed and to keep track of what is stored and where it is stored. If the inventory is bulky or heavy, forklifts may be necessary to move it around. Storage facility also requires heating, cooling, lighting and water. The company must pay taxes on the inventory and opportunity costs occur from the lost use of the funds that were spent on the inventory. Also obsolescence, theft and shrinkage are problems. All these add cost to holding or carrying inventory. A rough estimate is about 25 percent.

They are expenses such as storage, handling, insurance, taxes, obsolescence, theft, and interest on funds financing the goods. These charges increase as inventory levels rise. To minimise carrying costs, management makes frequent orders of small quantities. Holding costs are commonly assessed as a percentage of unit value, rather than attempting to derive monetary value for each of these costs individually. This practice is a reflection of the difficulty inherent in deriving a specific per unit cost, for example, obsolescence or theft.

(ii) **Set-up costs :** These are the costs incurred from getting a machine ready to produce the desired good. A technician, tools required for calibration and setting up the machine for smooth running, the time required for it as all the while the machine is idle and not producing anything. All these are included in set-up costs.

(iii) **Procurement or Ordering cost :** It is simply the cost of the purchased item itself. This would include the cost of calling quotations, processing tenders, placing supply orders, receiving and inspection costs, as well as the costs of verifying invoices and the payment of bills, etc. Ordering costs are those fees associated with placing an order, including expenses related to personnel in purchasing department, communications, and the handling of related paper work. Lowering these costs would be accomplished by placing small number of orders, each for a large quantity. Unlike carrying costs, ordering expenses are generally expressed as a monetary value per order.

(iv) **Shortage Costs:** When the stock of an item is depleted, an order for that item must either wait until the stock is replenished or be cancelled. There is a trade-off between carrying stock to satisfy demand and the costs resulting stock-out. This balance is sometimes difficult to obtain, because it may not be possible to estimate lost profits, the effects of lost customers or lateness penalties. Frequently, the assumed shortage cost is little more than a guess, although it is usually possible to specify a range of such costs.

While these costs may be calculated by an analysis of records from purchasing, material planning, receiving, their actual measurement will have to be done by proper systems of accounting and statistics.

∴ Total Inventory Cost = Holding or Carrying Cost + Set-up Cost + Purchasing Cost

4.3 Economic Order Quantity (EOQ)

As the name suggests, Economic Order Quantity (EOQ) model is the method that provides the company with an order quantity. This order quantity figure is where the record holding costs and ordering costs are minimised. By using this model, the companies can minimise the costs associated with the ordering and inventory holding. In 1913, **Ford W. Harris** developed this formula whereas **R. H. Wilson** is given credit for the application and in-depth analysis on this model. The economic order quantity (EOQ) is a model that is used to calculate the optimal quantity that can be purchased or produced to minimise the cost of both the carrying inventory and the processing of purchase orders or production set-ups.

The two major costs i.e. procurement cost and inventory holding/carrying cost, are diametrically opposite to each other. The right quantity to order will be the one that strikes an optimal balance between these two opposing costs. When these costs have been properly balanced, the total cost is minimised and the resultant quantity is termed as the economic order quantity and is commonly abbreviated as EOQ. It may be observed from the graph that the lowest total cost occurs at the intersection of the procurement cost curve and the carrying cost curve.

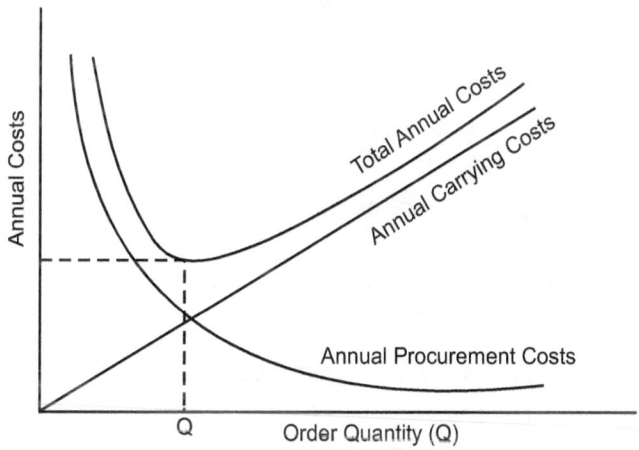

Fig 4.6: EOQ

There are different EOQ models. The most classical model was first proposed by **Wilson** in **1928**. It is popularly known as EOQ model or Wilson's Lot Size Formula. Three basic assumptions of Wilson formula are :

1. The replenishment of stock is instantaneous.
2. No shortage (or no back ordering) is allowed.
3. Price per unit is fixed and is independent of the order quantity.

Graphically, this model can be portrayed as shown.

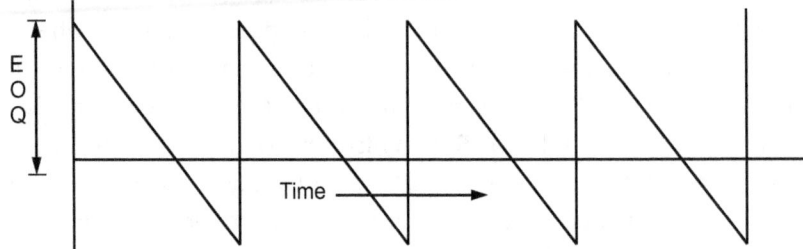

Fig 4.7: Instantaneous Replenishment of Stock

This model is also known as "EOQ model under infinite replenishment rate".

4.3.1 Assumptions Underlying the EOQ Model

(i) The demand of the item occurs uniformly over the period at the known rate.

(ii) The replenishment of the stock is instantaneous.

(iii) The time that elapses between the placing a replenishment order and receiving the item into stock, called lead time, is zero.

(iv) The price per unit is fixed and is independent of the order size.

(v) The cost to place an order and process the delivery is fixed and does not vary with the lot size.

(vi) The inventory carrying charges vary directly and linearly with the size of the inventory and are expressed as a percentage of average inventory investment.

(vii) The item can be procured in the quantities desired, there being no restriction of any kind.

(viii) The item has fairly long shelf life, there being no fear of deterioration or spoilage.

Let,

(i) Annual consumption of the item (units) be S,

(ii) Price per unit (₹) be C_u,

(iii) Procurement cost per order (₹) be C_p,

(iv) Inventory carrying cost as a percentage of average inventory investment (decimal) be i,

(v) Order quantity (units) be q,

(vi) Economic order quantity be q_o.

4.3.2 Preparation of the Model

Annual Procurement Cost = No. of Orders Per Year × Procurement Cost Per Order

$$= \frac{\text{Annual Consumption}}{\text{Order Quantity}} \times \text{Procurement Cost Per Order}$$

$$= \frac{S}{q} \times C_p \quad \quad \ldots \text{(i)}$$

Annual Inventory Carrying Out = $\frac{\text{Annual Inventory Investment}}{} \times$ Inventory Carry Cost

$$= \frac{1}{2} \text{ (Order Quantity} \times \text{Price Per Unit)}$$

$$\times \text{Inventory Carrying Cost}$$

$$= \frac{q}{2} \times C_u \times i \quad \quad \ldots \text{(ii)}$$

Annual Total Cost (ATC) $= \frac{S}{q} \times C_p + \frac{q}{2} \times C_u \times i \quad \quad \ldots \text{(iii)}$

To determine economic order quantity (q_o) that minimises the total cost, we must differentiate ATC with respect to decision variable q and set the first derivative to zero.

$$\therefore \quad \frac{d(ATC)}{dq} = \frac{-S \cdot C_p}{q^2} + \frac{C_u \cdot i}{2} = 0$$

$$\therefore \quad \frac{S \cdot C_p}{q^2} = \frac{C_u \cdot i}{2}$$

$$\therefore \quad q^2 = \frac{2 \cdot S \cdot C_p}{C_u \cdot i}$$

When order quantity equals EOQ, then $q = q_o$.

$$\therefore \quad q_o^2 = \frac{2 \cdot S \cdot C_p}{C_u \cdot i}$$

$$\therefore \quad q_o = \sqrt{\frac{2 \cdot S \cdot C_p}{C_u \cdot i}} \quad \quad \ldots \text{(iv)}$$

$\therefore$ Economic Order Quantity (EOQ)

$$= \sqrt{\frac{2 \times \text{Annual Consumption (Units)} \times \text{Procurement Cost Per Order}}{\text{Price Per Unit} \times \text{Inventory Carrying Cost}}}$$

4.3.3 Proof of Optimal Buying

To give proof of optimal buying, we must calculate annual procurement cost and annual inventory carrying cost, when quantity ordered per occasion equals Economic Order Quantity (EOQ).

$$\text{Annual Procurement cost} = \frac{S}{q} \times C_p$$

$$= \frac{S \times C_p}{q_o} \quad \text{Since at EOQ } q = q_o$$

$$= \frac{S \times C_p}{\sqrt{\frac{2 \cdot S \cdot C_p}{C_u \cdot i}}}$$

$$= \sqrt{\frac{S \cdot C_p \cdot C_u \cdot i}{2}} \quad \ldots \text{(v)}$$

$$\text{Annual inventory carrying cost} = \frac{q}{2} \times C_u \times i$$

$$= \frac{q_o}{2} \times C_u \times i \quad \text{since at EOQ, } q = q_o$$

$$= \sqrt{\frac{2 \cdot S \cdot C_p}{C_u \cdot i}} \times \frac{C_u \times i}{2}$$

$$= \sqrt{\frac{S \cdot C_p \cdot C_u \cdot i}{2}} \quad \ldots \text{(vi)}$$

It is evident from the above two equations (v) and (vi), that the best buying results when annual procurement costs equals annual inventory carrying cost.

Formula for EOQ when consumption is specified in Amount (Rupees):

At times, it is desirable to calculate order quantity in rupees instead of units.

Let, $\quad A$ = Annual Consumption in rupees

and $\quad Q_o$ = Economic Order Quantity in ₹

$$q_o = \sqrt{\frac{2 \cdot S \cdot C_p}{C_u \cdot i}}$$

$$\therefore \quad Q_o = q_o \times C_u$$

$$= \sqrt{\frac{2 \cdot S \cdot C_p}{C_u \cdot i}} \times C_u$$

$$= \sqrt{\frac{2 \cdot S \cdot C_p \cdot C_u^2}{C_u \cdot i}}$$

Now, S = Annual Consumption in units

$\therefore \quad S = \dfrac{A}{C_u}$

$\therefore \quad Q_o = \sqrt{\dfrac{2 \cdot A \cdot C_p \cdot C_u^2}{C_u \cdot C_u \cdot i}}$

$\therefore \quad Q_o = \sqrt{\dfrac{2 \cdot A \cdot C_p}{i}}$ ...(vii)

Formula for EOQ, when carrying/holding cost is specified in Rupees per unit :

$$q_o = \sqrt{\dfrac{2 \cdot S \cdot C_p}{C_u \cdot i}}$$

Let C_h be inventory holding cost or inventory carrying cost per unit per year.

$\therefore \quad C_h$ = Cost Per Unit $\times$ $\dfrac{\text{Inventory carrying cost per year}}{\text{(Percentages form or decimals)}}$

$\qquad\qquad = C_u \times i$

Replacing $C_u \times i$ by C_h, we get

$$q_o = \sqrt{\dfrac{2 \cdot S \cdot C_p}{C_h}}$$ ...(viii)

4.3.4 Economic Order Quantity with Price Discounts

Economic Order Quantity formula established under the basic EOQ model is based on the assumption that the price per unit is fixed irrespective of the quantity ordered. That is why total cost function then was assumed to be uniformly continuous. However, if the price per unit is variable (as in case of a quantity discount situation), the total cost function no longer remains uniformly continuous but becomes stepwise continuous. This implies that in order to establish optimum quantity, some of which may occur at price break level while others may occur within a price range.

In lieu of stepwise continuous nature of the total cost function, while making comparison on the basis of annual total cost, material cost should be considered in the cost calculations :

$\therefore \quad ATC = S \cdot C_u + \dfrac{S}{q} \cdot C_p + \dfrac{q}{2} \cdot C_u \cdot i$

Procedure for Computation:
1. Calculate EOQ at different price levels.
2. Decide the quantity to be purchased at each price level. (This equals EOQ or price break quantity. The latter being necessary if EOQ at a particular price level works out to be lower than corresponding price breaks quantity).

3. Calculate annual total cost at the quantities fixed under step (2).
4. Select an optimal purchase quantity, this being one which entails the lowest annual cost.

Numerical Problems on Economic Order Quantity:

Problem 1 :

A company uses 120 numbers of an item per month. Each unit costs the company ₹ 25/-. The cost of putting through each order is ₹ 36/- annual inventory carrying charges is 0.2. In what economic lots should the item be purchased to minimise annual total cost?

Solution :

$$EOQ = \sqrt{\frac{2 \cdot S \cdot C_p}{C_u \cdot i}}$$

where,
- S = Annual Consumption
  = 120 × 12
  = 1440 numbers
- C_p = Procurement Cost Per Order
  = ₹ 36/-
- C_u = Unit Cost
  = ₹ 25/-
- i = Inventory Carrying Cost Per Year
  = 0.2

$$\therefore EOQ = \sqrt{\frac{2 \times 1440 \times 36}{25 \times 0.2}}$$

$$= \sqrt{\frac{103680}{5}}$$

$$= \sqrt{20736}$$

$$= 144 \text{ numbers}$$

Problem 2 :

Rajesh Engineering buys a special pulley worth ₹ 28,800 each year. It has now entered into a contract with its manufacturer to supply it in staggered lots against the purchase order to be raised by Rajesh Engineering covering annual requirements. Cost of replenishing the stock per lot is ₹ 48/- and inventory carrying cost as percentage of average inventory investment is 12 percent. How many lots of those pulleys should be received by Rajesh Engineering and what should be the value of each consignment?

Solution :

Given
A = Annual usage of the item
 = ₹ 28,800
C_p = Procurement Cost Per Order
 = ₹ 48
i = Inventory Carrying Cost Per Year
 = 0.12

$$Q_o = \sqrt{\frac{2 \cdot A \cdot C_p}{i}}$$

$$= \sqrt{\frac{2 \times 28{,}800 \times 48}{0.12}}$$

$$= \sqrt{\frac{27{,}64{,}800}{0.12}} = \sqrt{2{,}30{,}40{,}000}$$

$$= 4800$$

No. of lots of be received in a year

$$= \frac{\text{Annual usage}}{Q_o}$$

$$= \frac{28{,}800}{4{,}800}$$

$$= 6$$

∴ The pulleys should be procured six times in a year and the value of each consignment should be ₹ 4.800.

Problem 3 :

Switches are procured by a panel manufacturer from a local firm and are consumed at an average rate of ₹ 125/- per month. If the procurement cost is ₹ 42/- per order, and the cost holding it in stock is ₹ 1.40 per switch per year. Determine the quantity that should be procured at a time to optimise the costs involved. If the consumption of the above item increases to 15 numbers per day its actual inventory cost is 0.20 per unit per day, what will be its revised EOQ ?

Solution :

EOQ when inventory carrying cost is specified in ₹ per unit,

$$q_o = \sqrt{\frac{2 \cdot S \cdot C_p}{C_h}}$$

where, S = Annual Consumption
$= 125 \times 12 = 1500$
C_p = Procurement Cost Per Order
$= 42$
C_h = Inventory holding cost or inventory carrying cost per year
$= 1.40$

$\therefore \quad q_o = \sqrt{\dfrac{2 \times 1500 \times 42}{1.40}}$

$= \sqrt{3000 \times 30}$

$= \sqrt{90000} = 300 \text{ number}$

Revised EQO :

Assuming 300 working days per year,

$S = 15 \times 300$
$= 4500$
$C_p = 42$
$C_n = 0.02 \times 300 = 6$

$q_o = \sqrt{\dfrac{2 \cdot S \cdot C_p}{C_h}}$

$= \sqrt{\dfrac{2 \times 4500 \times 42}{6}}$

$= \sqrt{4500 \times 14}$

$= \sqrt{63000}$

$= 250.998 \sim 251 \text{ numbers}$

Problem 4 :

The Precision Co. uses 72,000 values per year and the usage is fairly constant at 6,000 values per month. Each value costs the company ₹ 1.80. The carrying cost for the company has been estimated at 18 percent of the average inventory invested. The cost to place an order and process the delivery is ₹ 36.

(a) Calculate economic order quantity.

(b) What is the stock turn-over rate ignoring safety stock is EOQ is ordered frequently ?

(c) What will be the effect of total cost if stock turnover rate is reduced to one-third by infrequent ordering ?

Solution :

(a)
$$q_o = \sqrt{\frac{2 \cdot S \cdot C_p}{C_u \cdot i}}$$

where, S = annual consumption = 72,000

C_p = Procurement cost = ₹ 36

C_u = Unit Cost = ₹ 1.80

i = Inventory carrying cost = 0.18

$$\therefore Q_o = \sqrt{\frac{2 \times 72000 \times 36}{1.80 \times 0.18}}$$

$$= \sqrt{\frac{72 \times 72000}{0.324}}$$

$$= \sqrt{16000000}$$

$$= 4000 \text{ units}$$

(b) Stock turnover rate refers to the frequency of replenishment of stock of an item over a period of time, say a year. In the absence of safety stock, it may be expressed as :

$$n = \frac{S}{q_o}$$

$$= \frac{72000}{4000} = 18$$

(c) Annual Total Cost (ATC)

$$= \frac{S}{q} \times C_p + \frac{1}{2} \times q \times C_u \times i$$

when $q = q_o$ i.e. 4,000 units,

$n = 18$

$$ATC_{q_o} = \frac{72000}{4000} \times 36 + \frac{1}{2} \times 4000 \times 1.8 \times 0.18$$

$$= 648 + 648$$

$$= 1296$$

If stock turnover rate is reduced to $\frac{1}{3}$, then

$$n = \frac{q_o}{3} = \frac{18}{3} = 6$$

$$\therefore \quad q = \frac{72000}{6} = 12{,}000$$

$$ATC_q = \frac{72000}{12000} \times 36 + \frac{1}{2} \times 12000 \times 1.8 \times 0.18$$

$$= 216 + 1944 = 2160$$

From the annual total costs calculated above for different stock turnover rates, it can be concluded that the annual total cost will increase by ₹ 864/- (i.e. 2160 – 1296) when the stock turnover rate of the item is reduced to one-third.

Problem 5 :

The requirement of a particular size of oil seal at an automobile firm is estimated at 50,000 nos. next year. The oil seal is available locally with a lead time of 2 weeks and it costs ₹ 10 each. The cost of order writing, follow-up, primary inspection and in warding stores is computed at ₹ 60 per order. The holding cost is estimated at ₹ 3 per unit for storage plus 30 percent per unit per year on account of opportunity cost of the capital.

(a) How many units should the firm order at a time to optimise the inventory costs ?

(b) What are the annual inventory costs ?

Solution :

(a) $$q_o = \sqrt{\frac{2 \cdot S \cdot C_p}{C_h}}$$

where, S = annual consumption
$$= 50{,}000$$

C_p = Procurement Cost Per Order
$$= 60$$

C_h = ₹ 3 + 30% of ₹ 10
$$= 3 + \frac{30}{100} \times 10$$
$$= 6$$

$$\therefore \quad q_o = \sqrt{\frac{2 \times 50{,}000 \times 60}{6}}$$

$$= \sqrt{10{,}00{,}000}$$

$$= 1000 \text{ units}$$

(b) Annual Inventory Cost = Annual Total Cost

$$ATC = \frac{S}{q} \cdot C_p + \frac{1}{2} \cdot q \cdot \underline{C_u \cdot i} \qquad \text{where, } C_u \cdot i = C_h$$

$$= \frac{50{,}000}{1000} \times 60 + \frac{1000 \times 6}{2}$$

$$= 3000 + 3000$$

$$= 6000$$

Problem 6 :

An aircraft company buys an item in lots of ISO units which is six months requirements. The cost per unit is ₹ 80 and the ordering cost is ₹ 200 per batch order. The inventory carrying cost is estimated at 20 percent of the average inventory investment.

(a) What is the annual total cost of the existing inventory policy ?

(b) How much money can be saved by using economic order quantity ?

Solution :

(a) Annual Total Costing of existing Inventory (ATC)

$$= \frac{S}{q} \times C_p + \frac{1}{2} \times q \times C_u \times i$$

where,
S = Annual requirement
$= 750 \times 2$
$= 1500$ units

C_p = Procurement cost
$= 200$

C_u = Cost per unit
$= 80$

i = Inventory carrying cost per annum
$= 0.20$

q = Order quantity under existing policy
$= 750$ units

$$\therefore \quad ATC = \frac{1500}{750} \times 200 + \frac{1}{2} \times 750 \times 80 \times 0.20$$

$$= 400 + 6000$$

$$= 6400$$

(b) $$ATC_{q_o} = \frac{S}{q_o} \times C_p + \frac{1}{2} \times q_o \times C_u \times i$$

$$q_o = \sqrt{\frac{2 S \cdot C_p}{C_u \cdot i}}$$

$$= \sqrt{\frac{2 \times 1500 \times 200}{80 \times 0.20}}$$

$$= \sqrt{\frac{600000}{1.60}}$$

$$= \sqrt{37500}$$

$$= 193.649 \simeq 194$$

$$ATC_{q_o} = \frac{1500}{194} \times 200 + \frac{1}{2} \times 194 \times 80 \times 0.20$$

$$= 1546 + 1552$$

$$= 3098$$

∴ Annual saving if economic order quantity purchases are made in place of six-monthly purchases:

$$= ATC_q - ATC_q$$
$$= 6400 - 3098$$
$$= 3302$$

Problem 7 :

A manufacturer of control panels spends ₹ 34,000 p.a. on its purchasing activities. ₹ 67,200 are spent each year in maintaining inventory of ₹ 4.2 lakh (expenses referred above are only the variable portion of the total expenses). Around 850 orders are placed every year to replenish stocks of the various items.

One of the items whose annual consumption is 9600 nos. is bought by the company at the rate of ₹ 30 each. The company has entered into an annual contract with the supplier of the item based on the staggered deliveries. How frequently should the company receive the staggered deliveries and in what quantities ?

Solution :

Given S = Annual consumption
                = 9600 nos.

C_p = Procurement Cost Per Order to be calculated

$$= \frac{\text{Expenses on procurement activity}}{\text{No. of orders per year}}$$

$$= \frac{34{,}000}{850}$$

$$= 40$$

C_u = Cost per unit
= 30

i = Inventory carrying cost p.a. to be calculated

$= \dfrac{\text{Inventory carrying charges spent}}{\text{Average inventory investment p.a.}}$

$= \dfrac{67200}{4,20,000}$

= 0.16

$$q_o = \sqrt{\dfrac{2 \times S \times C_p}{C_u \times i}}$$

Substituting all the values, we get

$$q_o = \sqrt{\dfrac{2 \times 9600 \times 40}{30 \times 0.16}}$$

= 400 nos.

Problem 8 :

Sony Company buys assembly kits from its vendor. Each kit costs the company ₹ 50. The inventory carrying charges and the procurement cost have been estimated at 20 percent of the average inventory investment and ₹ 40 per order respectively.

(a) Calculate economic order quantity of the kit assuming annual production programme being fixed at 5000 no. of assemblies.

(b) "If the actual costs to place an order and execute the delivery and inventory carrying cost are ₹ 50 and 16 percent, the optimal policy would change". How much is the company losing per year because of imperfect cost information ?

Solution :

$$\text{EOQ, } q_o = \sqrt{\dfrac{2 \cdot S \cdot C_p}{C_u \cdot i}}$$

where,

S = Annual consumption
= 50000 nos.

C_u = Cost per unit
= ₹ 50

C_p = Procurement cost per order
   (i) estimated = ₹ 40
   (ii) actual = ₹ 50

i = Inventory carrying charges p.a.
(i) estimated = 0.20
(ii) actual = 0.16

Substituting these values, we get

$$q_o \text{ (at estimated costs)} = \sqrt{\frac{2 \times 5000 \times 40}{50 \times 0.20}}$$

= 200 nos.

$$q_o \text{ (at actual costs)} = \sqrt{\frac{2 \times 5000 \times 50}{50 \times 0.16}}$$

= 250 nos.

Now we will calculate annual total cost under both order quantities. For cost calculations, actual values/costs need to be considered to obtain true costs.

$$ATC_{q_o = 200} = \frac{S}{q} \times C_p + \frac{q}{2} \times C_u \times i$$

$$= \frac{5000}{200} \times 50 + \frac{200}{2} \times 50 \times 0.16$$

= 1250 + 800

= 2050

$$ATC_{q_o = 250} = \frac{S}{q_o} \times C_p + \frac{q_o}{2} \times C_u \times i$$

$$= \frac{5000}{250} \times 50 + \frac{250}{2} \times 50 \times 0.16$$

= 1000 + 1000

= 2000

Difference between annual total costs

= 2050 − 2000

= 50

∴ The company is losing ₹ 50 per year because of imperfect cost structure (wrong estimation).

Problem 9 :

A manufacturer of bicycle requires a special bearing at the rate of 300 nos. per year. Each bearing costs the company ₹ 36. The procurement cost and the inventory carrying cost have been calculated at ₹ 30 and 20 percent respectively.

If the supplier offers a discount of ₹ 2 bearing on an order of 200 or above, should higher quantity be purchased ?

Solution :

Given
S = Annual consumption = 300 nos.
C_p = Procurement cost per order = ₹ 30
C_{u_1} = Basic unit cost = ₹ 36
C_{u_2} = Discounted unit cost = ₹ 34
i = Inventory carrying out cost = 0.20

The above prices are valid for quantities as below :

Price	Range of quantity
₹ 36	0 < q < 200
₹ 34	200 ≤ q

Step 1 : EOQ at different price levels

(I) Price ₹	(II) EOQ	(III) Quantity to be purchased
₹ 36	$\sqrt{\dfrac{2 \cdot S \cdot C_p}{C_{u_1} \cdot i}} = \sqrt{\dfrac{2 \times 300 \times 30}{36 \times 0.20}}$ $= \sqrt{2500}$ $= 50$	50
₹ 34	$= \sqrt{\dfrac{2 \times 300 \times 30}{34 \times 0.20}}$ $= \sqrt{2647}$ $= 51$	200

Step 2 : Quantity to be purchased at each price level (Column III).

This equals EOQ or price-break-quantity the latter being necessary if EOQ at particular price levels works out to be lower than corresponding price break quantity.

Step 3 : ATC at the quantities fixed under step (2).

Cost Elements	Order quantity	
	50	200
Annual Cost of Materials $= S \times C_u$	300 × 36 = 10,800	300 × 34 = 10,200
Annual Procurement Cost $= \dfrac{S}{q} \times C_p$	$\dfrac{300}{50} \times 30 = 180$	$\dfrac{300}{200} \times 30 = 45$

Operations & Supply Chain Management — Inventory Planning & Control

Annual Inventory $= \dfrac{q}{2} \times C_u \times i$	$\dfrac{50 \times 36 \times 20}{2} = 180$	$\dfrac{200 \times 34 \times 20}{2} = 680$
Annual Total Cost (1 + 2 + 3)	= 11,160	= 10,925

Step 4 : Selecting an optimal purchase quantity. From the annual total cost figures calculated above, we find that cost incurred is the least when quantity purchased is 200 nos.

$$\therefore \quad EOQ = 200 \text{ Nos.}$$

Problem 10 :

A company uses 2000 numbers per annum of a special stud in the manufacture of its products. The studs are procured from a local manufacture at a basic price of ₹ 10 each. The inventory cost data is :

    Procurement cost per order   = ₹ 20

    Inventory carrying cost   = 20%

The suppliers offers following discounts on the basic price for order quantities of :

Order quantity	Discount
400 – 799	2%
800 – 1599	4%
1600 & above	5%

What quantity should the company order to optimise cost ?

Step 1 : EOQ at different price levels.

Price Level	EOQ	Quantity to be ordered
1. Basic price ₹ 10	$\sqrt{\dfrac{2 \times 2000 \times 20}{10 \times 0.20}} = 200$	200
2. Discounted price 2% ₹ 9.80	$\sqrt{\dfrac{2 \times 2000 \times 20}{9.80 \times 0.20}} = 202$	400
3. Discounted price 4% ₹ 9.60	$\sqrt{\dfrac{2 \times 2000 \times 20}{9.60 \times 0.20}} = 204$	800
4. Discounted price 5% ₹ 9.50	$\sqrt{\dfrac{2 \times 2000 \times 20}{9.50 \times 0.20}} = 205$	1000

Step 2 : Quantity to be purchased at each price level which equals EOQ or price break quantity calculated in column III above.

Step 3 : Annual total cost at the quantities fixed under step (2).

Cost Element	Price Discount			
	–	2%	4%	5%
	Quantity to be purchased			
	200	400	800	1600
(A) Annual Material Cost ($S \times C_u$)	20,000	19,600	19,200	19,000
(B) Annual Procurement Cost $\left(\dfrac{S}{q} \times C_p\right)$	200	100	30	25
(C) Annual Inventory Carrying Cost $\left(\dfrac{1}{2} \times q \times C_u \times i\right)$	200	392	768	1520
Annual Total Cost (A + B + C)	20,400	20,092	19,998	20,545

Step 4 : Selecting an optimal purchase quantity.

It may be observed that the most economic order quantity is 800 studs at which the supplier offers 4 percent discount.

4.4 Inventory or Material Control

Inadequate control of inventories can result in both under and overstocking of items. Under stocking results in missed deliveries, lost sales, dissatisfied customers, and production bottlenecks; overstocking unnecessarily ties up funds that might be more productive elsewhere. The price tag for excessive overstocking can be staggering when inventory holding costs are high.

Inventory management has two main concerns. One is the level of customer service, that is, to have the right goods in sufficient quantities, in the right place, at the right time. The other is the costs of ordering and carrying inventories.

The overall objective of inventory management is to achieve satisfactory levels of customer service while keeping inventory costs within reasonable bounds. Towards this end, the decision maker tries to achieve a balance in stocking.

Managers have a number of measures of performance to judge the effectiveness of inventory management. The most important is the customer satisfaction, which can be measured by the number and quantity of backorders and/or customer complaints. A widely used measure is inventory turnover, which is the ratio of annual cost of goods sold to average inventory investment. The turnover ratio indicates how many times in a year the inventory is sold. Generally, the higher the ratio, the better, because that implies more efficient use of inventories. However, the desirable number of turns depends on the industry and what the profit margins are. The higher the profit margins, the lower the acceptable number of inventory turns, and vice versa. Also, a product that takes a long time to manufacture, or a long time to sell, will have a low turnover rate. Also, a product that takes a long time to manufacture or along time to sell will have a low turnover rate. This is often the case with high-end retailers (high profit margins). Conversely, supermarkets (low profit margins) have a fairly high turnover rate. It should be noted that there should be a balance between inventory investment and maintaining good customer service. Managers often use inventory turnover to evaluate inventory management performance. Monitoring this metric over time can yield insights into changes in performance.

Another useful measure is days of inventory on hand, a number that indicates the expected number of days of sales that can be supplied from existing inventory. Here a balance is desirable; a high number of days might imply excess inventory, while a low number might imply a risk of running out of stock.

4.4.1 Classification of Material or Inventory

Selective treatment of inventories is based on the following basic philosophy of business.

"Neither one can control everything nor should one try to do so even if one can. Uniform control is rarely effective. Effectiveness results when important aspects of a problem are pursued more rigorously than others."

The above can effectively be applied in inventory so as to identify items which are more important than others. The classification enables managerial time being spent according to the importance of the item.

Selective control means variations in method of control from item to item, which is on selective basis. The criteria used for the purpose may be cost of the item, criticality, lead time, consumption, procurement difficulties or something else. Various classifications are employed to render treatment to different types of materials. These are given below:

Table 4.1: Types of Classification

Classification	Criterion employed
1. ABC analysis	Usage value (i.e. consumption per periodic price per unit)
2. HML analysis (High Medium Low).	Unit price (i.e. it does not take consumption into account)
3. VED analysis (Vital Essential Desirable).	Criticality of the item (i.e. loss of production)
4. SDE analysis (Scarce Difficult Easy).	Procurement difficulties
5. GOLF analysis (Government - Ordinary Local Foreign)	Source of procurement
6. S-OS analysis (Seasonal-Off Seasonal)	Seasonality
7. FSN analysis (Fast Slow Non-moving)	Issue from stores
8. XYZ analysis	Inventory Investment

4.4.1 (a) ABC Analysis

It is a system of inventory control where discriminating control is exercised over different items of stores classified on the basis of investment involved. Usually the items are divided into three categories according to their importance, namely their value and frequency of replenishment during a period.

(i) 'A' category of items consists of only a small percentage i.e. about 10 percent of the total items handled by the stores but require heavy investment (in Rupee value) about 70 percent of the total inventory value.

(ii) 'B' category of items (relatively less important) constitutes 20 percent of the total items handled by stores, having an investment (in Rupee value) of about 20 percent of the total inventory value.

(iii) 'C' category consists of large number of items handled by stores say 70 percent, having relatively small investment say 10 percent of the total inventory value.

'A' category of items is controlled effectively by using a regular system, which ensures neither over-stocking nor shortage of materials for production. The stocks of materials are controlled by fixing certain levels like maximum level, minimum level and reorder level. Reduction in inventory management costs is achieved by determining economic order quantity. To avoid shortage and to minimise heavy investment in inventories, the techniques of value analyses, variety reduction, standardisation etc. are used.

In case of 'B' category of items, less degree of control as applicable to 'A' category items is warranted. The orders for the items, belonging to this category, may be placed after reviewing the situation periodically.

For 'C' category of items, there is no need of exercising constant control. Orders for these items are placed either at 6 months interval or yearly interval depending on the consumption pattern. In this case, the objective is to economise on ordering and handling costs.

Example :

Category	Cost Range (₹)	Total No. of items	Total Cost (₹)
C	1-500	12,000	10,00,000
B	501-2000	2,000	15,00,000
A	2001-1,00,000	1,000	1,00,00,000
		15,000	1,25,00,000

Percentage of total items and costs:

Category	Percentage of total items	Cumulative % of total items	Percentage of total cost	Cumulative Percentage of the total cost
A	7	7	80	80
B	13	20	12	92
C	80	100	8	100

ABC Analysis is a method of material control according to value. The basic principle is that high value items are more closely controlled than the low value items. The materials are grouped according to the value and frequency of replenishment during a period. The inventories are arranged in order of magnitude and are classified in three classes as follows :

'A' Class items	Small percentage of the total items but having higher values.
'B' Class items	More percentage of the total items but having medium values.
'C' Class items	High percentage of the total items but having low values.

The following illustration summarises the above classification :

Example

A manufacturing concern is having 2,000 items of materials valuing ₹ 2,00,000 in total. Prepare the statement showing the classification of stock according to ABC Analysis.

Answer

Category	Quantity		Value		
	%	Number of Items	%	Amount ₹	Average Value ₹
'A' High value items	10%	200	70%	1,40,000 = (₹ 1,40,000 ÷ 200)	700
'B' Medium value items	20%	400	20%	40,000 = (₹ 40,000 ÷ 400) 20,000 = (₹ 20,000 ÷ 1,400)	100
'C' Low value items	70%	1,400	10%		14.29
Total	100%	2,000	100%	2,00,000	

For the sake of simplicity, the above percentages have been considered. But in practice, the percentages may vary between 5 percent and 10 percent, 10 percent and 20 percent and, 70 percent and 85 percent.

The report of Indian Productivity Team on 'Stores and Inventory Control in USA, Japan and West Germany, gives the following example of ABC Analysis.

Group	% of items	% of cost
A	8	75
B	25	20
C	67	5
Total	100	100

Principle of Pareto's Law :

ABC Analysis is based on the principle known as 'Pareto's Law' developed by Pareto, an Italian economists. According to this law, 'in any series of elements to be controlled, selected small fractions, in terms of numbers of elements, would always account for a large fraction in terms of effect'.

ABC Analysis is popularly known as **'Always Better Control'**. It is also known as **'Control by Importance and Exception'**. It is based on the concept of **Selective Inventory Management**. i.e. concentrate your efforts where the results are maximised.

In foreign countries, Bin Cards and Stores Ledger Cards are not maintained for 'C' class items. These are issued directly to the production foreman concerned and controlled through norms of consumption based on production targets. By doing this, 70 percent of the efforts required for maintaining the Bin Cards and Stores Ledger Cards is eliminated. With 30% of the efforts, an organisation will be able to exercise control on 90 percent of the inventory values. This reduces the clerical costs and ensures close control on costly items in which a large amount of capital is invested.

Advantages of ABC Analysis :

The important advantages of ABC Analysis are given below :

(i) To minimise purchasing cost and carrying cost i.e. holding cost.

(ii) Closer and stricter control on these items which represent a high portion of total stock value.

(iii) Ensuring availability of supplies at all times.

(iv) Clerical costs can be reduced.

(v) Inventory is maintained at optimum level and thereby investment in inventory can be regulated and will be minimum. 'A' items will be ordered more frequently and as such the investment in inventory is reduced.

(vi) Maintaining enough safety stock for 'C' items.

(vii) Equal attention to A, B and C items is not desirable as it is expensive.

(viii) It is based on the concept of Selective Inventory Management and it helps in maintaining a high stock turnover ratio.

The ABC classification process is an analysis of a range of items, such as finished products or customers into three categories : **A** - outstandingly important; **B** - of average importance; **C** - relatively unimportant as a basis for a control scheme. Each category can and sometimes should be handled in a different way, with more attention being devoted to category A, less to B, and less to C.

ABC analysis is based on the principle "Vital few : trivial many." This analysis segregates all the items into three categories, viz A, B and C. The few items, called A items hold the key to business, while many items, called B and C category. Categorisation so made enables one to pay the right amount of attention as merited by the items.

A items : Statistics reveal that just a handful of items (below 10 percent of total items) account for bulk of the annual expenditure on materials (approx. 70-75 percent of total expenditure on materials). These items require detailed and rigid control and need to be stocked in smaller quantities. These items should be procured frequently, the quantity per occasion being small. The inventory can be kept at minimum by frequent ordering. A healthy approach would be to enter into a contract with the manufacturers of A items and have their supply in staggered lots according to production planned.

B items : These items are generally 10-15 percent of the total items which account for 10-15% of the total expenditure items. The control on these items need not be as detailed and as rigid as applied to C items.

C items : These are numerous, as many as 70-75 percent of the total items which are not expensive and account for only 5-10 percent of the total expenditure. Hence insignificant items and do not require close control. These items should be procured infrequently and in sufficient quantities to avail price discounts, exactly reverse of A items.

Procedure of conducting ABC analysis :
1. Prepare the list of the items and estimate their annual consumption (units).
2. Determine unit price (or cost) of each item.
3. Multiply each annual consumption by its unit price (or cost) to obtain its annual consumption in rupees (annual usage).
4. Arrange items in the descending order of their annual usage starting with the highest annual usage down to the smallest usage.
5. Calculate cumulative annual usages and express the same as cumulative usage percentages. Also express the no. of items into cumulative items percentages.
6. Graph cumulative usage percentages against cumulative items percentages and segregate the items into A, B and C categories.
7. Decide the policies of control for the three categories.

Points to be remembered while doing ABC analysis :
- ABC curve is a lopsided distribution wherein a small percentage of items account for a major expenditure on materials. Therefore, ABC curve is similar in shape for different industries.
- All items that the company consumes should be considered together while doing ABC analysis. Separate classification of inventory is meaningless. Company manufacturing more than one product should also make only one ABC analysis. Separate ABC analysis for each product is error prone.
- Though generally annual consumption figures are considered for ABC analysis, yet it is not a rule. If convenient, then quarterly or six monthly consumption figures can be considered.

Though classification of items is done into three categories A, B and C, yet if required, items may be classified into more than three categories.

4.4.1 (b) HML Analysis

HML analysis is similar to ABC analysis except for the difference that instead of usage value, unit price is used. The items under this analysis are classified into three groups which are called High, Medium, and Low. To classify, the items are listed in the descending order of their unit price. The cut-off lines are then fixed by the management for deciding three categories. For example, the management may decide that all items of unit price above ₹1000 will be of H category, those with unit price between ₹100 to ₹1000 will be of M category and those having unit price below ₹100 will be of L category.

Objectives of HML analysis:
- Assess storage and security requirements (e.g. high priced items like bearings, worm shafts, worm wheels etc. require to be kept in the cupboards).

- To keep control over consumption at the departmental head level (e.g. indents of high and medium priced items are authorised by the departmental head after careful scrutiny of the consumption figures).
- Determine the frequency of stock verification e.g. high priced items is checked more frequently than low priced items.
- To evolve buying policies to control purchases, e.g. excess supply than the ordered quantity may not be accepted for H and M groups, while lot may be accepted for L group.
- To delegate authorities to different buyers to make petty cash purchases, e.g. H and M category of items may be purchased by senior buyers and L category of items by junior buyers.

4.4.1 (c) VED Analysis

VED ansalysis represents classification of items based on their criticality. The analysis classifies the items into three groups called Vital, Essential and Desirable.

Vital category encompasses those items for want of which production would come to halt. Essential group includes items whose stock outs cost is very high and Desirable group comprises of items which do not cause any immediate loss of production or their stock out entails nominal expenditure and causes minor disruptions for a short duration.

VED analysis is carried out to identify critical items. An item, which usage wise belongs to C category may be critical from production point of view if its stock out can cause heavy production loss.

An item may be vital for a number of reasons, namely-
- If the non-availability of the item can cause serious production losses.
- Lead-time for procurement is very large.
- It is non-standard item and is procured to buyer's design.
- The source of supply is only one and is located far off from the buyer's plant.

Steps involved in making VED analysis are as under :

(i) Identify the factors to be considered for VED analysis.
(ii) Assign points/weightages to the factors according to their importance to the company.
(iii) Divide each factor into three degrees and allocate points to each degree.
(iv) Prepare categorisation plan.
(v) Evaluate items one by one against each factor, assign points to the item depending upon the extent of presence of the factor in the item.
(vi) Place the items into V, E and D categories depending upon the points scored by them and basis of certification set under steps (iv).

Table 4.2 : Typical VED Analysis Categorisation Plan

Sr. No.	Factor	First degree	Second degree	Third degree
1.	Stock out cost in the event of non-availability (30)	Above ₹ x (30)	Between ₹ x to y (60)	Above ₹ y (90)
2.	Lead time for procurement (30)	1-4 weeks (30)	4-8 weeks (60)	Over 8 weeks (90)
3	Nature of the item (20)	Produced to commercial standard, or off the shelf availability (20)	Produced to suppliers design (40)	Produced to buyer's design or proprietary items (60)
4	Sources of supply (20)	Local (20)	Outstation (40)	Imported, quota items i.e. controlled supply (60)

Table 4.3: Typical Categorisation Plan

Points	Classification
100-160	Desirable
161-230	Essential
231-300	Vital

VED analysis is best suited for spares inventory. In fact, it is advantageous to use more than one method, e.g. ABC and VED analysis together would be helpful for inventory control of spares.

4.4.1 (d) SDE Analysis

SDE analysis is based on the problems of procurement namely:
- Non-availability,
- Scarcity,
- Longer lead-time,
- Geographical location of suppliers, and
- Reliability of suppliers.

S-D-E analysis classifies the items into three groups called "Scarce", "Difficult" and "Easy". The information so developed is then used to decide purchasing materials.

"Scarce" classification comprises of items which are in short supply, imported or channelised through government agencies. Such items are based to procure limited number of times a year in lieu of effort and expenditure involved in the procedure for import.

"Difficult" classification includes those items which are available indigenously but are not easy to procure. All items which come from long distance and for which reliable sources do not exist fall into this category. Even the items which are difficult to manufacture and only one or two manufacturers are available, belong to this group. Suppliers of such items require several weeks of advance notice.

"Easy" classification covers those items which are readily available, items produced to commercial standards, items where supply exceeds demand and others which are locally available fall into this group.

S-D-E analysis is employed by the purchase department:

(i) To decide on the method of buying, e.g. forward buying method may be followed for some of the items in the "Scarce" group, "scheduled buying" and "contract buying" for "easy" group.

(ii) To fix responsibility of buyers, e.g. Senior buyers may be given the responsibility of "S" and "D" groups while items in "E" groups may be handled by junior buyers or even directly by the storekeeper.

4.4.1 (e) GNGLF Analysis / Golf Analysis

GNGLF Analysis (or GOLF Analysis) like SDE analysis is based on the category of suppliers on the criteria of quality, lead time, terms of payment, continuity or otherwise of supply and administrative work involved. The analysis classifies the items into four groups namely GNGL and F.

"G" group covers items procured from "Government" suppliers such as the STC, MMTC and public sector undertakings. Transactions with this category of suppliers involve long lead time and payments in advance or against delivery.

"NG" (O in GOLF analysis) group comprises of items procured from "Non-Government" (or Ordinary) suppliers. Transactions with this category of suppliers involve moderate delivery time and availability of credit, usually in the range of 30 to 60 days.

"L" group contains items bought from "Local suppliers". The items bought from local suppliers are those which are cash purchased or purchased on blanket orders.

"F" group contains those items which are purchased from "foreign" suppliers. The transaction with such suppliers :

- Necessitate search of foreign suppliers.
- Require opening of letter of credit.
- Involve lot of administrative and procedural work.
- Require making of arrangement for shipping and port clearance.

4.4.1(f) S-OS Analysis

- SOS Analysis is based on seasonality of the items and it classifies the items into two groups S (Seasonal) and OS (i.e. Off seasonal).
- The analysis identifies items which are :
- (i) Seasonal and are only available only for a limited period. For example, agricultural produce like raw mangoes, raw materials for cigarette and paper industries etc. are available for a limited time and therefore such items are procured to last the full year.
- (ii) Seasonal but are available throughout the year. Their prices are lower during harvest time. The quantity of such items are required to be fixed after comparing the cost savings due to lower prices if purchased during season against higher cost of carrying inventories if purchased throughout the year.
- (iii) Non-seasonal items whose quantity is decided on different considerations.

4.4.1 (g) MNG Analysis

MNG Analysis is based on stock turnover rate and it classifies the items into M (moving item), N (non-moving item) and G (Ghost items).

M (moving items) are those items which are consumed from time to time. N (non-moving items) are those which are not consumed in the last one year, G (Ghost items) are those items which had nil balance both in the beginning and at the end of the last financial year and there were no transactions (receipts or issues) during the year.

Analysis mainly helps to identify non-existing items for which the store keeps bin-cards or waste computer stationary while preparing stores ledger. Stores department even might have ear-marked space for these non-existed items.

All pending/open purchase orders (if any) of such items should be cancelled.

4.4.1 (h) FSN Analysis

FSN Analysis is based on consumption figures of the items and is classified into three groups : F (fast moving), S (slow moving) and N (non-moving).

To conduct the analysis, the last date of receipt or the last date of issue whichever is later is taken into account and the period, usually in terms of number of months, that have elapsed since the last movement are recorded. Such an analysis helps to identify :

(i) Active items which require to be reviewed regularly.
(ii) Surplus items whose stocks are higher than their rate of consumption; and
(iii) Non-moving items which are not being consumed. The last two categories are reviewed further to decide on disposal action to deplete their stocks and thereby release company's productive capital.

Further detailed analysis is made of the third category in regard to their year-wise stocks and items can be classified as non-moving for 2 years, non-moving for 3 years, non-moving for 5 years and so on.

4.4.1 (i) XYZ Analysis

XYZ Analysis is based on value of stocks on hand (i.e. investment on inventory). Items whose inventory values are high are called X items while those whose inventory items are low are called Z items and Y items are those which have moderate inventory stocks.

Usually XYZ analysis is used in conjunction with either ABC analysis or HML analysis.

Table 4.4: XYZ Analysis when Combined with ABC Analysis

Class of items	A	B	C
X	Efforts to be made reduce stocks to Z category	Efforts to be made / convert these to Y category	Steps to be taken to dispose to off surplus stocks
Y	Efforts to be made convert these to Z category	*	Control may be further tightened
Z	*	Stock levels may be reviewed twice a year.	*

XYZ analysis when combined with FSN analysis helps to formulate more specific strategies.

Table 4.5: XYZ and JSN Analysis Combined

Class of items	F	S	N
X	Tight control	Deplete stocks to very low level	Dispose - off immediately at optimum price.
Y	*	Deplete the stocks further at good price	Dispose - off as early as possible
Z	Liberal control (to reduce clerical cost)	*	Dispose - off as early as possible even at lower prices.

Note : * items are within control. No further action is necessary.

XYZ, therefore, helps to identify a few items which account for large amount of money locked up in stock and take steps for their liquidation/reduction.

XYZ when combined with FSN analysis helps to classify non-moving items into XN, YN and ZN group and thereby identify a handful of non-moving items which account for bulk of non-moving stock. These can be studied individually in details to take decision on their disposal or retention.

4.4.2 Inventory Turnover Ratios

This is also one of the useful methods of exercising material control. The inventory ratios can be calculated by the following formula :

(i) Turnover of Stores Materials : Inventory Turnover Ratio i.e. Stock Turnover is usually measured in terms of the ratios of the value of materials consumed to the average stock held during the period.

$$\text{Stock Turnover} = \frac{\text{Value of Materials Consumed during the period}}{\text{Cost of Average Stock held during the period}}$$

(ii) Inventory Turnover in days $= \dfrac{\text{Number of Days during the period}}{\text{Stock Turnover Ratio}}$

$$\text{Average Stock} = \frac{\text{Opening Stock + Closing Stock}}{2}$$

$$\text{Inventory Performance Index} = \frac{\text{Actual Stock Turnover Ratio}}{\text{Standard Stock Turnover Ratio}} \times 100$$

A high ratio indicates fast-moving stock whereas a low ratio indicates slow-moving stock. It is, therefore, advantageous to compare the stock turnover of the different grades and kinds of materials in order to find out the slow-moving items thus, enabling the management to avoid blocking up of capital in such slow-moving stocks. If stock turnover ratio for a particular item is zero, it means that the item had not been used during the period.

FORMULAE TO REMEMBER

(i) Inventory Turnover Ratio expressed in Number of Times :

$$= \frac{\text{Cost of Materials Consumed during the period}}{\text{Cost of Average Stock held during the period}}$$

(ii) Inventory Turnover Ratio expressed in Number of Days :

$$= \frac{\text{Number of Days during the period}}{\text{Inventory Turnover Ratio}}$$

where,

- Inventory Turnover = Material Turnover = Turnover of Stores Material
- Cost of Materials Consumed = Opening Stock + Purchases – Closing Stock
- Cost of Average Stock = Average Inventory = $\dfrac{\text{Opening Stock + Closing Stock}}{2}$

Indications :

(i) Inventory Turnover Ratio expressed in Number of Times :

(a) Low Ratio indicates slow moving stock, accumulation of obsolete stock, carrying of too much stock, i.e. those items of stores which are not issued frequently, their issue is irregular and at large intervals. It leads to the disadvantages arising out of over-stocking. Hence, every attempt should be made to reduce the amount of capital locked up and prevent over stocking of slow moving items. Losses and costs arising from slow moving stocks can be reduced by reducing their quantity in the store. Smaller quantity of such material should be purchased keeping in view their consumption rate and lead period. To reduce the quantity of such stores, efforts should be made to increase their consumption by finding out their alternative uses and increasing the production by creating more demand in the market.

(b) High Ratio indicates fast moving stock and less investment in stock i.e. those items of stock which are issued frequently and their issue is very regular.

(c) Zero Ratio means the item of stock had not been used at all during the period and hence it should be disposed off immediately, otherwise the quality and value of such item will be deteriorated. Such dormant stocks are very rarely issued from the store and their consumption is almost nil. Losses and costs arising from these stocks can be reduced by purchasing only those items which are very much necessary for the continuous production.

(ii) Inventory Turnover Ratio expressed in Number of Days :

Inventory turnover ratio can also be expressed in terms of number of days for which the inventory will be sufficient. This period should be as minimum as possible. Shorter the period better is the management.

ILLUSTRATIONS

ILLUSTRATION 1

Calculate Inventory Turnover Ratio from the following for Material 'X'.

Particulars	₹
Stock on hand 1-4-2007	20,000
Closing Stock on 31-3-2008	15,000
Purchases during year 2007-2008	70,000

SOLUTION

(i) **Calculation of Inventory Turnover Ratio (in times):**

$$= \frac{\text{Cost of Materials Consumed}}{\text{Cost of Average Stock}}$$

$$= \frac{\text{Opening Stock + Purchases – Closing Stock}}{\frac{\text{Opening Stock + Closing Stock}}{2}}$$

$$= \frac{₹\,20{,}000 + ₹\,70{,}000 - ₹\,15{,}000}{\frac{₹\,20{,}000 + ₹\,15{,}000}{2}}$$

$$= \frac{₹\,75{,}000}{₹\,17{,}500}$$

$$= 4.3 \text{ i.e. 4 times.}$$

(ii) **Calculation of Inventory Turnover Ratio (in days):**

$$= \frac{\text{Number of Days during the year}}{\text{Inventory Turnover Ratio}}$$

$$= \frac{366 \text{ days}}{4.3 \text{ times}}$$

$$= 85.12 \text{ i.e. 85 days}$$

Working Notes:

(i) 2007-2008, being a Leap Year, the number of days during the year are 366.

ILLUSTRATION 2

The following information is available from the books of Xansa Ltd., Pimpri for the year 2008. Calculate Material Turnover Ratio and determine which of the material is **fast moving**.

Particulars	Material 'A' ₹	Material 'B' ₹
Opening Stock	1,400	2,000
Purchases	23,000	3,600
Closing Stock	1,000	2,400

SOLUTION

(1) Calculation of Material Turnover Ratio (in times) :

$$= \frac{\text{Cost of Materials Consumed}}{\text{Cost of Average Stock}}$$

$$= \frac{\text{Opening Stock + Purchases – Closing Stock}}{\frac{\text{Opening Stock + Closing Stock}}{2}}$$

Material 'A' $= \dfrac{₹\,1,400 + ₹\,23,000 - ₹\,1,000}{\dfrac{₹\,1,400 + ₹\,1,000}{2}}$

$= \dfrac{₹\,23,400}{₹\,1,200}$

$= 19.5$ i.e. 19 times

Material 'B' $= \dfrac{₹\,2,000 + ₹\,3,600 - ₹\,2,400}{\dfrac{₹\,2,000 + ₹\,2,400}{2}}$

$= \dfrac{₹\,3,200}{₹\,2,200}$

$= 1.45$ i.e. 1 time

(ii) Calculation of Material Turnover Ratio (in days) :

$$= \frac{\text{Number of Days during the year}}{\text{Inventory Turnover Ratio}}$$

Material 'A' $= \dfrac{366 \text{ days}}{19.5 \text{ times}} = 18.77$ i.e. 19 days

Material 'B' $= \dfrac{366 \text{ days}}{1.45 \text{ times}} = 252.41$ i.e. 252 days

Working Notes :

(i) 2008, being the Leap Year, the number of days during the year are 366.

Conclusion :

In case of Material 'A', the Material Turnover Ratio of 19 times shows that an Average Stock is being held for 19 days, on the other hand in case of Material 'B', the Material Turnover Ratio of 1 time shows that an Average Stock is being held for 252 days. As Material Turnover Ratio of Material 'A' (i.e. 19 times) is high as compared to Material 'B' (i.e. 1 times), Material 'A' is a fast moving material.

ILLUSTRATION 3

From the following data, calculate the Inventory Turnover Ratio for 2008-2009.

Particulars	₹
Purchases during the year 2008-2009	1,10,000
Stock as on 31-3-2008	15,000
Stock as on 01-4-2009	25,000

Also comment upon the **inventory position**.

SOLUTION

(i) Calculation of Cost of Materials Consumed :

$$= \text{Opening Stock + Purchases - Closing Stock}$$
$$= ₹\,25,000 + ₹\,1,10,000 - ₹\,15,000$$
$$= ₹\,1,35,000 - ₹\,15,000$$
$$= ₹\,1,20,000.$$

(ii) Calculation of Cost of Average Stock :

$$= \frac{\text{Opening Stock + Closing Stock}}{2}$$
$$= \frac{₹\,25,000 + ₹\,15,000}{2}$$
$$= \frac{₹\,40,000}{2}$$
$$= ₹\,20,000$$

(iii) Calculation of Inventory Turnover Ratio :

$$= \frac{\text{Cost of Materials Consumed}}{\text{Cost of Average Stock}}$$
$$= \frac{₹\,1,20,000}{₹\,20,000}$$
$$= 6 \text{ times}$$

Comment :

The Inventory Turnover Ratio is 6 times, it means that the stock has been turned over six times during the year 2008-2009 or on an average the stock has been held for two months.

ILLUSTRATION 4

From the following information in respect of Material 'A' calculate Inventory Turnover Ratio.

Issue of Material 'A' during the year 2008-2009 - 8,000 units
Re-order Quantity – 3,000 units
Minimum Level of Stock – 500 units

Also put forward your comments upon the **inventory position**.

SOLUTION

(i) Calculation of Material Consumed i.e. Issue of Material during the year – 8,000 units

(ii) Calculation of Average Stock = $MN \cdot L + \frac{1}{2} RQ$

= Minimum Level of Stock + ½ of Re-order Quantity
= 500 units + ½ × 3,000 units
= 500 units + 1,500 units
= 2,000 units.

(iii) Calculation of Inventory Turnover Ratio :

$$= \frac{\text{Material Consumed in units}}{\text{Average Stock in units}}$$

$$= \frac{8,000 \text{ units}}{2,000 \text{ units}}$$

= 4 times

(iv) **Comment :**

The Inventory Turnover Ratio of Material 'A' is 4 times it means that the stock has been turned over 4 times during the year 2008-2009 or on an average, the stock has been held for three months.

ILLUSTRATION 5

The following information is available from the books of M/s Royal Traders, Sholapur, for the year 2008-2009.

Particulars	Material	
	X ₹	Y ₹
Stock as on 31-3-2009	3,000	3,500
Purchases	26,000	7,000
Stock as on 1-4-2008	2,000	3,000

Calculate Inventory Turnover Ratio and determine which material is **fast moving**.

SOLUTION

(i) Calculation of Cost of Materials Consumed :

$$= \text{Opening Stock + Purchases} - \text{Closing Stock}$$

X = ₹ 2,000 + ₹ 26,000 − ₹ 3,000
  = ₹ 28,000 − ₹ 3,000
  = ₹ 25,000

Y = ₹ 3,000 + ₹ 7,000 − ₹ 3,500
  = ₹ 10,000 − ₹ 3,500
  = ₹ 6,500

(ii) Calculation of Cost of Average Stock :

$$= \frac{\text{Opening Stock + Closing Stock}}{2}$$

X $= \dfrac{₹\,2{,}000 + ₹\,3{,}000}{2}$

$= \dfrac{₹\,5{,}000}{2}$

= ₹ 2,500

Y $= \dfrac{₹\,3{,}000 + ₹\,3{,}500}{2}$

$= \dfrac{₹\,6{,}500}{2}$

= ₹ 3,250

(iii) Calculation of Inventory Turnover Ratio:

$$= \frac{\text{Cost of Materials Consumed}}{\text{Cost of Average Stock}}$$

X $= \dfrac{₹\,25{,}000}{₹\,2{,}500}$

= 10 times

Y $= \dfrac{₹\,6{,}500}{₹\,3{,}250}$

= 2 times

(iv) Conclusion : As Inventory Turnover Ratio of Material 'X' (i.e. 10 times) is high as compared to Material 'Y' (i.e. 2 times), Material X is a Fast Moving Material.

ILLUSTRATION 6

Calculate the Inventory Turnover Ratio expressed in Number of Times and in Number of Days separately for the year ended 31-03-2008 and determine which of the two materials is **fast moving**.

Particulars	Material M (₹)	Material N (₹)
Opening Balance of Stock as on 1-4-2007	20,000	30,000
Average Stock	16,000	25,000
Purchases during the year 2007-2008	72,000	90,000

SOLUTION

(i) Calculation of Value of Closing Stock :

$$\text{Average Stock} = \frac{\text{Opening stock} + \boxed{\text{Closing Stock}}}{2}$$

∴ 2 × Average Stock = Opening Stock + $\boxed{\text{Closing Stock}}$

∴ $\boxed{\text{Closing Stock}}$ = (2 × Average Stock) − Opening Stock

M = (2 × ₹ 16,000) − ₹ 20,000
 = ₹ 32,000 − ₹ 20,000
 = ₹ 12,000

N = (2 × ₹ 25,000) − ₹ 30,000
 = ₹ 50,000 − ₹ 30,000
 = ₹ 20,000

(ii) Calculation Cost of Materials Consumed :

= Opening Stock + Purchases − Closing Stock

M = ₹ 20,000 + ₹ 72,000 − ₹ 12,000
 = ₹ 92,000 − ₹ 12,000
 = ₹ 80,000

N = ₹ 30,000 + ₹ 90,000 − ₹ 20,000
 = ₹ 1,20,000 − ₹ 20,000
 = ₹ 1,00,000

(iii) Calculation of Inventory Turnover Ratio expressed in number of times :

$$= \frac{\text{Cost of Materials Consumed}}{\text{Cost of Average Stock}}$$

$$M = \frac{₹\,80{,}000}{₹\,16{,}000}$$

$$= 5 \text{ times}$$

$$N = \frac{₹\,1{,}00{,}000}{₹\,25{,}000}$$

$$= 4 \text{ times}$$

(iv) Calculation of Inventory Turnover Ratio expressed in Number of Days :

$$= \frac{\text{Number of Days during the year}}{\text{Inventory Turnover Ratio}}$$

$$M = \frac{366 \text{ days}}{5 \text{ times}} = 73.2 \text{ i.e. 73 days,}$$

$$N = \frac{366 \text{ days}}{4 \text{ times}} = 91.50 \text{ i.e. 91 days.}$$

Working Notes :

(i) 2007-2008, being a Leap Year, the number of days during the year are 366.

Conclusion :

In case of material M, the Inventory Turnover Ratio of 5 times shows that an Average Stock is being held for 73 days, on the other hand in case of Material N, the Inventory Turnover Ratio of 4 times shows that an Average Stock is being held for 91 days. As Inventory Turnover Ratio of Material M (i.e. 5 times) is high as compared to Material N (i.e. 4 times), Material M is a Fast Moving Material.

ILLUSTRATION 7

From the following data for the year 2007-2008 calculate the Inventory Turnover Ratio and determine which material is **Slow-Moving**.

Particulars	Material A (₹)	Material B (₹)
Stock of Material as on 1-4-2007	40,000	60,000
Stock of Material as on 31-3-2008	24,000	20,000
Yearly Purchases	2,08,000	2,00,000

Solution :

(i) Calculation of Cost of Materials Consumed :

$$= \text{Opening Stock} + \text{Purchases} - \text{Closing Stock}$$

$$A = ₹40,000 + ₹2,08,000 - ₹24,000$$

$$= ₹2,48,000 - ₹24,000$$

$$= ₹2,24,000$$

$$B = ₹60,000 + ₹2,00,000 - ₹20,000$$

$$= ₹2,60,000 - ₹20,000$$

$$= ₹2,40,000$$

(ii) Calculation of Cost of Average Stock :

$$= \frac{\text{Opening Stock} + \text{Closing Stock}}{2}$$

$$A = \frac{₹40,000 + ₹24,000}{2}$$

$$= \frac{₹64,000}{2}$$

$$= ₹32,000$$

$$B = \frac{₹60,000 + ₹20,000}{2}$$

$$= \frac{₹80,000}{2}$$

$$= ₹40,000$$

(iii) Calculation of Inventory Turnover Ratio :

$$= \frac{\text{Cost of Materials Consumed}}{\text{Cost of Average Stock}}$$

$$A = \frac{₹2,24,000}{₹32,000}$$

$$= 7 \text{ times}$$

$$B = \frac{₹2,40,000}{₹40,000}$$

$$= 6 \text{ times}$$

(iv) Conclusion :
As Inventory Turnover Ratio of Material B (i.e. 6 times) is low as compared to Material A (i.e. 7 times), Material B is a Slow Moving Material.

ILLUSTRATION 8

From the following information calculate Inventory Turnover Ratio and Inventory Turnover period for the year 2007-2008 and determine which of the materials is **fast moving**.

Particulars	Material C (₹)	Material D (₹)
Materials in Hand on -		
(i) 1-4-2007	50,000	50,000
(ii) 31-3-2008	30,000	1,00,000
Materials Purchased during the year 2007-2008	3,80,000	3,50,000

SOLUTION

(i) Calculation of Cost of Materials Consumed :

= Opening Stock + Purchases − Closing Stock

C = ₹ 50,000 + ₹ 3,80,000 − ₹ 30,000
 = ₹ 4,30,000 − ₹ 30,000
 = ₹ 4,00,000

D = ₹ 50,000 + ₹ 3,50,000 − ₹ 1,00,000
 = ₹ 4,00,000 − ₹ 1,00,000
 = ₹ 3,00,000

(ii) Calculation of Cost of Average Stock :

$$= \frac{\text{Opening Stock + Closing Stock}}{2}$$

$$C = \frac{₹\,50{,}000 + ₹\,30{,}000}{2}$$

$$= \frac{₹\,80{,}000}{2}$$

$$= ₹\,40{,}000$$

$$D = \frac{₹\,50{,}000 + ₹\,1{,}00{,}000}{2}$$

$$= \frac{₹\,1{,}50{,}000}{2}$$

$$= ₹\,75{,}000$$

(iii) Calculation of Inventory Turnover Ratio :

$$= \frac{\text{Cost of Materials Consumed}}{\text{Cost of Average Stock}}$$

$$C = \frac{₹\,4,00,000}{₹\,40,000}$$

= 10 times

$$D = \frac{₹\,3,00,000}{₹\,75,000}$$

= 4 times

(iv) Calculation of Inventory Turnover Period :

$$= \frac{\text{Number of Days during the year}}{\text{Inventory Turnover Ratio}}$$

$$C = \frac{366 \text{ days}}{10 \text{ times}}$$

= 36.6 i.e. 37 days

$$D = \frac{366 \text{ days}}{4 \text{ times}}$$

= 91.50 i.e. 91 days

Working Notes :

(i) 2007-2008, being a Leap Year, the number of days during the year are 366.

(v) Conclusion :

In case of material C, the Inventory Turnover Ratio of 10 times shows that an Average Stock is being held for 37 days, on the other hand in case of Material 'D', the Inventory Turnover ratio of 4 times shows that an Average Stock is being held for 91 days. As Inventory Turnover Ratio of Material C (i.e. 10 times) is high as compared to Material D (i.e. 4 times), Material 'C' is a Fast Moving Material.

ILLUSTRATION 9

From the following information relating to two materials C and D for the year 2008-2009, determine which of the two materials **is to be disposed off immediately**.

Particulars	Material	
	C ₹	D ₹
Material in Hand on 1-4-2008	25,000	20,000
Materials Purchased during the year 2008-2009	50,000	40,000
Material in Hand on 31-3-2009	75,000	20,000

SOLUTION

(i) Calculation of Cost of Materials Consumed :

$$= \text{Opening Stock + Purchases – Closing Stock}$$

$$C = ₹\,25,000 + ₹\,50,000 - ₹\,75,000$$

$$= ₹\,75,000 - ₹\,75,000$$

$$= \text{NIL.}$$

$$D = ₹\,20,000 + ₹\,40,000 - ₹\,20,000$$

$$= ₹\,60,000 - ₹\,20,000$$

$$= ₹\,40,000$$

(ii) Calculation of Cost of Average Stock :

$$= \frac{\text{Opening Stock + Closing Stock}}{2}$$

$$C = \frac{₹\,25,000 + ₹\,75,000}{2}$$

$$= \frac{₹\,1,00,000}{2}$$

$$= ₹\,50,000$$

$$D = \frac{₹\,20,000 + ₹\,20,000}{2}$$

$$= \frac{₹\,40,000}{2}$$

$$= ₹\,20,000$$

(iii) Calculation of Inventory Turnover Ratio :

$$= \frac{\text{Cost of Materials Consumed}}{\text{Cost of Average Stock}}$$

$$C = \frac{\text{Nil}}{₹\,50,000}$$

$$= \text{Nil}$$

$$D = \frac{₹\,40,000}{₹\,20,000}$$

$$= 2 \text{ times}$$

(iv) Conclusion : As Material 'C' indicates Zero Inventory Turnover Ratio, it is to be disposed off immediately.

Operations & Supply Chain Management   **Inventory Planning & Control**

ILLUSTRATION 10

The following information is available from the books of Utkal Enterprises, Nashik for the year 2007-2008.

Particulars	Material		
	A ₹	B ₹	C ₹
Opening Stock on 1-4-2007	10,000	10,000	25,000
Material Consumption Cost	40,000	90,000	60,000
Closing Stock on 31-3-2008	30,000	20,000	15,000

You are required to calculate,
(i) Cost of Materials Consumed,
(ii) Cost of Average Stock,
(iii) Inventory Turnover Ratio
(iv) Inventory Turnover Period and
(v) Determine which of the three materials is **Fast Moving**.

SOLUTION

(i) **Calculation of Cost of Material Consumed i.e. Material Consumption Cost :**

$$A = ₹40,000$$
$$B = ₹90,000$$
$$C = ₹60,000$$

(ii) **Calculation of Cost of Average Stock :**

$$= \frac{\text{Opening Stock + Closing Stock}}{2}$$

$$A = \frac{₹10,000 + ₹30,000}{2}$$

$$= \frac{₹40,000}{2}$$

$$= ₹20,000$$

$$B = \frac{₹10,000 + ₹20,000}{2}$$

$$= \frac{₹30,000}{2}$$

$$= ₹15,000$$

$$C = \frac{₹\,25{,}000 + ₹\,15{,}000}{2}$$

$$= \frac{₹\,40{,}000}{2}$$

$$= ₹\,20{,}000$$

(iii) Calculation of Inventory Turnover Ratio :

$$= \frac{\text{Cost of Materials Consumed}}{\text{Cost of Average Stock}}$$

$$A = \frac{₹\,40{,}000}{₹\,20{,}000}$$

$$= 2 \text{ times}$$

$$B = \frac{₹\,90{,}000}{₹\,15{,}000}$$

$$= 6 \text{ times}$$

$$C = \frac{₹\,60{,}000}{₹\,20{,}000}$$

$$= 3 \text{ times}$$

(iv) Calculation of Inventory Turnover Period :

$$= \frac{\text{Number of Days during the year}}{\text{Inventory Turnover Ratio}}$$

$$A = \frac{366 \text{ days}}{2 \text{ times}}$$

$$= 183 \text{ days}$$

$$B = \frac{366 \text{ days}}{6 \text{ times}}$$

$$= 61 \text{ days}$$

$$C = \frac{366 \text{ days}}{3 \text{ times}}$$

$$= 122 \text{ days}$$

Working Notes :

(i) 2007-2008, being a Leap Year, the number of days during the year are 366.

(v) Conclusion :

As Inventory Turnover Ratio of Materials B (i.e. 6 times) is higher as compared to Material A (i.e. 2 times) and Material C (i.e. 3 times), and Inventory Turnover Period of Material B (i.e. 61 days) is Shorter as compared to Material A (i.e. 183 days) and Material C (i.e. 122 days), Material B is a Fast Moving Material. The control has to be exercised more strictly over purchases of Material A.

ILLUSTRATION 11

The following information is available from the books of Vanita Enterprises, Varanasi for the year ended 31st March, 2008.

Particulars	Material	
	X ₹	Y ₹
Stock of Material in hand on 1-4-2007	10,000	9,000
Stock of Material in hand on 31-3-2008	6,000	11,000
Purchases during the year 2003-2008	52,000	32,000

Which material requires **Strict Control over the Purchases** ? Comment.

SOLUTION

(i) Calculation of Cost of Materials Consumed :

$$= \text{Opening Stock} + \text{Purchases} - \text{Closing Stock}$$

$$X = ₹\,10{,}000 + ₹\,52{,}000 - ₹\,6{,}000$$
$$= ₹\,62{,}000 - ₹\,6{,}000$$
$$= ₹\,56{,}000$$

$$Y = ₹\,9{,}000 + ₹\,32{,}000 - ₹\,11{,}000$$
$$= ₹\,41{,}000 - ₹\,11{,}000$$
$$= ₹\,30{,}000$$

(ii) Calculation of Cost of Average Stock :

$$= \frac{\text{Opening Stock} + \text{Closing Stock}}{2}$$

$$X = \frac{₹\,10{,}000 + ₹\,6{,}000}{2}$$
$$= \frac{₹\,16{,}000}{2}$$
$$= ₹\,8{,}000$$

$$Y = \frac{₹\,9{,}000 + ₹\,11{,}000}{2}$$
$$= \frac{₹\,20{,}000}{2}$$
$$= ₹\,10{,}000$$

(iii) Calculation of Inventory Turnover Ratio :

$$= \frac{\text{Cost of Material Consumed}}{\text{Cost of Average Stock}}$$

$$X = \frac{₹\,56{,}000}{₹\,8{,}000}$$

$$= 7 \text{ times}$$

$$Y = \frac{₹\,30{,}000}{₹\,10{,}000}$$

$$= 3 \text{ times}$$

(iv) Calculation of Inventory Turnover Period :

$$= \frac{\text{Number of Days in a year}}{\text{Inventory Turnover Ratio}}$$

$$X = \frac{366 \text{ days}}{7 \text{ times}}$$

$$= 52.29 \text{ i.e. } 52 \text{ days}$$

$$Y = \frac{366 \text{ days}}{3 \text{ times}}$$

$$= 122 \text{ days}$$

Working Notes :

(i) 2007-2008 being a Leap Year, the number of days during the year are 366.

(v) Comment :

As Inventory Turnover Ratio of Material Y (i.e. 3 times) is lower as compared to Material X (i.e. 7 times) and Inventory Turnover Period of Material Y (i.e. 122 days) is longer as compared to Material X (i.e. 52 days), Material Y is a Slow Moving Material which requires strict control over their purchases.

4.4.3 Fixed Order Quantity Model

The number of units that the company should include to the inventory in order to minimise the total expense that is involved in the inventory is referred to as the **economic order quantity**.

The cost of inventory includes the order cost, the holding cost, and even the shortage costs. When the inventory level attains particular reorder point then a fixed quantity is ordered. This economic order quantity plays a vital role in calculating the accurate reorder point.

The fixed order quantity is mainly the arrangement which helps a continuous monitoring and ordering of the replenishment stock. The replenishment stock would be ordered whenever the stock at hand attains the reorder point.

The fixed order quantity model can be used when the inventory is very expensive or when the inventory becomes more important to you than you would never take chance to have stock out for the particular inventory. This is also used when there is too much of expense in maintaining the inventory.

On the other hand, the POQ which is expanded as the production order quantity is a particular kind of model that finds an answer for the questions when to order and how much to produce. The holding cost in the EOQ can be lowered by using the materials immediately which are produced.

The main focus of the fixed order quantity is to reorder points in the order quantities. The basic question what is inventory should be clearly understood before taking a look at the Fixed-order quantity model. When a quantity or a particular store of goods are kept for some sort of purpose, then that is called inventory. Either it be kept in-house or it is kept in a distant warehouse or even it be kept in a distribution center. The main purpose of the inventory is to keep things in hold. There are firms that hold inventories that are excess in order to ensure the operation of the firm. Inventory management is an art which has got several functions. This art is taught in several schools of thoughts.

The other names of the fixed order quantity are the economic order quantity, the EOQ and the Q model. The fixed order quantity is the source for initiating the order. It is like a trigger that trigger up the order when the order reaches a specific reorder level. The remaining inventory is needed to be monitored continuously in order to make the fixed – order quantity effective. It needs to be updated regularly in order to reach a particular order.

POINTS TO REMEMBER

- *The word inventory basically means the total of goods and services that businesses hold in stock.*
- **Inventories are classified as:**
    - Productive,
    - Non-productive,
    - In-process Materials,
    - Finished Goods Inventories,
    - Scrap, Obsolete Materials.
- **Inventory planning** is the method and procedures companies use to determine the amount of products they should have on hand for meeting consumer demand. This planning may involve several steps, depending on the company's inventory management system and business operations.
    1. The first step of inventory planning is to estimate future sales.
    2. The next step in inventory planning is to purchase the necessary products for business locations.

3. Companies may also make plans for moving inventory quickly before new items must be purchased for upcoming seasons.

- **Inventory control** is the process of managing an inventory so that the business derives the most overall benefit from the existence of the inventory.
- These categories, based on the aspect of regularity of demand have been discussed ahead.
    1. Continuous Demand System
    2. Intermittent Demand System
- In the continuous production system, goods are produced constantly as per demand forecast. Goods are produced on a large scale for stocking and selling. They are not produced on customer's orders. Here, the inputs and outputs are standardised along with the production process and sequence.
- **The characteristics of a continuous production system** are listed as follows:
    - The flow of production is continuous. It is not intermittent.
    - The products are standardised.
    - The products are produced on predetermined quality standards.
    - The products are produced in anticipation of demand.
    - Standardised routing sheets and schedules are prepared.
    - In the intermittent production system, goods are produced based on customer's orders. The **characteristics of an intermittent production system** are listed as follows:
        - The flow of production is not continuous. It is intermittent.
        - Wide varieties of products are produced.
        - The volume of production is small.
        - General purpose machines are used. These machines can be used to produce different types of products.
        - The sequence of operation goes on changing as per the design of the product.
        - The quantity, size, shape, design, etc. of the product depends on the customer's orders.
- The **need for Inventory Management** can be summarised as follows:
    1. Meet variation in Production Demand
    2. Cater to Cyclical and Seasonal Demand
    3. Economies of Scale in Procurement
    4. Earn advantage of Price Increase and Quantity Discounts

5. Reduce Transit Cost and Transit Times
6. Long Lead and High demand items need to be held in Inventory

- **Types of Inventory:**
    1. Seasonal
    2. Decoupling
    3. Cyclic
    4. Pipeline
    5. Safety Inventory or Safety Stock

- The impacts of the implications of the Inventory Control Methods have been discussed ahead;
    1. Protects from fluctuations in demand
    2. Better services to customers
    3. Continuity of production operations
    4. Reduces the risk of loss
    5. Minimises the administrative workload
    6. Protects fluctuation in output
    7. Effective use of working capital
    8. Check on loss of materials
    9. Facilitates cost accounting activities

- **Four types of inventory costs:**
    (i) Holding or carrying costs.
    (ii) Set-up costs.
    (iii) Purchasing costs.
    (iv) Shortage Costs

- **Total Inventory Cost** = Holding or Carrying Cost + Set-up Cost + Purchasing Cost

- **Economic order quantity (EOQ)** model is the method that provides the company with an order quantity. This order quantity figure is where the record holding costs and ordering costs are minimised.

- **Economic Order Quantity (EOQ)**

$$\sqrt{\frac{2 \times \text{Annual Consumption (Units)} \times \text{Procurement Cost Per Order}}{\text{Price Per Unit} \times \text{Inventory Carrying Cost}}}$$

- **Classification of Material or Inventory**
  1. ABC Analysis
  2. HML Analysis
  3. Ved analysis
  4. SDE Analysis
  5. GNGLF Analysis / Golf Analysis
  6. S-OS Analysis
  7. MNG Analysis
  8. FSN Analysis
  9. XYZ Analysis
- **Inventory Turnover Ratio expressed in Number of Times :**

  $$\frac{\text{Cost of Materials Consumed during the period}}{\text{Cost of Average Stock held during the period}}$$

Questions for Discussion:

1. What is EOQ? Explain the different assumptions considered in EOQ model? Discuss EOQ as a inventory control technique.
2. What is meant by selective control of inventories? What are the different methods for selective control of inventory items?
3. A diesel engine manufacturers buys an item in lots of 500 units which is a three month requirements. The cost per unit is ₹ 90 and the ordering cost is ₹ 180 per batch order. The inventory carrying cost is estimated at 20% of the average inventory investment.
   (a) What is the annual total cost of the existing inventory policy?
   (b) How much money can be saved by using EOQ?
   (c) Profitability of a company depends to a large extent on effectiveness of its purchase function. Discuss.
4. Materials requirement planning is both an inventory control and scheduling technique. Discuss.
5. Write short notes on:
   (i) EOQ
   (ii) Inventory costs
   (iii) Inventory control
   (iv) Types of inventory
   (v) Need of inventory

Questions from Previous Examinations

Note: Since the chapter is new, there are no University Questions.

Chapter **5**...

Supply Chain Management

Contents ...

5.1 Supply Chain Management
    5.1.1 Generalised Supply Chain Management Model
    5.1.2 Key Issues in Supply Chain Management
5.2 Customer Service
    5.2.1 Supply Chain Management and Customer Service Linkages
    5.2.2 Availability, Service Reliability, Perfect Order
    5.2.3 Customer Satisfaction
    5.2.4 Enablers of SCM
• Points to Remember
• Questions for Discussion

Learning Objectives:
➢ To study and understand the concept of Supply Chain Management and the key issues surrounding it.
➢ To study the current trends and preferences of organisations to mitigate such key issues faced in supply chain management.
➢ To define and link the knowledge and concept of Supply Chain Management with the Customers and the markets and identify the linkages which influence the same.

Introduction

Supply chain management is a paradigm driving many businesses, and in turn business relationships, today. Customers are dictating how their orders and shipments will be handled. They want to drive out excess inventory and costs. They want their orders shipped complete, accurate, on time and in the manner they require. Compliance means continued business. Non-compliance means financial penalties and possible loss of business. This is significant in terms of sales revenues and operating costs for their suppliers. Supply chain management competence can build competitive advantage.

Supply chains encompass the companies and the business activities needed to design, make, deliver, and use a product or service. Businesses depend on their supply chains to provide them with what they need to survive and thrive. Every business fits into one or more supply chains and has a role to play in each of them. The pace of change and the uncertainty about how markets will evolve has made it increasingly important for companies to be aware of the supply chains they participate in and to understand the roles that they play. Those companies that learn how to build and participate in strong supply chains will have a substantial competitive advantage in their markets.

The term "supply chain management" arose in the late 1980s and came into widespread use in the 1990s. Prior to that time, businesses used terms such as "logistics" and "operations management" instead.

A supply chain is the network of organisations that are involved through upstream and downstream linkages in the different processes and activities that produce value in the form of products and services in the hands of ultimate customers. It is also called as a value chain.

It consists of all parties involved directly or indirectly, in fulfilling a customer request. The supply chain includes not only the manufacturer and suppliers, but also transporters, warehouses, retailers, and even customers themselves.

Within each organisation, such as a manufacturer, the supply chain includes all functions involved in receiving and filling a customer request. These functions include, but are not limited to, new product development, marketing, operations, distribution, finance and customer service.

Supply chain management is an application of a total systems approach to manage the entire flow of information, materials, and services from raw materials suppliers through factories and warehouses to the end customer. The linkages may be observed between suppliers that provide inputs, manufacturing and service support operations that transform the inputs into products and services, and the distribution and local service providers that localise the product. Localisation can involve just the delivery of the product or some more involved process that tailors the product or service to the needs of the local market.

5.1 Supply Chain Management

A **supply chain** is a system of organisations, people, activities, information, and resources involved in moving a product or service from supplier to customer. Supply chain activities transform natural resources, raw materials, and components into a finished product that is delivered to the end customer. In sophisticated supply chain systems, used products may re-enter the supply chain at any point where residual value is recyclable. Supply chains link value chains.

For more details Refer Chapter No. 1, Article 1.1.3.

5.1.1 Generalised Supply Chain Management Model

The general concept of an integrated supply chain is typically illustrated by the diagram that has been discussed ahead. The Fig. 5.1 demonstrates a generalised model adapted from the supply chain management programme at Michigan State University.

The framework of an integrated supply chain is a multi-firm relationship management within the framework characterised by capacity limitations, information management, core competencies, capital, and human resource constraints.

Within this context, supply chain structure and strategy results from efforts to operationally link an enterprise with customers as well as the supporting distributive and supplier networks to gain competitive advantage. Business operations are hence integrated from initial material purchase to delivery of products and services to the end customers.

A value results from the cooperation among firms comprising the supply chain with respect to five critical flows which influence the efficiency. These flows are:

- Information
- Product
- Service
- Financial and
- Knowledge (see the bidirectional arrow at the top of the figure 5.1).

Logistics is the primary channel of product and service flow within a supply chain arrangement. Each firm engaged in supply chain management is involved in performing the functions of logistics. Such logistical activity may or may not be integrated within that firm and within overall supply chain performance.

Achievement of logistical integration is the focus of this concept. The generalised supply chain arrangement illustrated in the Figure logically and logistically links a firm and its distributive and supplier network to end customers. The message conveyed in the figure is that the integrated value-creation process must be managed from material procurement to end-customer product/service delivery.

The integrated supply chain perspective shifts traditional channel arrangements from loosely linked groups of independent businesses that buy and sell inventory towards a managerially coordinated initiative to increase market impact, overall efficiency, continuous improvement, and competitiveness.

In reality, many difficulties work to cloud the simplicity of illustrating supply chains as directional line diagrams. For example, many individual firms simultaneously participate in multiple and competitive supply chains. To the degree that a supply chain becomes the basic unit of competition, firms participating in multiple arrangements may confront loyally issues related to confidentially and potential conflict of interest. Another factor that serves to add complexity to understanding supply chain structure is the high degree of mobility and change observable in typical arrangements.

It's interesting to observe the fluidity of supply chains as firms enter and exit without any apparent loss of essential connectivity. For example, a firm and/or service supplier may be actively engaged in a supply chain structure during selected times, such as a peak selling season, and not during the balance of a year.

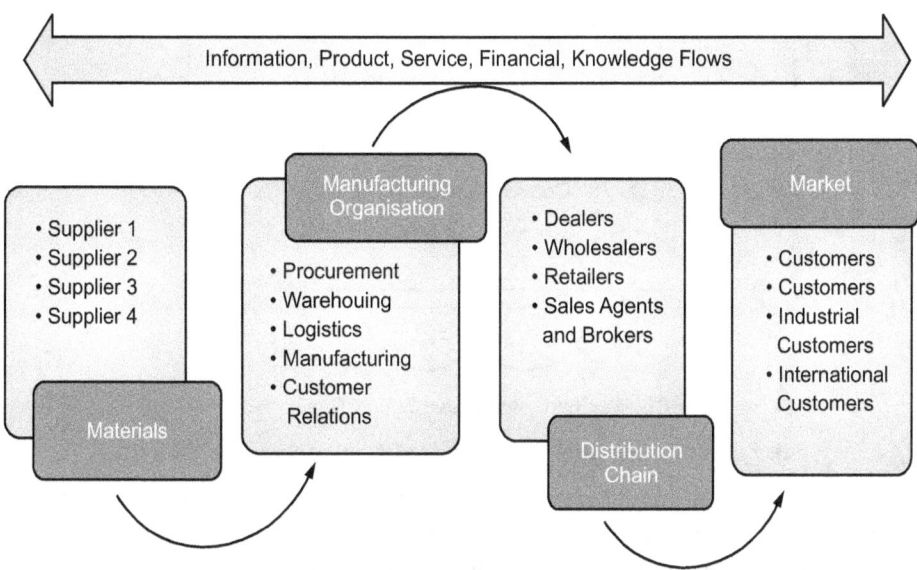

Fig. 5.1: Supply Chain Management Critical Flows

The overarching enabler of supply chain management is information technology. In addition to information technology, the rapid emergence of supply chain arrangements is being driven by four related forces:

1. Integrative management;
2. Responsiveness;
3. Financial sophistication; and
4. Globalisation.

These forces will continue, for the foreseeable future, to drive supply chain structure and strategy initiatives across most industries.

5.1.2 Key Issues in Supply Chain Management

Across all aspects of business operations, attention is focused in achieving improved integrative management. The challenge to achieve integrated management results from the long standing tradition of performing and measuring the work on a functional basis. Since industrial revolution the managerial attention has been focused on achieving functional specialisation. A blind belief which worked till now was that "better the specialisation of a specific function, better is the efficiency of the overall process".

In terms of management, firms have traditionally been structured into departments to facilitate work focus, standardisation, reutilisation and control. Accounting practices on the other hand were developed to measure departmental performance. Most of this performance measurement focused on individual functions. However, the cross functional measurements were sidelined in the process of specialised measurement of activities.

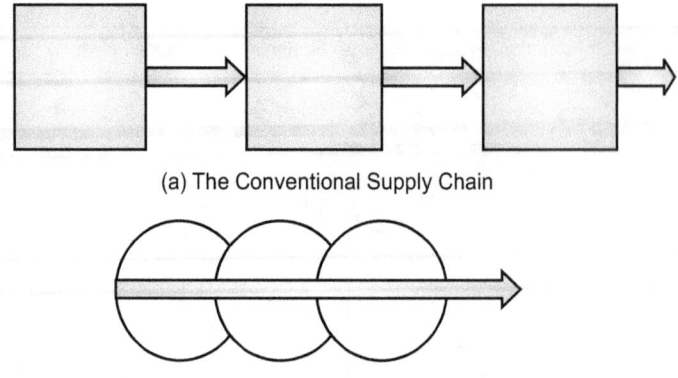

(a) The Conventional Supply Chain

(b) The Shorter Integrated Supply Chain

Fig. 5.2: Conventional and Shorter Integrated Supply Chain

The basic and fundamental challenge of integrated management is to achieve the overall process performance than achieving any specialised task performance. Over the past few years, it has been observed that functions which are individually performed may be the best in class. However, they do not contribute to the efficiency of the process or for gaining a low cost advantage.

Integrative process management seeks to identify and achieve lowest total cost by capturing tradeoffs that exist between functions. The primary aim of integrated management is to achieve lowest total process cost, which may not necessarily mean achieving the lowest cost for each function included in the process.

The quest for achieving this lowest cost and highest efficiency for a process through Integrated Management has opened up three facets for development. These facets are:

1. Collaboration
2. Enterprise Extension, and
3. Integrated Service Providers

We shall see each of these facets in brief ahead.

5.1.2.1 Collaboration

Under the facet of Collaboration, the Supply Chains of various competitive organisations and their departments are collaborated in order to gain the mutual benefit of cost minimisation. The processes where a few functions perform similar tasks are collaborated and the costs thus are saved and the total cost is minimised. This eases the overall process as well thus making the final product in less time, less cost and greater efficiency.

Collaboration can also be seen through competitive organisations as an effort to reduce cost and increase efficiency. The organisations which have similar functions outsource such functions to the specialised agencies which are formed in mutual understanding.

For example, we may purchase a product from any online portal such as flipkart, snapdeal, myntra, jabong or any other website. The delivery system at times is a single agency for all the portals. This agency performs a function which is similar within these competitors. It does not influence their competition. Rather, it helps in reducing their overall setup, costs and increasing the efficiency of their process.

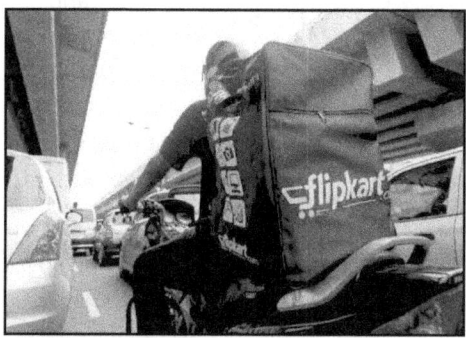
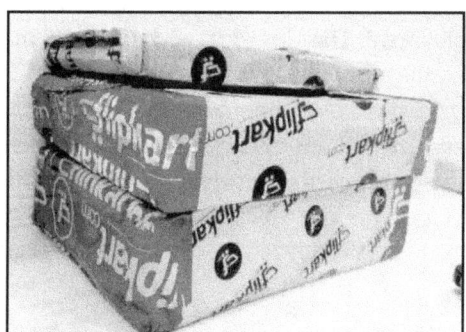

5.1.2.2 Enterprise Extension

The concept of enterprise extension implies the expansion of managerial influence and control beyond the ownership boundaries of a single enterprise to facilitate joint planning and operations with customers and suppliers. The basic understanding of Enterprise Extension is to collaborate the behaviour between firms that integrate the processes will maximise customer impact, reduce overall risk, and greatly improve efficiency.

Firms participating in Supply Chain come up with specific roles and share similar strategic goals. Sharing information and joint planning can help in reducing the risks that prevail in the process. Collaboration can eliminate duplicate and redundant work such as repetitive quality inspection through lined up processes. It gets clear that challenges of collaboration and enterprise extension constitute greater managerial horizons. The third contributing factor towards integrated supply chain development is the rapidly changing managerial attitude towards the integrated service providers.

Fig. 5.3: Enterprise Extension

5.1.2.3 Integrated Service Providers

As discussed earlier, the similar and demanding functions are outsourced by firms in order to attain the cost benefit in the process. Also, it helps the organisation in concentrating on the main objects of the business. The functions which are typically outsourced by the businesses are the services which require setup cost and more employment. This does not add up to the main process of expanding the operations. In such cases, these services are outsourced by the firms to the Integrated Service Providers in order to gain the cost benefit in the process. For example, the tele-calling function of sales management is outsourced by many organisations to the BPOs. Typically, manufacturing firms outsource the activities of transportation and warehousing to the integrated service provider channels.

5.1.2.4 Responsiveness

After understanding the working of a Supply Chain, the efforts taken to integrate the functions in order to achieve the lowest cost and highest efficiency within the supply chain, now it is an important factor to link this integrated supply chain decisions with the market in an attempt to acquire a greater market share. Efficiency of supply chains will be judged if they reap out sufficient benefits for the firm. These benefits may come out of cost reductions or profit maximisations. Cost Reduction as we saw earlier is achieved through Integrated Supply Chain design. However, Profit Maximisation is achieved through greater market share, increased sales and the success of the company's revenues. To achieve this, the firm has to respond effectively to the market forces. This responsiveness of the firm to the market demand determines the success of a supply chain.

With the great intensity of the rate at which the world changes today, it has become extremely important for organisations to consider their responsiveness strategies in order to gain benefits from this change. Two such strategies have been identified under this science. They are:

1. **Anticipatory Responsiveness:** Under Anticipatory Responsiveness, the firm anticipated the changes in the tastes, preferences, fashions and styles in the market, and undertakes the activities accordingly. All the activities of the firm are reorganised

based on such anticipatory models framed by the organisation. If the forecasts and anticipations prove to be correct, firms enjoy the competitive advantage in the market in respect to timing and initiator to respond to the changing requirements. This helps the firm in acquiring greater market shares, sales and customer loyalty at times.

2. **Normal Responsiveness:** Anticipations may not always prove to be perfect and hence may demand great designing and execution costs for the company. If these anticipations fail, the organisation may suffer great setbacks on grounds of infrastructure and implementation costs. Hence, some organisations do not anticipate any changes in the market. They just identify the current needs and work on satisfying them. The basic belief amongst these organisations is that anticipatory models merely work for branding purposes. They willingly lose the competitive advantage of being the first entrant of the product in the market. However, they gain market shares as well once their setups are functional in the competition.

5.1.2.5 Cash to Cash Conversion

Through the normal course of business, companies acquire inventory on credit, which they in turn use to create products. These products are then sold, oftentimes on credit. These actions generate accounts payable and accounts receivable, with no cash exchanged until the company collects accounts receivable and settles the accounts payable.

The cash conversion cycle (CCC) measures the time in days that it takes for a company to convert resource inputs into cash flows. In other words, the cash conversion cycle reflects the length of time it takes a company to sell inventory, collect receivables, and pay its bills. As a rule, the lower the number, the better. This is because, as the cash conversion cycle shortens, cash becomes free for a company to invest in new equipment or infrastructure or other activities to boost investment return. Also, the cash conversion cycle can be useful in comparing close competitors and assessing management efficiency.

The cash conversion cycle (CCC) is one of several measures of management effectiveness. It measures how fast a company can convert cash on hand into even more cash on hand. The CCC does this by following the cash as it is first converted into inventory and accounts payable (AP), through sales and accounts receivable (AR), and then back into cash. Generally, the lower this number is, the better for the company. Although it should be combined with some other metrics such as return on equity and return on assets, it can be especially useful for comparing close competitors, because the company with the lowest CCC is often the one with better management.

The cash conversion cycle is the measurement of the amount of time it takes inventory to sell and cash to be available. Consequently, cash flow cycle analysis examines the inventory, accounts receivable and accounts payable ledgers. Positive cash conversion cycles occur when the time in inventory and accounts receivable is greater than the time it takes to pay the supplier. Positive numbers aren't necessarily a good sign, and low numbers indicate a more effectively managed operation – the money isn't tied up for long in inventory or accounts receivable.

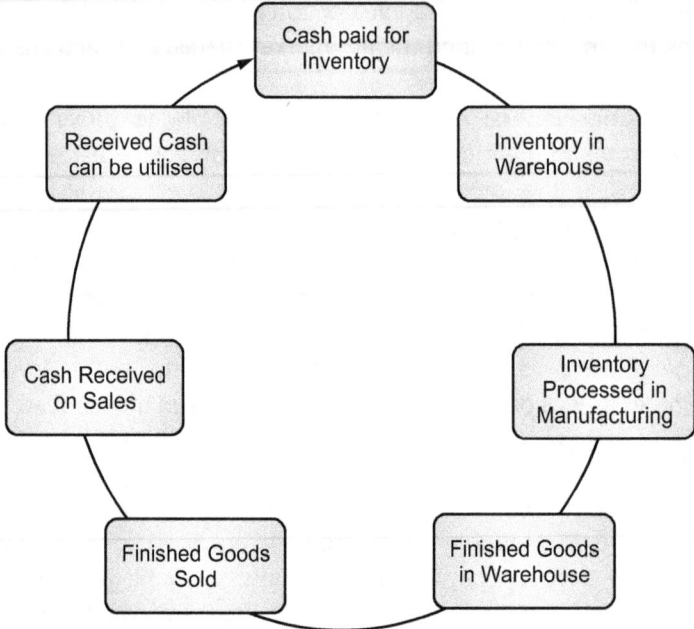

Fig. 5.4: Cash Conversion Cycle

1. **Inventory:** Inventory is an asset that becomes a burden if it doesn't sell. Slow turnover of inventory is an indication of a problem. If the product isn't selling, it means that the customer doesn't find it useful, or it's priced too high for the marketplace. The company may have to reduce the price below the original cost of goods to clear the shelves and make room for more desirable products. Companies want to minimise the time a product remains in inventory.
2. **Accounts Payable:** Companies want to maximise the amount of time it takes to pay a supplier. This allows more time to make productive use of the cash on hand. Once the company pays the supplier, that money is unavailable to purchase additional inventory or other types of investments. A company may be able to negotiate the payment due date when it initially contacts a supplier.
3. **Accounts Receivable:** The faster a company receives payment for its own products or services, the better. It's of little practical benefit to a company to have a large outstanding balance in accounts receivable. It may be an indication of future profitability, but it needs to be converted to cash before it can truly affect the bottom line. A short collection time is one indicator of efficient management.
4. **Cash Conversion Cycle:** A simple formula for calculating the cash conversion cycle is: average number of days in inventory + average number of days in accounts receivable - average number of days in accounts payable. A smaller result indicates a

healthier cycle. Negative totals reflect a business model for companies such as Dell or Amazon, in which suppliers are not paid until the company receives payment from the customer. However, that business model is not the norm for most companies. Analysts do consider downward historical trends in the cash conversion cycle as a good sign; the company is selling its products faster, collecting payments quicker or taking longer to pay its vendors.

5.2 Customer Service

Supply chains consist of a company, its suppliers, its distributors and its customers. Customer service entails delivering products to customers for their complete satisfaction and delight. Satisfied customers are the desired result of any supply chain management strategy. The importance for consideration of Customer Service is as follows;

1. **Referrals and Testimonials:** A satisfied customer can be an ambassador for the company. Word-of-mouth advertising from a customer through referrals and testimonials will ensure that other people know about the customer's good experience with the company.

2. **Returning Customers:** The Small Business organisation states that every year, businesses lose between 10 and 50 percent of their customers. According to Ohio State University, it costs five times more to find a new customer than to keep an existing one. Satisfied customers will not move to a different supplier, but will establish a relationship with the current suppliers and continue to do business with them.

3. **Customer Lifetime Value:** The lifetime value of a customer is the sum of all the transactions over times that occur. This is a much higher cost than the cost incurred for a single purchase. Good customer service will entice the customer to return repeatedly.

4. **Customers' Customers:** Excellent customer service should extend to customers' customers. Making it easy for the customer to deliver products to their customers will ensure that they return to do further business.

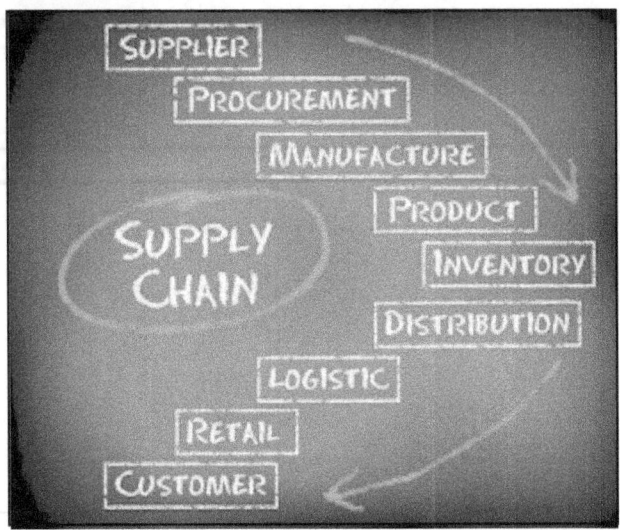

5.2.1 Supply Chain Management and Customer Service Linkages

Supply chain management strategies enable companies to ensure the business has the materials, information and financial resources it needs to produce quality goods and services in a timely manner. By coordinating the flow of work from vendors to manufacturers and then from distributors to retailers, effective supply management techniques reduce inventory and ensure product availability when required.

Customer relationship management programmes are used to ensure parts and service get to customers when needed after sales are completed by automating business processes used for sales, service and support. Integrated supply chain management and customer relationship management functions to maximise the operations of a company.

1. **Differences:** Supply chain management personnel ensure that all departments in the business get the raw materials they need to complete their work, while customer relationship management personnel deal with customers to make sure they get the support and services they need. Supply chain personnel work with vendors, while customer relationship personnel work with customers. For example, at a small veterinary hospital, the supply chain management personnel make sure the veterinarians and technicians have the medical supplies required to conduct routine examinations, perform surgeries and treat medical conditions for clients' animals at the hospital, while customer relationship management personnel work with customers to make sure they get the right medications to administer to their animals at home.

2. **Product Flow:** The supply chain management function ensures that movement of resources from suppliers to manufacturing occurs smoothly. For example, at a small brochure printing business, supply chain management personnel buy and distribute the paper products and ink required to run the business. The customer relationship management function takes and transmits orders and ensures that product returns and customer support needs are handled. At the small brochure printing business, customer relationship personnel take orders from customers who want brochures printed by the business. Supply chain management software applications facilitate planning and track the management of materials. Ideally, these applications share data across the business, including suppliers and business partners to ensure the smooth flow of products from development through delivery. When customer relationship management personnel take a large order for brochure printing, for example, the vendor supplying the paper gets an alert that the company needs more paper than usual. This expedites service for the customer.

3. **Information Flow:** Supply chain management professionals use data generated from software applications to ensure their suppliers provide the right raw materials to create products and services. Accurate analysis and interpretation allows them to improve the production schedules, reduce costs, and eliminate bottlenecks and plan for future work. Customer relationship management professionals also need access to data regarding spare parts availability to support consumers. Customer relationship management personnel work with customers to take orders, solve problems and get new business. For example, at a small catering business, supply chain management personnel make sure that the cooks have all the raw ingredients required to make meals for events. They inform the customer relationship management personnel if problems arise in obtaining the required products, such as flour, sugar or fresh produce.

4. **Considerations:** Supply chain management personnel need accurate manufacturing and inventory data from suppliers. This enables them to ensure that the small business has the raw materials it needs to conduct business in a cost-effective manner. For example, supply chain management personnel at a small computer repair business need parts from suppliers, such as Apple, IBM, Dell and HP, to support the business but typically they cannot afford to stock all part to all computers. By contrast, customer relationship management personnel need to be able to respond quickly to customer needs. By establishing good relationships with suppliers to obtain access to current spare parts availability and pricing information, small businesses can get the information they need to run a profitable operation.

5.2.2 Availability, Service Reliability, Perfect Order

Availability

Availability is the capability to have inventory when a customer desires it. It is not at all uncommon for an organisation to spend considerable time, money, and effort to create customer demand and then fail to have product available to fill customer orders. The traditional practice in many organisations is to stock inventory in expectation of customer orders. Characteristically an inventory stocking plan is based on forecasted demand for products and may include differential stocking policies for specific items as a result of sales popularity, profitability, or significance of an item to the overall product line.

Achieving high levels of inventory availability requires a large deal of planning. The key is to attain these high levels of availability while minimising overall investment in inventory and facilities. Availability is typically based on three performance measures: stockout frequency, fill rate, and perfect orders shipped.

Service Reliability

Service reliability includes the combined attributes of logistics and is concerned with a firm's capability to carry out all order-related activities, as well as offer customers with important information regarding logistical operations and status. Attributes of reliability may mean that shipments arrive damage-free; invoices are accurate and error-free; shipments are sent to the correct locations; and the exact amount of product ordered is included in the shipment. While these and numerous other aspects of overall reliability are difficult to enumerate, the point is that customers demand that a wide variety of business details be handled routinely by suppliers. Additionally, service reliability involves a capability and a willingness to provide accurate information to customers regarding operations and order status. Research indicates that the ability of a firm to provide accurate information is one of the most significant attributes of a good service programme. Increasingly, customers indicate that advanced notification of problems such as incomplete orders is more critical than the complete order itself. Customers hate surprises! More often than not, customers can adjust to an incomplete or late delivery if they have advanced notification.

Perfect Order

The perfect order is a simple concept which means an order that is shipped complete, on time, damage-free, to the correct destination. It is an indicator of an organisation's commitment to zero-defect logistics. Delivery of perfect orders is the ultimate measure of quality in logistics operations. A perfect order measures the effectiveness of the firm's overall integrated logistical performance rather than individual functions. It measures whether an order proceeds faultlessly through every step—order entry, credit clearance, inventory availability, accurate picking, on-time delivery, correct invoicing, and payment without deductions—of the order management process without fault, be it expediting, exception processing, or manual intervention. In fact, as many as 20 different logistic service elements may impact a perfect order. From a measurement perspective, perfect order performance is computed as the ratio of perfect orders during a given time period to the total number of orders completed during that period.

5.2.3 Customer Satisfaction

Customer satisfaction is a term frequently used in marketing. It is a measure of how products and services supplied by a company meet or surpass customer expectations. Customer satisfaction is defined as "the number of customers, or percentage of total customers, whose reported experience with a firm, its products, or its services (ratings) exceeds specified satisfaction goals.

It is seen as a key performance indicator within business and is often a part of a Balanced Scorecard. In a competitive marketplace where businesses compete for customers, customer satisfaction is seen as a key differentiator and increasingly has become a key element of business strategy. Therefore, it is essential for businesses to effectively manage customer satisfaction. To be able do this, firms need reliable and representative measures of satisfaction.

"In researching satisfaction, firms generally ask customers whether their product or service has met or exceeded expectations. Thus, expectations are a key factor behind satisfaction. When customers have high expectations and the reality falls short, they will be disappointed and will likely rate their experience as less than satisfying. For this reason, a luxury resort, for example, might receive a lower satisfaction rating than a budget motel—even though its facilities and service would be deemed superior in 'absolute' terms."

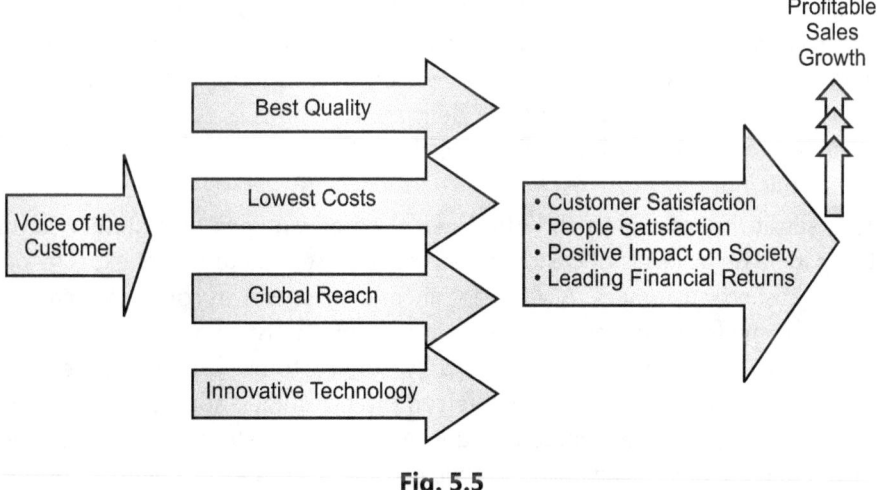

Fig. 5.5

The importance of customer satisfaction diminishes when a firm has increased bargaining power. For example, cell phone plan providers, such as Idea and Airtel, participate in an industry that is an oligopoly, where only a few suppliers of a certain product or service exist. As such, many cell phone plan contracts have a lot of fine print with provisions that they would never get away if there were, say, a hundred cell phone plan providers, because customer satisfaction would be far too low, and customers would easily have the option of leaving for a better contract offer.

The advantages of customer satisfaction to a business are hard to overestimate. They may be grouped into four categories:

- Customer retention,
- Advertising savings,
- Pricing buffers and
- Business intelligence.

These benefits are available to managers who actively cultivate a positive customer experience. A high degree of customer retention is usually a major goal of a company. To implement a customer-retention programme takes company-wide participation. Many businesses spend a significant part of the marketing budget attempting to capitalise upon the advantages of customer satisfaction. Customer retention statistics may be difficult to obtain, and these studies may be misinterpreted.

Business experts often state that the costs to sell to an existing customer are less than those to acquire a new customer. Established customers are already aware of the business and do not need to change established buying habits. Customer service is a key cornerstone of the maturation of the new customer status to that of an established customer.

About 20 percent of annual growth may be attributed to the careful nurturing of existing customers. Explosive growth rates, in the range of 50 percent to 100 percent per year, require multiple advertising and promotional efforts geared at the new customer. The benefits of customer satisfaction surface to the top in these fast-growth companies. Social media marketing alone can make or break a new product as thousands of unknown people provide an endorsement or point out the deficiencies of the latest market entry. A high-approval rating from a well-connected user can send the provider's stock soaring and the cash registers ringing.

Pricing sensitivity, as one of the often perceived advantages of customer satisfaction, may actually increase as levels of customer satisfaction rise, due to higher expectations from established, satisfied customers. A decrease in pricing sensitivity or an increased priced tolerance may come from noticeable changes in customer satisfaction levels. Customers who observe a company's increased efforts to improve the customer experience are more likely to accept price increases. Often, customers can offer a unique source of feedback to the business owner. If appropriate communications means exist, customers will feel free to make constructive criticism. Business intelligence could come from the comments or observations of customers.

Consumers are often the first to know of new competitors, new techniques, or new technologies that can threaten the core products and services of a company. Focus groups may reveal this underlying knowledge as well as polling, data mining, and other market research methods. Business owners can frequently acquire at least some of this information by communicating with their own customers. Complaints should always be resolved as quickly as possible to maintain the advantages of customer satisfaction.

5.2.4 Enablers of SCM

A basic supply chain management system has five components:

1. The **plan**, which refers to the over-all strategy of the SCM programme including the development of SCM metrics to monitor; Companies need a plan that is efficient in that it is cost effective, valuable to its customers, and provides high quality products or services.
2. The **source**, which refers to the suppliers who'll provide you with goods and services necessary for you to run your business; Finding a reliable source to deliver the goods is challenging and takes time
3. The **make** or manufacturing component, which refers to the execution of processes needed to produce, test, and package your products or services; Making the product requires testing, packaging and preparation before it can be delivered.
4. The **delivery**, which refers to the system for receiving orders from customers, developing a network of warehouses; getting the products to the customers; invoicing customers and receiving payment from them; and
5. The **return**, which is the system for processing customer returns and/or supporting customers with problems with the products they received.

5.2.4.1 Facilities or Location

Facilities or Location refers to the geographical sitting of supply chain facilities. It also includes the decisions related to which activities should be performed in each facility. When making location decisions, managers need to consider a range of factors that relate to a given location including the cost of facilities, the cost of labour, skills available in the workforce, infrastructure conditions, taxes and tariffs, and proximity to suppliers and customers.

Facilities decisions tend to be very strategic decisions because they commit large amounts of money to long-term plans. Location decisions depend on market demands and determination of customer satisfaction. Strategic decisions must focus on the placement of production plants, distribution and stocking facilities, and placing them in prime locations to the market served. Once customer markets are determined, long-term commitment must be made to locate production and stocking facilities as close to the consumer as is practical. In industries where components are lightweight and market driven, facilities should be located close to the end-user. In heavier industries, careful consideration must be made to determine where plants should be located so as to be close to the raw material source. Decisions concerning location should also take into consideration tax and tariff issues, especially in inter-state and worldwide distribution.

Location decisions have strong impacts on the cost and performance characteristics of a supply chain. Once the size, number, and location of facilities is determined, that also defines the number of possible paths through which products can flow on the way to the final customer. Location decisions reflect a company's basic strategy for building and delivering its products to market.

5.2.4.2 Inventory

Inventory is the stock of any item or resource used in an organisation. An inventory system is the set of policies and controls that monitor levels of inventory and determine what levels should be maintained, when stock should be replenished and how large orders should be.

By convention, manufacturing inventory generally refers to items that continue to or become part of a firm's product output. Manufacturing inventory is classified into raw materials, finished products, component parts, supplies and work-in-process. In services, inventory generally refers to the tangible goods to be sold and the suppliers necessary to administer the service.

The basic purpose of inventory analysis in manufacturing and storekeeping services is to specify

1. When items should be ordered and
2. How large the orders should be.

Inventory is spread throughout the supply chain and includes everything from raw material to work in process to finished goods that are held by the manufacturers, distributors, and retailers in a supply chain. Further, strategic decisions focus on inventory and how much product should be in-house. A delicate balance exists between too much inventory, which can cost anywhere between 20 and 40 per cent of their value, and not enough inventory to meet market demands. This is a critical issue in effective supply chain management. Operational inventory decisions revolve around optimal levels of stock at each location to ensure customer satisfaction as the market demands fluctuate. Control policies must be looked at to determine correct levels of supplies at order and reorder points. These levels are critical to the day to day operation of organisations and to keep customer satisfaction levels high.

There are three basic decisions to make regarding the creation and holding of inventory :

(a) **Cycle Inventory:** This is the amount of inventory needed to satisfy demand for the product in the period between purchases of the product. Companies tend to produce and to purchase in large lots in order to gain the advantages that economies of scale can bring. However, with large lots also comes increased carrying costs. Carrying costs come from the cost to store, handle, and insure the inventory. Managers face the trade-off between the reduced cost of ordering and better prices offered by purchasing product in large lots and the increased carrying cost of the cycle inventory that comes with purchasing in large lots.

(b) **Safety Inventory:** Inventory that is held as a buffer against uncertainty. If demand forecasting could be done with perfect accuracy, then the only inventory that would be needed would be cycle inventory. But since every forecast has some degree of uncertainty in it, we cover that uncertainty to a greater or lesser degree by holding additional inventory in case demand is suddenly greater than anticipated. The trade-off here is to weigh the costs of carrying extra inventory against the costs of losing sales due to insufficient inventory.

(c) **Seasonal Inventory:** This is inventory that is built up in anticipation of predictable increases in demand that occur at certain times of the year. For example, it is predictable that demand for anti-freeze will increase in the winter. If a company that makes anti-freeze has a fixed production rate that is expensive to change, then it will try to manufacture product at a steady rate all year long and build up inventory during periods of low demand to cover for periods of high demand that will exceed its production rate. The alternative to building up seasonal inventory is to invest in flexible manufacturing facilities that can quickly change their rate of production of different products to respond to increases in demand. In this case, the trade-off is between the cost of carrying seasonal inventory and the cost of having more flexible production capabilities.

Many firms are tending to enter into longer-term relationships with vendors to supply their needs for the entire year. This changes the "when" and "how many to order" to "when" and "how many to deliver". All firms (including JIT operations, keep a supply of inventory, for the following reasons :

1. **To maintain independence of operations:** A supply of materials at a work center allows the center flexibility in operations. For example, because there are costs for making each new production setup, the inventory allows management to reduce the number of setups.

2. **To meet variation in product demand:** If the demand for the product is known precisely, it may be possible (though not necessarily economical) to produce the product to exactly meet the demand. Usually, however demand is not completely known and a safety or buffer stock must be maintained to absorb variations.

3. **To allow flexibility in production scheduling:** A stock of inventory relieves the pressure on the production system to get the goods out. These cause longer lead times, which permit production planning for smoother flow and lower-cost operation through larger lot-size production. High setup costs, for example, favour producing a larger number of units once the setup has been made

4. **To provide a safeguard for variation in raw material delivery time:** When material is ordered from a vendor, delay can occur for a variety of reasons; a normal variation in shipping time, a shortage of material at the vendor's plant causing backlogs, an unexpected strike at the vendor's plant or at one of the shipping companies, a lost order or a shipment of incorrect or defective material.

5. **To take advantage of economic purchase order size:** There are costs to place an order: labour, phone calls, typing, postage and so on. Therefore the larger each order is, the fewer the orders that need be written. Also shipping costs favour large orders - the larger the shipment, the lower the per-unit cost.

6. **To hedge against price increase:** Occasionally a firm will foresee that a substantial price increase is on the cards and therefore purchase larger-than-normal amounts. The ability to store extra goods also allows firm to take advantage of price discounts for large orders.

7. **To take advantage of quantity discounts:** Suppliers may give discounts on large orders.

5.2.4.3 Transportation

This refers to the movement of everything from raw material to finished goods between different facilities in a supply chain. In transportation the trade-off between responsiveness and efficiency is manifested in the choice of transport mode. Fast modes of transport such as airplanes are very responsive but also more costly. Slower modes such as ship and rail are very cost efficient but not as responsive. Since transportation costs can be as much as a third of the operating cost of a supply chain, decisions made here are very important.

There are six basic modes of transport that a company can choose from :

(i) The ship which is very cost efficient but also the slowest mode of transport. It is limited to use between locations that are situated next to navigable waterways and facilities such as harbours and canals.

(ii) The rail which is also very cost efficient but can be slow. This mode is also restricted to use between locations that are served by rail lines.

(iii) Pipelines can be very efficient but are restricted to commodities that are liquids or gases such as water, oil, and natural gas.

(iv) Trucks are a relatively quick and very flexible mode of transport. Trucks can go almost anywhere. The cost of this mode is prone to fluctuations though, as the cost of fuel fluctuates and the condition of roads varies.

(v) Airplanes are a very fast mode of transport and are very responsive. This is also the most expensive mode and it is somewhat limited by the availability of appropriate airport facilities.

(vi) Electronic Transport is the fastest mode of transport and it is very flexible and cost efficient. However, it can only be used for movement of certain types of products such as electric energy, data, and products composed of data such as music, pictures, and text.

Strategic transportation decisions are closely related to inventory decisions as well as meeting customer demands. Using air transport obviously gets the product out quicker and to the customer expediently, but the costs are high as opposed to shipping by boat or rail. Yet using sea or rail often times means having higher levels of inventory in-house to meet quick demands by the customer. It is wise to keep in mind that since 30% of the cost of a product is encompassed by transportation, using the correct transport mode is a critical strategic decision. Above all, customer service levels must be met, and this often times determines the mode of transport used. Often times this may be an operational decision, but strategically, an organisation must have transport modes in place to ensure a smooth distribution of goods.

Transportation is used in distribution channels for moving goods from one place to another. The way products are transported has two major implications on the distribution channel performance – transportation time and cost. The total cost of transportation in India works out to be in the range of one tenth of the GNP. The longer it takes to transport the goods from manufacturers to the end customers, the higher is the investment tied up in the material-in-transit. The level of service provided to customers by distribution reduces as the speed of transportation reduces. However, as the speed of transportation is increased, the costs also go up. On the other hand, the channel members have another way of increasing the level of customer service – that is by maintaining a stock of products near to the customers. This also requires additional expenditure. Therefore, it becomes essential to settle down at less than one hundred per cent level of service.

The two most important characteristics of the transportation systems "modes of transport" and "transport networks" have a major impact on transport speed and cost. Faster transportation has a large impact on both responsiveness and efficiency. Products can be transported using many different modes of transports like Air, Road, Rail, Water, Pipelines, Others (e.g. conveyors).

A transport network refers to the design of routes and intermediate bulk breaking and assorting locations for transportation of products from manufacturers to end customers, designed to economise the cost using principle of economies of scale in transportation. There are three basic types of transportation networks : Point-to-Point, Hub and Spoke, Milk Route. In a point-to-point network, the material is transported from manufacturer to a customer directly in a single transportation. In hub and spoke network, a number of transport routes are connected to a central node (warehouse, distribution centres, trans-shipment, cross-docking.) Milk route network involves a transport vehicle starting from one point and moving along a loop or circular route covering several locations where smaller lots of material is need to be collected or delivered. A typical distribution channel uses transportation networks that combine several of these basic network types.

5.2.4.4 Information

Information is the basis upon which one has to make decisions regarding the other four supply chain drivers. It is the connection between all of the activities and operations in a supply chain. To the extent that this connection is a strong one, (i.e., the data is accurate, timely, and complete), the companies in a supply chain will each be able to make good decisions for their own operations. This will also tend to maximise the profitability of the supply chain as a whole. That is the way how the stock markets or other free markets work and supply chains have many of the same dynamics as markets.

Information is used for two purposes in any supply chain :

(i) Co-ordinating daily activities related to the functioning of the other four supply chain drivers : production; inventory; location; and transportation. The companies in a supply chain use available data on product supply and demand to decide on weekly production schedules, inventory levels, transportation routes, and stocking locations.

(ii) Forecasting and planning to anticipate and meet future demands. Available information is used to make tactical forecasts to guide the setting of monthly and quarterly production schedules and timetables. Information is also used for strategic forecasts to guide decisions about whether to build new facilities, enter a new market, or exit an existing market.

Effective supply chain management requires obtaining information from the point of end-use, and linking information resources throughout the chain for speed of exchange. Overwhelming paper flow and disparate computer systems are unacceptable in today's competitive world. Fostering innovation requires good organisation of information. Linking computers through networks and the internet, and streamlining the information flow, consolidates knowledge and facilitates velocity of products. Account management software, product configurators, enterprise resource planning systems, and global communications are key components of effective supply chain management strategy.

5.2.4.5 Sourcing/Purchasing

Order processing is the primary activity before sourcing for an organisation. Hence, we shall first study order processing and then the activities which precede it.

A customer order is the message that sets the supply chain process in motion. An Order processing starts with the receiving of a customer's order and ends with the final delivery of goods to him along with the transfer of title. In other words, order processing is a set of activities for receiving, recording, assembling of products for dispatch to fill the customer order. The customer order cycle time is the total time consumed in order preparation and its transmittal, order receipt, order entry, order processing, warehouse picking and packing, preparation of invoices and shipping documents, transportation and delivery and unloading of goods at the customer's end. Order processing is key to achievement of logistics and supply chain objective in terms of achievement of required level of customer service, reduction in order cycle time, point-to-point information apart from fulfillment of legal formalities for movement and transfer of title.

The total order processing system can be described with a flow-chart as shown in Fig. 5.6

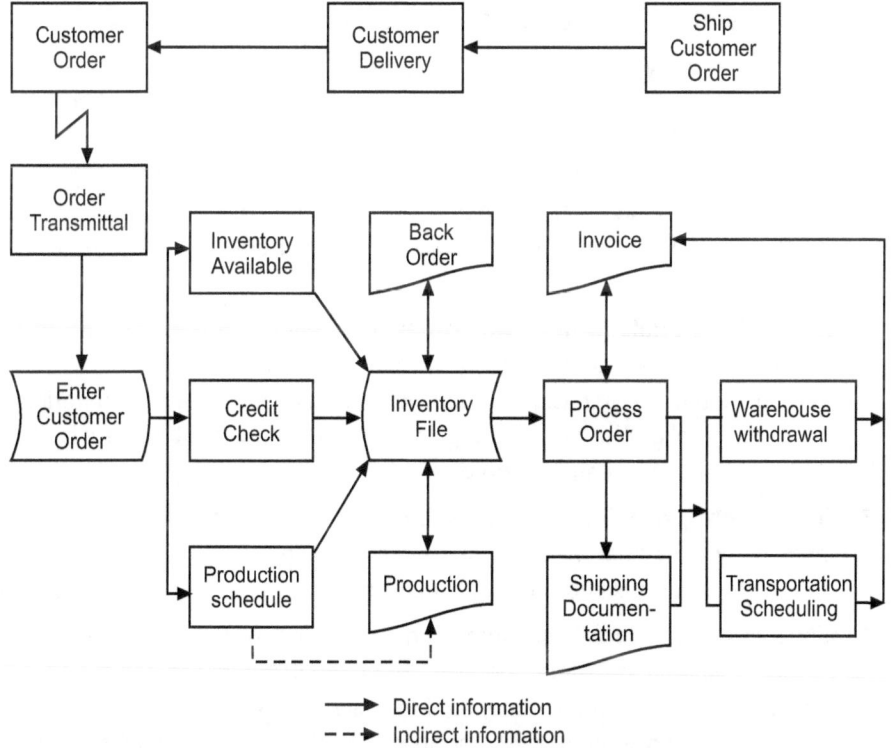

Fig. 5.6: Total Order Processing System

Purchasing is of extreme importance particularly to a manufacturing concern, because it has its bearing on every vital factor concerning the manufacture, i.e. quality, quantity, cost, volume of production, prompt delivery, efficiency, economy etc. It is by the **Purchasing Department** that much money can be saved or lost. The work of purchasing materials should be handled by a separate Purchase Department, under an official designated as Purchase Manager.

The **Purchasing Department** obtains the required materials, supplies, machines, tools etc. at the most favourable terms, consistent with maintaining the desired standard of quality and continuity in service. In order to ensure procurement of materials of requisite quantity at economic prices, following points should be noted :

(a) Purchasing should be centralised i.e. no purchases should be made except by the Purchasing Department.
(b) Full co-operation between Purchase Department and other departments is necessary.
(c) The Purchasing Officer should have a good technical knowledge of the industry.
(d) No purchases should be made unless the Purchasing Department receives a duly signed purchase requisition.

Following are the **Functions of Purchase Department** in a manufacturing concern.

1. **Purchase of quality materials:** While purchasing, Purchasing Department should kept in mind that raw materials should be of proper quality to meet the requirements of the market for which the final product is intended. For different kinds of products, different types of material is needed. Unnecessary increase in quality of raw materials or components increases the cost of product. So, purchase manager must know the exact specification of materials which are used in the production.

2. **Purchase of materials in right quantities:** Material cost may account for as much as 50 percent to 70 percent of the total cost of producing a product. Hence, while purchasing material, Purchasing Department should purchase the materials strictly as per requisition of the various departments. It means that materials should be purchased in required quantities only.

3. **Buying at right price:** The price to be paid for the purchases of materials must be reasonably low, but quality must not be sacrificed in doing so. This will be secured from market quotations and reports, catalogue prices issued by different suppliers.

4. **Timely supply of materials:** Time element is an important factor in purchase procedure. It should be remembered that material purchased for a particular job must be obtained in the right time, so that there should not be delay in production. So, while doing an agreement with supplier, Purchasing Department must mention that timely supply of material will be one of the important condition of the agreement. While specifying the time limit, lead time should also be considered.

5. **Determination of Purchase Budget:** Preparation of a Purchase Budget is one of most important function of Purchasing Department. While preparing purchase budget, requisitions and specification of materials should be taken from various departments. For prompt and correct payment of purchase bills, there should be close liason with the accounts department and stores department. This purchase budget guides the purchase manager in knowing what he has to buy, what should be the quality, quantity and size and also when he has to buy.

6. **Selection of suppliers:** After receiving the purchase requisition, the Purchase Department starts exploring the sources of materials and suppliers. Various sources are examined for the purpose of securing the best materials at the lowest possible price. Due consideration is also given to factors like terms of payments, date of delivery and reliability of suppliers.

7. **Issue purchase orders to suppliers:** After selecting the supplier the purchase manager prepares a Purchase Order and places them to the selected supplier. Once the Purchase Order is issued to a supplier, it is obligatory on the part of the Purchase Manager to take delivery of materials and arrange for the payment of invoice. The purchase order must be carefully prepared including all essential elements of purchases to be made.

8. **Verification of quality and quantity of materials received:** On receipt of materials purchasing department should verify the materials obtained in respect of quality and quantity and ensure that it is as per the purchase order only.

9. **Approving Invoices:** After verifying materials received, Purchasing Department should verify and check the invoices and approve them for payment.

10. **Maintenance of proper record:** Keeping up-to-date information about the best markets, best seasons, new and improved material, spare parts, components, equipments etc. is also one of the important function of the purchasing department. It is necessary for efficient operation of the purchase department.

11. **Co-ordination with other departments:** For smooth and efficient functioning of purchase department it must be co-ordinated with stores, accounts and industrial engineering departments. Purchase Manager should also take part in departmental conferences for planning, formulation of policies and other purposes.

5.2.4.6 Pricing

In general terms price is a component of an exchange or transaction that takes place between two parties and refers to what must be given up by one party (i.e., buyer) in order to obtain something offered by another party (i.e., seller). Yet this view of price provides a somewhat limited explanation of what price means to participants in the transaction. In fact, price means different things to different participants in an exchange:

- **Buyers' View:** For those making a purchase, such as final customers, price refers to what must be given up to obtain benefits. In most cases what is given up is financial consideration (e.g., money) in exchange for acquiring access to a good or service. But financial consideration is not always what the buyer gives up. Sometimes in a barter situation a buyer may acquire a product by giving up their own product. For instance, two farmers may exchange cattle for crops. Also, as we will discuss below, buyers may also give up other things to acquire the benefits of a product that are not direct financial payments (e.g., time to learn to use the product).

- **Sellers' View:** To sellers in a transaction, price reflects the revenue generated for each product sold and, thus, is an important factor in determining profit. For marketing organisations price also serves as a marketing tool and is a key element in marketing promotions. For example, most retailers highlight product pricing in their advertising campaigns.

Price is commonly confused with the notion of cost as in "I paid a high cost for buying my new plasma television." Technically, though, these are different concepts. Price is what a buyer pays to acquire products from a seller. Cost concerns the seller's investment (e.g., manufacturing expense) in the product being exchanged with a buyer. For marketing organisations seeking to make a profit the hope is that price will exceed cost so the organisation can see financial gain from the transaction.

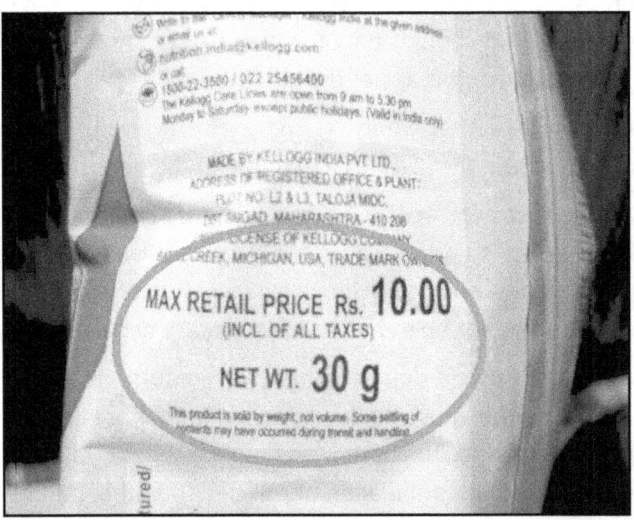

Finally, while product pricing is a main topic for discussion when a company is examining its overall profitability, pricing decisions are not limited to for-profit companies. Not-for-profit organisations, such as charities, educational institutions and industry trade groups, also set prices, though it is often not as apparent. For instance, charities seeking to raise money may set different "target" levels for donations that reward donors with increases in status (e.g., name in newsletter), gifts or other benefits. While a charitable organisation may not call it a price in their promotional material, in reality these donations are equivalent to price setting since donors are required to give a contribution in order to obtain something of value.

How you set your prices can have a host of implications for your business. Not every price you set needs to maximise your margins. Many small businesses use price to compete, change market share or create different revenue scenarios. Understanding how pricing affects your business model, not just your bottom line, will help you better choose price levels.

1. **Profit Margins:** The price you set affects your profit margin per unit sold, with higher prices giving you a higher profit per item if you don't lose sales. However, higher prices that lead to lower sales volumes can decrease, or wipe out, your profits, because your overhead costs per unit increase as you sell fewer units.

2. **Sales Volumes:** One of the most obvious affects pricing will have on your business is an increase or decrease in sales volume. Economists study price elasticity, or the response of consumer purchasing to a price change. Increasing your prices might lower your sales volume only slightly, helping you make up for decreased volume with higher total profits generated by higher margins. Lowering your prices can increase your profits if your sales jump significantly, decreasing your overhead expense per unit. Test the market's response to price increases by changing prices in targeted areas before instituting an across-the-board price increase.

3. **Position:** The price you set sends a message to some consumers about your business, product or service, creating a perceived value. This affects your brand, image or position in the marketplace. For example, higher prices tell some consumers that you have higher quality, or you wouldn't be able to charge those prices. Other consumers look for low-priced products and services, believing they'll get the quality they need at a low price. Offering sales, discounts, rebates and closeouts can send the message you can't sell your products or services at your regular price, or tell buyers they have a short-term opportunity to get a bargain.

4. **Market Share:** The price you set makes you more or less competitive in the marketplace, affecting your share of the market's volume. Some businesses lower prices temporarily to gain market share from competitors, who can't respond to and meet a price decrease. After consumers have had time to try your product and develop a brand preference or loyalty, you can raise your prices again to a level that won't cause them to leave you. Predatory pricing is the practice of selling a product or service below cost for the specific purpose of taking market share away from a competitor or closing it down, then raising prices on consumers when they have fewer, or no options after that competitor is gone. This is illegal.

5. **Loss Leaders:** Some businesses price products or services at or below cost to get customers into their businesses, who then spend more money elsewhere. For example, big-box retailers might buy large quantities of tennis balls, selling them at or below cost to entice affluent tennis players who use many cans of balls during the year into their stores. By placing the low-cost balls at the back of the store, they

hope to generate impulse buys as the shopper walks to the sports area and back to the front. Restaurants offer low-margin specials to offer a change-of-pace to regular diners to keep their normal business, or to let regulars bring friends who want upscale dishes at a moderately priced eatery.

POINTS TO REMEMBER

A value results from the cooperation among firms comprising the supply chain with respect to five critical flows which influence the efficiency. These flows are:
- Information
- Product
- Service
- Financial and
- Knowledge

The quest for achieving this lowest cost and highest efficiency for a process through Integrated Management has opened up three facets for development. These facets are:
1. Collaboration
2. Enterprise Extension, and
3. Integrated Service Providers

Cash Conversion Cycle:
1. Cash paid for inventory.
2. Inventory in warehouse.
3. Inventory processed in manufacturing.
4. Finished goods in warehouse.
5. Finished goods sold.
6. Cash received on sales.
7. Received cash can be utilised.

Customer Service:
1. Referrals and Testimonals.
2. Returning Customers.
3. Customer Lifetime Value.
4. Customers' Customers.

Supply Chain Manageme4nt and Customer Service Linkages:
1. Differences.
2. Product flow.
3. Information flow.
4. Considerations.

Enablers of SCM:
1. Plan

2. Source
3. Make
4. Delivery
5. Return.

Inventory:

There are three basic decisions to make regarding the creation and holding of inventory:
1. Cycle inventory.
2. Safety inventory.
3. Seasonal inventory.

All firms (including JIT operations, keep a supply of inventory, for the following reasons:
1. To maintain independence of operations.
2. To meet variation in product demand.
3. To allow flexibility in production scheduling.
4. To provide a safeguard for variation in raw material delivery time.
5. To take advantage of economic purchase order size.
6. To hedge against price increase.
7. To take advantage of quantity discounts.

Questions for Discussion

1. What is Supply Chain Management ?
2. State the Objectives of Supply Chain Management.
3. Explain the Various ENABLERS OF Supply Chain Management.
4. Explain : Generalised Supply Chain Management Model.
5. Describe the Various Key Issues in Supply Chain Management.
6. Explain : Supply Chain Management and Customer Service Linkages.
7. Write short notes on:
   (a) Service Reliability
   (b) Collaboration
   (c) Perfect Order
   (d) Cash to Cash Conversion
   (e) Enterprise Extension

Questions from Previous Examinations

Note: Since the chapter is new, there are no University Questions.

Case Studies

Case Study - 1

Introduction

Supply chain management is a paradigm driving many businesses, and in turn business relationships, today. Customers are dictating how their orders and shipments will be handled. They want to drive out excess inventory and costs. They want their orders shipped complete, accurate, on time and in the manner they require. Compliance means continued business. Non-compliance means financial penalties and possible loss of business. This is significant in terms of sales revenues and operating costs for their suppliers. Supply chain management competence can build competitive advantage.

Inventory management basically deals with the effectively and efficiently controlling the inventories or the stock by any organisation. Nowadays, many concepts and techniques are available for controlling inventories.

There are very remarkable examples for controlling inventories like some models to determine order quantities, techniques for forecasting demands, etc. Basically the concept and techniques that are mainly used in controlling and effectively managing the inventory is based on mathematical assumptions and modelling inventory situations. Although this approach to inventory control has proved to be very valuable in determining inventory parameters and planning resources but its value can be questioned in dealing with practical inventory control problems.

This case study is divided into various parts. First of all the purpose of the inventory management, why do we need to study it, what all areas are taken under consideration of the inventory control (i.e. its scope), then the technology used by the Harish Bakers (Shop in Gurgaon) to efficiently manage their inventory. Then we will deal with the system on which they are currently working with, what were their requirements, who all are going to use that system, what are its constraints, what were the problems faced by them when they were not having the system and what requirements were put by them to the people who made their project.

System Analysis

1. Purpose or Identification of the Need

Within the area of inventory we found traditionally few topics that played an important role in the inventory control management.

First of all inventory management basically deals with the order quantities, order intervals and finally the complete inventory control systems.

The first topic is concerned with regards to order quantities or how much we order. In order to determine economic order quantities, several costs associated with inventories play a part, such as ordering costs and inventory carrying costs. The second topic regards the order interval or when to order. In this respect demand and lead time processes are important. Finally, the topic regards the inventory control system.

Common subjects concerning systems for controlling inventories are information systems. These three aspects represent the traditional characteristics of an inventory situation. In addition to that they are considered to be starting points for improving the inventory system. Below are some of the advantages and disadvantages of manual processing as compared to using automated system for managing inventory.

(a) Disadvantages :
 1. Time consuming.
 2. It is very tedious.
 3. All information is not placed separately.
 4. Lot of paper work.
 5. Slow data processing.
 6. Not user-friendly environment.
 7. It is difficult to find records due file management system.

(b) Advantages :
 1. Manually system changes into computerised system.
 2. Friendly user interface.
 3. Time saving.
 4. Save paper work.
 5. Connecting to database so we use different type of queries, data report.
 6. Give facility of different type of inquiry.
 7. Formatted data.
 8. Data's are easily approachable.

2. Scope of Inventory Management

A significant example concerning inventory management is allocation of responsibilities and authorities. Inventory control problems can easily arise when for instance nobody in the organisation is responsible for the inventory or the responsible person has insufficient authorities to carry out the task.

Likewise, high inventory values indicating a lack of control may just be the result of inaccurate inventory records or of a reporting system that doesn't function well.

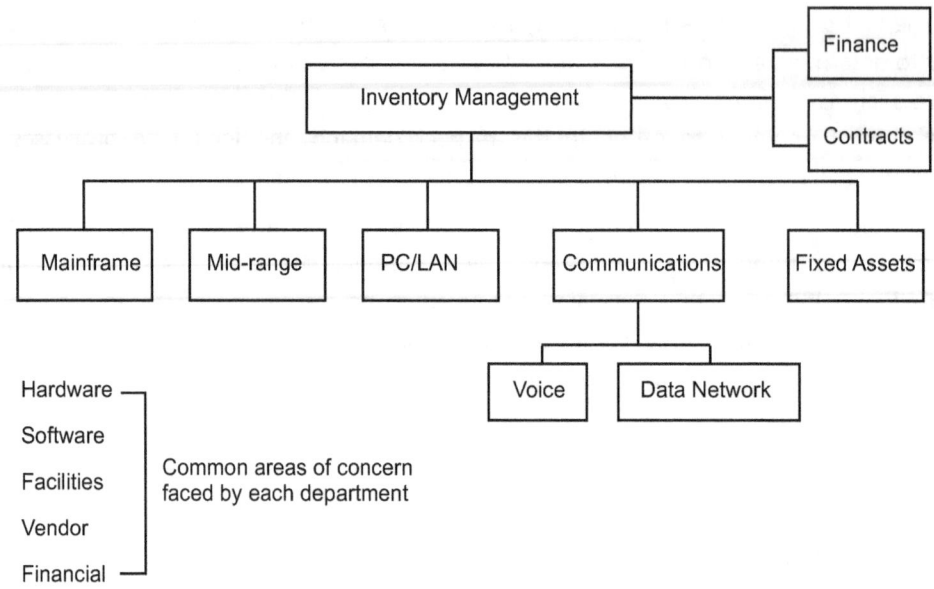

Scope of Inventory Management

All functional areas listed above utilises the information contained with the inventory management control system and asset repository of information.

The inventory management discipline encompasses all system and data elements from the mainframe to the server level throughout the enterprise. All mainframe and data network based hardware and software assets must be identified and entered into the inventory system. Any changes to these environments must be reflected in the inventory system. Financial and technical product information must be available through the inventory system, as needed to support the functional responsibilities of personnel within the finance and contracts management department.

3. **Preliminary investigation :**

This part has further three categories :

(a) Request clarification

(b) Feasibility study

(c) Request approval

(a) Request Clarification :

We all know that many requests originate from the side of users, employees in the organisation but these requests are not clearly indicated or stated. Therefore before any system is developed to fulfil such requests we must understand what the originator of the requests wants from the system. All this is studied under the category of the request clarification. In our case of inventory management of a bakery shop in Gurgaon after going through their documents we found the below mentioned framework that arouse for solving the inventory control and management problems.

Inventory control management deals with the controlling stock, orders, daily, weekly and monthly orders of how much company purchases the stocks and utilises the stock. So using all this data an analysis carried out on how the inventory system should be modified or redesigned to meet its requirement.

(b) Feasibility Study :

First of all in feasibility analysis we take into account whether the proposed system would be feasible by performing various feasibility analysis tests like technical feasibility, operational feasibility, economic feasibility, etc. So in order to study all this, let us have an overview of the goals of proposed system or see what all objectives people had when they approached some company to develop the system to manage their inventory shop.

Goals or Objectives of Proposed System :

1. Ensure efficient and timely identification of vital corporate assets (commodities).
2. Provide common repository for asset protection.
3. To indentify and trace all data processing assets in an inventory system repository.
4. To provide inventory system access to all necessary personnel (data entry, update data, delete data).
5. To provide full range of reports that will satisfy informational requirements.
6. To document the inventory management system with standards and procedures manual.
7. To provide training to the personnel responsible for supporting the inventory management system.

Based upon these objectives of the system to be developed the inventory management system was studied under the three aspects of the feasibility analysis :

Technical feasibility :

This states that whether the project or the system can be developed with the existing technology available in the market or would it require some training or expertise to develop the system. All the objectives were put forward to the company making their project so that they can check whether it is technically feasible or not. Documents shown by the store manager indicates that at the time when the system to manage inventory was developed the technology that was available and which could be used for the development of the system was Windows Server 2003 32-bit, Min 512 Mb of RAM and the programming language that could be used was Visual Basic in addition to the database storage using MS Access. It was found that with these tools or software's the inventory management system could be formulated.

After this the system was tested for the Economic Feasibility discussed below :

Economic Feasibility :

This test of feasibility analysis was performed by the company as well as by the shop owner. Under this test they judged whether the project was economically feasible i.e. whether the software they will be using or the tools required in making the project will benefit the shopkeeper cost wise or in other words whether the shop owner will be able to recover the cost or money spent in making the project and will have faster processing now at his shop unlike he had before the system.

Operational Feasibility :

This test judge whether the project or the system developed for that shop would be used by the users or their will be reluctance or resistance from the user to use that system to manage their inventory.

Looking and analysing the documents provided by the shop it was found that in the initial or earlier phases their was lot of resistance from the users or the employees working in that shop like they were not able to handle that system to add or delete the inventory commodities when it was purchased or sold to the customers. One more problem that aroused was when some customer returned a product stating that the product has expired or is not up to the mark, the employees didn't know how to add the already sold product entry again in the database and return their money using that system of inventory management.

(c) Request Approval :

As we all know that all requested projects are not desirable or feasible. Some organisations receive so many requests from the employees that only few of them can be implemented. In some cases development can start immediately. When this happens management decide which project are most important and schedule them accordingly.

In our case the project of inventory management was approved by the management of the shop considering the cost of project, benefit they will get, completion time of the project and other functional and non functional requirements.

4. Interview Questionnaire :

1. What does the existing system include in it or what all functions it performs?

The system we are using has 3 major tasks to be performed i.e.

  (a) **Order Processing :** It consists of the following functions :
   - Order Creation
   - Order Release
   - Reporting
   - Inquiries
   - Control Automatic Pricing

(b) **Inventory Management :** This part of the system maintains the minimum level of the inventory to ensure profitability while still satisfying management consideration for the customer's service. It provides for recording and reporting stock movement.

(c) **Sales Analysis :** Maintains sales history, report sales activity and providing decision making information are the major tasks of the sales analysis.

2. **Why do you use this automated system?**

   We use this automated system because of the below mentioned reasons :
   - Provide fast order turn-around.
   - Offer flexibility in automatic pricing and discounting.
   - Making timely price changes.
   - Reduce man hours cost in managing inventory.
   - Improved cash flow.
   - Improve customer service.
   - Calculates tax by total items.

   In addition to the invoice, the system prints a detail or summary invoice register and item margin analysis report and removes invoiced or cancelled orders from the open order file.

3. **What are the various reports generated by the system?**
   - Order entry report.
   - Order hard copy inquiry report.
   - Open order status report.
   - Back order status reports.
   - Daily business summary.
   - Item margin analysis.

4. **What is the benefit of daily business summary?**
   - Make better management decisions.
   - Improve profits.
   - Provides better customer service.

5. **Why do you think that inventory management is important?**
   - Assists in maintaining minimum levels of inventory without jeoparding customer deliveries.
   - Provides central file inventory management capability.
   - Provides an important tool for making timely purchase decisions.

- Highlights under-stocked items requiring immediate action.
- Automates prices, discounts, quality breaks to maintain an effective pricing strategy.
- Aids in planning cash requirements for payables.

Software Engineering Paradigm

Under this sub topic we are going to discuss the waterfall model used in system analysis and development of the inventory management system

The stages of "The Waterfall Model" are :

1. **Requirement Analysis and Definition :**

All possible requirements of the system to be developed are captured in this phase. Requirements are set of functionalities and constraints that the end-user (who will be using the system) expects from the system. The requirements are gathered from the end-user by consultation, these requirements are analysed for their validity and the possibility of incorporating the requirements in the system to be developed is also studied. Finally, a Requirement Specification document is created which serves the purpose of guideline for the next phase of the model.

2. **System and Software Design :**

Before starting for actual coding, it is highly important to understand what we are going to create and what it should look like? The requirement specifications from first phase are studied in this phase and system design is prepared. System Design helps in specifying hardware and system requirements and also helps in defining overall system architecture. The system design specifications serve as input for the next phase of the model.

3. **Implementation and Unit Testing :**

On receiving system design documents, the work is divided in modules/units and actual coding is started. The system is first developed in small programmes called units, which are integrated in the next phase. Each unit is developed and tested for its functionality; this is referred to as Unit Testing. Unit testing mainly verifies if the modules/units meet their specifications.

4. **Integration and System Testing :**

As specified above, the system is first divided in units which are developed and tested for their functionalities. These units are integrated into a complete system during integration phase and tested to check if all modules/units coordinate between each other and the system as a whole behaves as per the specifications. After successfully testing the software, it is delivered to the customer.

5. **Operations and Maintenance :**

This phase of "The Waterfall Model" is virtually never ending phase (very long). Generally, problems with the system developed (which are not found during the development life cycle) come up after its practical use starts, so the issues related to the system are solved after deployment of the system. Not all the problems come in picture directly but they arise time to time and needs to be solved; hence this process is referred as Maintenance.

There are some Disadvantages of the Waterfall Model.
1. As it is very important to gather all possible requirements during the Requirement Gathering and Analysis phase in order to properly design the system, not all requirements are received at once, the requirements from customer goes on getting added to the list even after the end of "Requirement Gathering and Analysis" phase, this affects the system development process and its success in negative aspects.
2. The problems with one phase are never solved completely during that phase and in fact many problems regarding a particular phase arise after the phase is signed off, this result in badly structured system as not all the problems (related to a phase) are solved during the same phase.
3. The project is not partitioned in phases in flexible way.
4. As the requirements of the customer goes on getting added to the list, not all the requirements are fulfilled, this results in development of almost unusable system. These requirements are then met in newer version of the system; this increases the cost of system development.

Questions:
1. Analyse the system analysis of this case.
2. Give a suitable title to this case.

Case Study - 2

The transportation and distribution management of food and beverages has always been a challenge for logistic managers. The task becomes much more complex and tricky if the product is perishable or has a very short shelf life. Think of a distribution for ice creams, for instance!

The new-age enterprise software applications such as supply chain management (SCM) have been of great help in handling operations which used to take days earlier. Before SCM system was implemented, it used to be a tedious process to collaborate and comprehend information from thousand of tables, before any action could be taken. But organisations soon realised that monthly or weekly planning was also not enough to optimise resources. This is because most of the software system was not able to take care of unexpected developments or demand fluctuations within the planned time frame.

The importance of optimising resources and incorporating last minute demand/supply fluctuations into planning resulted in a need to deploy resource optimisation software tools on top of enterprise applications. In an effort to take care of the problem, Bharat Ice creams

Limited (BIL) has adopted an optimisation resource system for manufacturing and distribution planning for its ice cool ice creams. The company wanted to figure out the best options for manufacturing, warehousing and distribution, depending on the demand fluctuations.

"They had a problem of sourcing and distribution optimisation," said the executive director of Integrated Software System (a state of the art solution company for SCM) that helped BIL in implementing the optimisation system. They wanted answers to questions such as how to plan production in terms of which factory should make what, depending on the demand and how to optimise distribution to best balance the service levels with inventory.

BIL manufactures and sells a variety of brands like Cool-Feast, Brando etc. These brands are very popular amongst the youth segment. The large number of flavours, variations in pack sizes, location of markets and placement of manufacturing facilities have made the task of managing supply chain a complex job. The optimisation model was required to allocate indents to factories to take decision on distribution plan like which factory should service which depot using which carrying agent. The purpose was to optimize the cost of distribution. The further distribution of products to service stockists from depots by routing and scheduling of vehicles also needed to be optimised to save cost. "We actually mathematically modelled the problem, capturing all constraints and objective functions," said the SCM manager, Mr. Arora. He claimed that the pilot model helped in identifying opportunities towards substantial savings for the company. "The live data was available and it was easy to find out as to which production units were actually below capacity and where manually taken distribution decisions were proving to be sub-optimal. Big savings were available by just addressing these anomalies," he said.

Mr. Arora said that companies might be having sound business methodology and processes, but they need to have the tools to gather information to take optimum scheduling decision.

Questions:
1. How will the supply chain of ice creams be different from say an automobile or any such engineering product? What is the complexity in the supply chain of ice creams?
2. Analyse the optimisation resource system used the Bharat Ice Cream Ltd.

A SPECIAL CASE STUDY - 3

An important and special case-study of Unconventional Marketing which is adopted by State Government to enhance the welfare of people is given below :

Scenario for Home Delivery Scheme of Foodgrains :

World Scenario :

1. Around 850 million people are chronically hungry worldwide due to extreme poverty. According to recent FAO figures, in the year 2009-10 alone 40 million more people have been pushed into hunger primarily due to increase in food prices.

By the end of 2007, increased acreage in the cultivation of bio fuels, rise in oil prices the world over, population explosion, climate change, loss of agriculture land to residential and industrial development and growing consumer demand have pushed up the prices of grain.

2. UN Food and Agriculture Organisation (FAO) defines food security as –when all people, at all times, have physical and economic access to sufficient, safe and nutritious food to meet their dietary needs and food preference for an active and healthy life.

3. Globally enough food is produced to feed the entire world population at a level adequate to ensure that everyone can be free of hunger and fear of starvation. That no one should live without enough food because of economic constraints or social inequalities is the basic goal. This approach is often referred to as food justice and views food security as a basic human right. It advocates fairer distribution of food, particularly grain crops, as a means of ending chronic hunger and malnutrition. The core of the Food Justice movement is the belief that what is lacking is not food, but the will to fairly distribute food regardless of the recipient's ability to pay.

4. The food crisis is being called a 'silent tsunami' – since it is threatening over 100 million people, including 20 million of the world's poorest children. Rising prices for staples like rice means that fewer people are getting the food that they need, pushing more people into poverty, and causing violence and instability. All countries which have legislated the right to food, have involved Civil Society Organisations, not just in local structure, but also in the national-level oversight bodies.

Indian Scenario :

1. The Public Distribution System is the largest food subsidy programme in India, and perhaps in the world. It reaches out to nearly 10.5 crore households in the country and provides subsidised foodgrains through a network of Fair Price Shops (FPS).

2. Despite this, India continues to have one of the worst track records globally, as far as the commitment to tackle hunger and malnutrition is concerned. The last round of the National Family Health Survey in 2006 confirmed that the child malnutrition rate in India is 46 percent, almost double that of Sub-Saharan Africa. India, the world's second fastest growing economy, ranks 66th among the 88 countries surveyed by the International Food Policy Research Institute (IFPRI) in the Global Hunger Index (2008), below Sudan, Nigeria and Cameroon, and slightly above Bangladesh.

3. As per the Planning Commission's evaluation of Targeted Public Distribution System (TPDS), 28 percent of subsidised foodgrains do not reach the BPL families, whereas 22 percent reaches Above Poverty Line (APL) and 36 percent is sold in black.

According to the study, for one rupee worth of income transfer to the poor, the Government of India (GoI) spends ₹ 3.65, indicating that one rupee of budgetary consumer subsidy is worth only 27 paise to the poor. The implementation of TPDS is plagued by targeting errors, prevalence of ghost cards and unidentified households. Homeless often do not have ration cards and only 57 percent of the other poor households have ration cards. FPSs are not viable; they remain in business through leakages. The key problems with TPDS shown in the evaluation are Inadequate Storage Capacity with FCI, poor condition of the State Food Corporations, states do not have food infrastructure, GOI quota lapses after one month, politics in the allotment of APL quota, shopkeepers lease out their shops to contractors, the shop does not open for more than 2-3 days in a month, ration cards being mortgaged to ration shop owners, too many intermediaries between the shopkeeper and the FCI.

4. Keeping the above facts in mind, an alternative method of periodical one-time distribution of foodgrains, openly before the community, either quarterly, half yearly and annually was tried in Nashik district by Additional Collector, Shri Shekhar Gaikwad,. This scheme is, popularly called 'Gharpoch Dhanya Yojana', the 'Home Delivery of Foodgrains Scheme.'

Home Delivery Scheme of Foodgrains

Introduction:

Despite various efforts made by the government to ensure that the poor get foodgrains under its Public Distribution Scheme (PDS), a number of difficulties still exist in providing the foodgrains directly to the beneficiaries.

In the existing system foodgrains are distributed through Fair Price Shops. Every month foodgrains are carried from Food Corporation of India (FCI) godowns to Taluka places and from Taluka godowns distributed to the Fair Price Shops.

A pilot scheme of periodical home delivery of foodgrains was proposed by, Shekhar Gaikwad, then Additional Collector Nashik in 2006 and received approval of Government of Maharashtra in April 2007.

Nature of Scheme :

This scheme proposed that beneficiaries of the PDS will get quota foodgrains of three, six and twelve months, instead of monthly basis directly at their doorsteps. Thus grains should be distributed only three to four times a year. Actual need of the consumers is taken into account and ration card holders are asked to make payment in advance. The consumers are asked to be ready with the money to pay for the required amount of foodgrains. On a date pre-decided by the administration, the amount is collected from consumers by the

Supply Officer / Village Talathi in advance. This amount collected for the entire village is deposited in the Government treasury under the proper account head. The place and date are fixed for distribution of foodgrains and grains are distributed to the ration card holders before the Gram Sabha, the village community. Foodgrains are distributed in the form of standardised sacks of 50 kg each. Instead of prevailing system of distribution through Fair Price Shops (FPS) followed by occasional inspection by Supply Officers, the scheme ensures a transparent distribution system in front of the village community.

Amount to be paid :

No.	Scheme	Maximum Grain for 3 months (kg)		Amount to be paid	Maximum Grains for 6 months (kg)		Amount to be paid
		Wheat	Rice		Wheat	Rice	
1.	Annapurna	15	15	Free	30	30	Free
2.	Antyoday	50	50	250	100	100	500
3.	B.P.L.	50	50	550	100	100	1100
4.	A.P.L.*	50	50	825	100	100	1650

*If the norms are changed, actual quota can vary and can be in multiple of 50 kg.

Implementation :

- **Pilot Scheme:** Initially the scheme was proposed as pilot scheme in three Talukas of Nashik district namely Surgana (tribal), Dindori (tribal) and Niphad (non-tribal).

- **Planned Programme of Distribution:** The Tehsildar should prepare a detailed programme of distribution of foodgrains considering the rainy season, cropping season, road conditions etc. Social factors such as festivals, period during which people normally get employment, the peak period during which the need of foodgrains is highest should also be considered. The Scheme is expected to reach up to the hamlets with even 50 houses.

- **Consent and payment in Advance:** Depending on the need of foodgrains every family is expected to give consent for the period for which the family is ready to pay money in advance. This period has to be 3 months, 6 months or 1 year.

    Ration card holders should make payment to Talathi or Supply Officer on the scheduled day. This is for ensuring that amount of all the needy persons is collected on one day and grains are distributed on a single day in a village. This saves lot of time while implementing Home Delivery Scheme.

- **Actual Distribution:** The distribution of foodgrains in the form of 50 kg sacks is done before villagers at a community place. Publicity is given to the programme so that other villagers also attend and get inspiration and adopt the scheme. The distribution is done before the Gram Sabha (Community) and local representatives.

Principles of the Scheme :

- Scheme of purchase of foodgrains from FCI (Food Corporation of India) godown remains the same as the regular PDS.
- Transport arrangements and cost of transport from FCI godown to Tahsil godown remains the same as PDS.
- Foodgrains from Taluka godown are not to be taken to Fair Price Shops. Instead they are taken to a village site directly for distribution. This transport and distribution are carried on the same day as per pre-decided schedule.
- Transport of foodgrains is carried out either by Government vehicle or FPS vehicle, since FPS is allowed transport rebate as per government rules.
- The distribution of foodgrains is organised at a centrally located place convenient to everyone in the village, vasti or hamlet.
- As distribution is done in the form of sacks of 50 kg each as are standardised in godown, it takes hardly one or two hours.
- Distribution is done before Media, NGOs, MLA, ZillaParishad members, other Panchayatraj functionaries and the entire village community.
- Any NGO or independent organisation can inspect and verify the implementation and effects of scheme. So also the effects on livelihood, storage methods, nutrition etc. can be studied.

Advantages of the Scheme :

- **One Time Distribution:** Foodgrains are distributed once in three, six months or one year. Therefore there is no necessity to distribute foodgrains again for next 3 / 6 months / 1 year period.
- **Food Security:** Traditionally farmers have been storing grains in various types of local storage devices in India. Therefore storage of foodgrains for 6 months is not a big problem for the ration card holders. The decentralised system of storage of foodgrain in thousands of households would ultimately bring about food security.
- **Transparency in Distribution:** Since the programme of distribution of foodgrains takes place before community, malpractices in distribution are eliminated.
- **Monitoring:** Once grains are distributed, independent agencies, NGOs can verify whether the grains are properly utilised.
- **Sustainable Scheme:** Since the new scheme reduces the expenditure on transport and guarantees 100 percent delivery of foodgrains, this scheme is more sustainable.

- **Cost Saving:** In the existing system, foodgrains are transported from Tehsil office to village 12 times a year. In the new scheme, the minimum period prescribed is 3 months and therefore the transportation is required for maximum 4 times a year. This saves the transport cost.

- **Family's Control:** The new scheme has become more pro-family because there is complete control of family members over the foodgrains received. The lady of the house has food security for longer period and she controls the utilisation of foodgrains.

- **Boon to the poor:** Government is spending huge funds in tribal areas separately for fighting malnutrition in addition to food subsidy programme. The new scheme would reduce the malnutrition and under nourishment as well. The foodgrains for next 3 or 6 months will give sufficient food security to the poorest families. They can instead concentrate on their employment and welfare once the concern of foodgrains is over.

- **Foodgrains to Actual Residents:** Many a time people take ration cards only as evidence of ordinary residence, which is useful for them for social / political reasons. But the new scheme expects money to be deposited in advance by actual residents and therefore foodgrains would also go to the actual residents, who are genuine beneficiaries.

- **Prohibition to Organised Black Marketing:** Every year many offences are registered against FPS for violations under Essential Commodities Act and yet organised black marketing has not been effectively stopped. The new scheme will check the organized black marketing of grains because once the grains reach the consumers; it is difficult to repurchase them.

- **Increase in purchasing power:** The new scheme will help in increasing the purchasing power of the poor.

- **Satisfaction to Consumers and Time Saving:** The scheme gives more satisfaction to consumers and saves their time.

- **Grains to the needy:** Instead of storing grains in large quantity in Government godowns, this scheme would ensure decentralised storage of foodgrains in thousands of households.

- **Saving in Administrative costs and time:** The new scheme saves a lot of time of supply staff on account of recurring activities such as filling up of chalans, permits, bills etc. The human resources in Government can best be utilised in the new scheme because the work load gets reduced once we shift to one time food distribution mechanism.

Progress of the Scheme (Till March 2010)

Sr. No.	Name of Taluka	No. of Villages/ Shops	No. of Beneficiaries	Distributed Foodgrain for 3 months (Qtl.)
1.	Nashik	9	820	820
2.	Igatpuri	38	10396	10396
3.	Sinnar	8	861	861
4.	Dindori	24	3173	3173
5.	Peth	41	3399	3399
6.	Surgana	50	4578	2005
7.	Niphad	4	1910	1910
8.	Trimbakeshwar	36	3710	3710
9.	Nandgaon	3	214	214
10.	Satana	20	2380	2380
11.	Chandwad	23	2396	2970
12.	Kalwan	46	3272	3272
13.	Devla	2	166	166
14.	Yewla	1	437	339
15.	Malegaon	9	1449	1449
	Total	**314**	**39161**	**37064**

(Source: Shri Shekhar Gaikwad, Additional Collector/Registrar, YASHADA.)

Case Study - 4

Branchwater :

The marketing management of Branchwaterwere reviewing the next year's marketing plan. It would concentrate on how changes to the physical distribution system could help the company achieve greater profitability so that resources could be allocated elsewhere : on trade and consumer divisions; or on making the product more price competitive; or on improving the level of customer service via better availability; or a combination of all three.

Branchwater had started operations in the early 1980s as a regional bottled water company in the north western part of the United States. As market demand grew, the company increased the volume it sold within the existing area and expanded its area of supply. It achieved a turnover of $10 million in the previous year. As Branchwater grew, it faced steadily greater problems of profitability and customer service. Though the company had a number of enquiries from new customers in three areas adjacent to the current sales area, it was uncertain as to how these could be profitably exploited, given the steadily rising distribution costs involved in servicing more distant market areas.

The Company:

Branchwater had a spring, high up in the Appalachian mountains, about 10 miles from the nearest main town which had an interstate highway, and one of the main railway lines in the country. The spring was 80 miles inland from a sea port serving the eastern seaboard of the United States. It was approximately 100 miles from the nearest point at which there was a navigable river, which could be used for the transport of product within the country. The spring water met all the government regulations concerning purity and had been certified satisfactory by the public health authorities ever since the company had started manufacturing. Near the spring, the company had a simple bottling plant and warehouse. Clear plastic bottles with attached labels were filled with spring water, sealed with tamper proof tape, collected and stacked in cardboard cartons. A sample of each production batch was removed for bacteriological inspection. Each of the cartons passed from the bottling plant into the warehouse by conveyor belt. Here the cartons were stacked onto pallets and stored by fork lift trucks on simple racking systems. The variable costs of manufacture were $0.10 cents for each bottle.

The advantage of the site used by Branchwater was that it was very cheap, could be extended easily should sales require it, and provided continuous volumes of high quality spring water. But the site was poorly situated for distribution of the product, and this had meant that costs tended to be higher than the competition. Overall fixed costs of the operation, including all manufacturing labour, bank interest on the outstanding loan, was $2.7 million.

The Market:

With the increase in disposable income and growing awareness of some of the contaminates in municipal water, the market for pure bottled water had grown substantially. Year on year volume increase were around 5 per cent, though consumption patterns were erratic with substantial seasonal variations.

There were two separate components of the bottled water market, the restaurant/cafe sector and retail. The restaurant sector was dominated by premium brands, like Perrier, which were often imported. Packaging and attitudinal investment was all important in this sector, and consumers were prepared to pay substantial prices for premium products. The retail market, which made up the bulk of the total volume sold in the United States, was by contrast, characterised by steep price and distribution elasticities. Consumers bought mainly on price and availability. They tended not to be willing to pay premium prices for products and would purchase those products that were available, rather than buy specific brands. As might be expected in this price sensitive retail market, a substantial proportion of total sales occurred during special offer periods. Purity of supply remained an important promotional element, with the authorities providing certification of water content, which was vital to achieve a reasonable level of sale. Large pack sizes were commonplace, with gallon - 3.6 litre - plastic containers the favourite size

The Competition:

The retail market was dominated by three brands, each with over 15 per cent of the market :Deer Park, Appalachian Spring, and Mountain Dew. All three had a target $0.99 retail for a gallon, but each discounted heavily during sales promotions. The average discount offer was for $0.10, or 5 gallons for the price of 4. Branchwater with its 5 per cent market share in the areas where it was sold, aimed for a target price of $1.10 based around a superior product benefit. It was believed that the price elasticity in the market was high, around 7 to 10 which meant that pricing and cost control was vital to a successful product.

Product Benefit :

Branchwater had detailed market research for its sales areas. This had shown that in addition to price and availability there were two other important influences on purchasing. The first was purity. The typical bottled water customer was interested in the source of the water and the certification. The detail on the packaging was also perceived as another part of the product benefit, confirming the quality of the water and its purity. The management of Branchwater had taken this concept further and had introduced a clear plastic bottle - the competition, in contrast, continued to bottle product in mottled or blue containers. The choice of clear plastic had a minor, but unimportant effect on shelf life. Bottled water generally had a long shelf life, in excess of 8 months, but clear plastic meant that the taste of product might alter if exposed to strong sunlight over a long period of time. This change reduced the shelf life by approximately 5 weeks, but had little real effect on the product because of the normal speed of sale. The second important element of the product benefit was attitudinal. In the restaurant/cafe sector the attitudinal component emphasised sophistication, while in the retail sector traditional values were more important. The name Branchwater was largely a result of this research. Branchwater was associated with pure spring water, only available high up in the hills before it joined another stream (above the branch, or branchwater).

Distribution Channels:

Supermarkets accounted for 95 per cent of all bottled water sold in the United States. Volumes were highest in suburban locations, which served the main bottled water segment, the ABC1 households, particularly those with younger children. Supermarkets required frequent deliveries into their central depots. Though there were considerable variations, the majority of outlets could hold 2-3 days' stock but not more. Most outlets also demanded suppliers support their products with an annual listing fee. For each of the 30 depots that Branchwater supplied this averaged $10,000 per depot per year. A small, but growing percentage of the market was supplied by home delivery to households with in-home water coolers. Market surveys suggested that this part of the market was likely to grow rapidly in the main urban centres. Retail margins were typically around 15 per cent of the retail price.

Current Physical Distribution Structure :

At present, the company used five of its own trailers to distribute product in the six states in which it operated. Its network of 30 delivery sites were the depots of the main supermarket outlets that the company supplied. These were all based in main centres of population. Details of the market sizes in millions of value, the road distance in miles (one way), and the rail-link in miles (if in existence) are provided in Table 1A.

Table 1A : Branchwater Market Analysis

Centre	Market size $ million	Deliveries No/ year	Distance miles	Rail miles	Water (miles)
A	55	250	75	125	N/A
B	35	164	80	140	300
C	40	155	40	55	150
D	65	283	90	200	300
E	25	127	45	60	n/a

Each lorry carried 40,000 kilos of water - about 11,500 bottles. Between them, they had driven 138,000 miles in the last year. Average travel speeds were fairly high at around 45 mph (speed limits on highways in the US being 55 mph maximum). Though there were no limitations on the total number of hours per employee, the company had a general rule that drivers should not work more than 10 hours a day. This meant a daily round trip limitation of 450-500 miles. Maintenance costs had risen over the last 2 years as breakdown rates increased with extra mileage. As a result, the company used subcontractors in emergencies. The overall annual costs of the current operation were : vehicles - including depreciation - $150,000; drivers $120,000; fuel $20,000; maintenance $60,000; and emergency delivery $45,000 per annum.

Future plans :

The company had identified four new areas for sales expansion, each of which had been extensively researched. Three of the four areas were west of the factory, (Areas F-H), the other (Area I) was far to the south. The main statistics of these areas are in Table 1B.

Table 1B : New Centres for Development

Centre	Population million	Market ($million)	Deliveries	Distance (miles)	Rail-link (miles)	Water (miles)
F	85	150	155	225	450	650
G	65	130	180	240	N/A	330
H	60	155	240	355	270	N/A
I	105	170	490	470	600	1000

The problems of supplying these areas would be acute. On the basis of the salesforce volume forecast, additional vehicle mileage would be in excess of an extra 250,000 miles. The company would have to invest in more vehicles, more drivers, more maintenance, and incur far higher delivery charges unless it chose an alternative distribution method, or combination of methods.

Distribution alternatives :

A number of distribution alternatives had been identified. The first option was to investigate the use of rail. Rail speeds were lower than road averaging 20 mph, but the network could, and did, operate over 24 hours. Yet rail delivery was far less reliable than road with no guarantee - unless the company paid premium rates - that delivery would occur under 72 hours to any point on the network. Rail costs were based on mileage and volume carried. Normally around $3 per ton per 100 miles of track. Because the company would have to deliver to the local rail-head near the factory, and then transport product from the railway at the destinations, additional costs - storage and onward shipment - would be incurred. Storage would cost around $1 per ton, per 24 hours, in third party warehousing organised by the rail shipper, with an average delivery cost to the railhead of $50 and a collection cost at the destination point of $100 dollars per 40 tonne load.

It was possible to use either sea freight - appropriate for the new market area I (Table 1B) - or inland waterways for particular market areas. There was information about the distances involved in servicing particular markets - given in Tables 1A and 1B. Water freight was slower than rail and less reliable in delivery times, but was much cheaper than rail and road. Costs per tonne/100 miles were about $0.5, with journey speeds of 12 miles per hour. Additional costs would include delivery to the river (approximately $100 per 40 tonne load), storage and onward delivery charges similar to those of rail.

A final option was subcontracting the road transport operation. Five small to medium sized road haulage companies had supplied quotes - based on full loads to the various centres - to service particular market areas (Table 1C). Subcontracting road haulage had proved difficult for many American manufacturers; many road hauliers had recently gone bankrupt as a result of intense competition.

Table 1C : Costs of Road Haulage to New Areas in $ by Haulage Company

Market area	1	2	3	4	5
A	450	500	370	400	500
B	400	525	525	420	430
C	120	150	135	170	80
D	600	530	500	550	540
E	250	300	320	270	230
F	900	1150	1200	1050	1000
G	1200	1400	1250	1300	1150
H	1500	1300	1450	1650	1700
I	3000	2800	3700	3300	3300

Promotional planning :

Branchwater had ambitious plans to increase its level of promotional investment in the following year. In the previous year, the company had spent $0.03 per bottle on average in sales promotion, and in the current year planned to increase this to $0.05 per bottle. On the basis of the price elasticity in the market, market share was likely to increase by around 20 per cent with 6 rather than 5 per cent of the market in each region. Accompanying the growth in expenditure and the plans to expand to new areas, the company had decided to recruit additional sales staff. Total staff was likely to rise to 8, costing $400,000 in the next year.

Action :

How should the marketing management of Branchwater approach the choice of physical distribution alternatives?

What criteria are important?

How does the choice of physical distribution fit into the overall marketing mix?

Case Study - 5

While the 2001 global overhaul of Whirlpool's supply chain systems remains a work in progress today, managers say its success to date is encouraging the remaining systems work.

The supply chain at Whirlpool in 2000 was broken. Indeed, a manager there at the time quipped that among the four major appliance makers in the U.S., Whirlpool ranked fifth in delivery performance.

"We had too much inventory, too little inventory, wrong inventory, right inventory/wrong place, any combination of those things," says J. B. Hoyt, who was then supply chain project director. He says a sales vice president approached him one day and said he'd accept even worse performance from supply systems if they would just be consistent rather than wildly bouncing back and forth between good and poor production and shipping plans.

So in 2001, Whirlpool embarked on a multiproject global overhaul of its supply chain systems. The metaproject remains a work in progress today, with a number of systems yet to be rolled out and some major technical issues to be resolved. But managers at Whirlpool say its success to date - including huge improvements in customer service and reduced supply chain costs - is providing the psychological and financial impetus to drive the remaining systems work.

Whirlpool CIO Esat Sezer says that by 2000, the company had grown by acquisition and geographic expansion to the point that old systems, stitched together by spreadsheets and manual procedures, couldn't cope with the exploding complexity. "Our supply chain was becoming a competitive disadvantage for us," he says. Availability - the percentage of time a product is in the right place at the right time - was an unacceptably low 83 percent, even as inventories remained too high overall.

The homegrown supply systems were primitive and not well integrated with the company's SAP ERP system, which had been installed in 1999, or with a legacy production scheduling system, Sezer says. And they weren't integrated with the systems of major wholesale customers or suppliers of parts and materials. "The plans we were creating weren't linking back into reality," he says.

In particular, Sezer says, supply chain systems weren't fine-grained enough, nor were they very good at juggling priorities and constraints except through slow and cumbersome manual methods. Often, they would optimise locally a single product line at one location, for example, but not for the supply chain as a whole.

Here's what Whirlpool was using for its North American supply chain in 2000:

- A homegrown production scheduling system, the Whirlpool Manufacturing Control System (WMCS), which was developed in the mid-1980s and extensively modified over the years.

- SAP's R/3 ERP system, which was installed in 1999 and used for transaction-processing applications such as accounting and order processing.

- i2 Technologies' Demand Planner (now called Demand Manager), which was installed in 1997 and used for demand forecasting.

- A system for distribution planning that was custom-developed for Whirlpool in the 1980s that used optimisation software from ILOG.

Then, in 2001, Whirlpool began to implement an Advanced Planning and Scheduling (APS) system. It included a suite of supply chain integration and optimisation tools from i2 - Supply Chain Planner for Master Scheduling, Deployment Planning and Inventory Planning. Those three modules, the heart of Whirlpool's efforts to fix its supply chain, went live in three phases over 2001 and 2002.

In mid-2002, Whirlpool installed the i2 Trade Matrix Collaborative Planning, Forecasting and Replenishment (CPFR) system, a Web-based collaboration tool for sharing and combining the sales forecasts of Whirlpool and its major trade partners - Sears, Roebuck and Co., Lowe's and Best Buy Co.

The rollout of a component for Web-based collaboration with suppliers, based on SAP's Inventory Collaboration Hub, is just getting under way. And Whirlpool continues to use the old WMCS for production scheduling but plans to replace that with SAP's Production Planning module.

It's available :

By all accounts, the supply chain overhaul was a smashing success for the US$13 billion company. CPFR cut forecasting errors in half. APS boosted availability in North America from 83 percent to 93 percent (it's at 97 percent today), reduced finished-goods inventories by more than 20 percent and trimmed 5 percent from freight and warehouse costs. Whirlpool declined to discuss the cost of the projects.

Managers at Whirlpool give much of the credit for the success of these projects to a close partnership between the IT department and the business units. Says Hoyt, "It was one of the first times the IT community didn't say, 'OK, here's your tool.' We said the tool had to do x, y and z. We did the requirements analysis together."

Whirlpool considered standardising completely on SAP for all ERP and supply chain systems in North America, but i2 ultimately got the nod for the APS system, the critical part needed to fix the company's availability and inventory problems. "There was a lot of back and forth, but after a long harangue and discussion of our business requirements, we settled on the i2 tool set in North America," Hoyt says.

But while i2 was seen as being more capable than SAP for handling the fine-grained optimisation, constraint-based planning and prioritisation that the business units wanted, it was far from ideal from an IT perspective. The APS system would cost IT, whose budget is about US $ 190 million, more than an all-SAP supply chain because there would be less integration, more systems interfaces and more skills to maintain in-house. Plus, IT was worried about i2's deteriorating financial condition.

Whirlpool had already standardised on IBM AIX application servers and zSeries mainframe database servers for supply chain systems and had put systems for all its global operations in a single data center in Benton Harbor. Now it was time to standardise on software.

So in 2001, a mandate came from the CIO, via Whirlpool's Executive Committee, that supply chain modernisations henceforth would be based entirely on SAP. In particular, new systems planned for Europe for 2003 and Latin America would use SAP's Advanced Planner and Optimiser rather than the more capable but costly i2-based APS system used in North America. And they were to use SAP's NetWeaver for Web collaboration with suppliers and trade partners rather than North America's TradeMatrix CPFR.

Vivek Mehta, a lead supply chain analyst at Whirlpool, says SAP may catch up with i2 in its optimisation capabilities, but in the meantime, i2's financial condition is worrisome. "There were 10 guys at i2 that we interacted with, and some of them are gone now," he says. "There's lack of continuity."

"We have this challenge, where the IT organisation is pushing for everything to be SAP, but the business, on the other hand, is going for whatever brings them value," Mehta says. "They are now used to the optimal plan, the high service levels, the lower inventories. So if we bring in something and say their availability will go down by a couple of points, no way will they buy that."

Sezer says Whirlpool will probably replace i2 with SAP "eventually" but is in no hurry. "We'd like to get the return out of that investment before making any platform decisions," he says.

Sezer says that in the four years since Whirlpool standardised on IBM and SAP as "strategic partners," revenue has increased on average US$1 billion per year and IT expenses have fallen 6 percent per year. He says there are several joint development projects under way involving all three companies.

But for the time being, the combination of SAP and i2 works well for Whirlpool, far better than the legacy tools of a few years ago. Sezer says the company's supply chain is now a competitive advantage. "On a global scale, to be able to manage all your operating platforms, I'm not aware that any of our competitors have that today," he says.

Think globally, act locally :

When the time came for Whirlpool Europe to overhaul its supply chain, the company decided not to go with i2 optimisation products, as North America had done, but with SAP's Advanced Planner and Optimiser (APO) for demand and supply-network planning.

Vivek Mehta, a lead supply chain analyst involved in both projects, says Europe was starting from a more primitive systems base, with even more manual procedures and less-integrated systems than had been the case in North America. So for Europe, "APO was a huge step forward," he says.

The integration of Whirlpool Europe's supply chain systems around APO, though not quite complete, has already boosted inventory availability from less than 80 percent to more than 90 percent, says Walter Manfredi, supply chain director in Whirlpool's Comerio, Italy, operations center.

"Today, our supply chain is integrated -- processes and systems," he says. "Now, demand from a trade partner or customer is integrated into production planning. We can look into production plans and see if this item for this date in this quantity is for this customer. So we can now give priority depending on the type of demand."

For example, he says, priority is always given to production orders earmarked for specific customers - for which availability is now 97 percent - over orders to simply replenish stock.

Still, improvements need to be made, especially at the level of individual factories, Manfredi says. Some factory managers, in an attempt to tweak system rules and parameters to optimise their operations, make the systems so complex that they become maintenance nightmares. And, he adds, attempts by factories to optimise their own performance can be at odds with optimising the European supply chain overall.

Finally, Manfredi says, while production can be varied daily by altering system rules and parameters, some production modifications require workforce changes or changes in line and equipment capacities, which can take weeks to accomplish. "That's very difficult," he notes.

Source : Gary H. Anthes (Computer world)

Case Study - 6

Nikon Focuses on Supply Chain Innovation and Makes New Product Distribution a Snap

Top consumer goods manufacturers now recognise that success requires more than just making market-leading products. Having the right distribution network is just as critical. Nikon Inc. is the world's leader in precision optics, 35 mm and digital imaging technology. So it's no surprise that when the company saw the next big trend in photographic technology, digital cameras, they were ready to deliver with some of the most advanced product designs in the marketplace. But to ensure that retailers could meet the demand of tech-hungry consumers and professional photographers, Nikon, with the help of UPS Supply Chain Solutions, reengineered its distribution network to keep them well supplied.

Client Challenge :

To support the launch of its new digital cameras, Nikon knew that customer service capabilities needed to be completely up to speed from the start and that distributors and retailers would require up-to-the-minute information, about product availability. While the company had previously handled new product distribution in-house, this time Nikon realised that burdening its existing infrastructure with a new, demanding, high-profile product line could impact customer service performance adversely.

"In our business, it's not enough just to produce leading-edge products," said Arnold Kamen, Nikon's Vice President of Operations and Customer Service. "Having the ability and visibility to predict how much merchandise is available and when it can be distributed makes the difference in staying ahead of customers' needs."

For Nikon, that meant applying its well-known talent for innovation to creating an entirely new distribution strategy and taking the rare step of outsourcing distribution of an entire consumer electronics product line. With UPS Supply Chain Solutions on board, Nikon was able to quickly execute a synchronised supply chain strategy that moves product to retail stores throughout the United States, Latin America and the Caribbean, and allows Nikon to stay focused on the business of developing and marketing precision optics.

Our Solution

Starting at Nikon's manufacturing centers in Korea, Japan and Indonesia, UPS Supply Chain Solutions manages air and ocean freight and related customs brokerage. Nikon's freight is directed to Louisville, Kentucky, which not only serves as the all-points connection for UPS's global operations, but also is home to the UPS Supply Chain Solutions Logistics Center main campus. Here, merchandise can either be "kitted" with accessories such as batteries and chargers, or repackaged to in-store display specifications. Finally, the packages are distributed to literally thousands of retailers across the U.S., or shipped for export to Latin American or Caribbean retail outlets and distributors, using any of UPS's worldwide transportation services to provide the final delivery.

With the UPS Supply Chain Solutions system in place, the process calibrates the movement of goods and information by providing SKU-level visibility within complex distribution and IT systems. UPS also provides Nikon advance shipment notifications throughout the U.S., Caribbean and Latin American markets. The result : a "snap shot" of the supply chain that rivals the performance of a Nikon camera.

Nikon has already seen the results of its innovation in both digital technology and product distribution. The consumer digital camera sector is one of Nikon's fastest growing product lines. In addition, supply chain performance and customer service are measurably improved. Products leaving Nikon manufacturing facilities in Asia can now be on a retailer's shelf in as few as two days. While products are en route, Nikon also has the ability to keep retailers informed of delivery times and to adjust them as needed, so that no retailer needs to miss sales opportunities due to lack of product availability.

UPS Supply Chain Solutions is forging a broad spectrum of creative solutions to support the Nikon supply chain, including logistics, transportation, freight and customs brokerage services. Synchronising those pieces to work together gives Nikon a significant advantage in leveraging the competitive strengths of UPS Supply Chain Solutions.

"Through a combination of UPS services, we have been able to greatly shorten our supply chain," Kamen said. "Although we are achieving greater speeds, we have better visibility of our products, which enables us to provide a higher level of service to retailers and ultimately, the final customer." Once again, Nikon leads the market in leveraging the latest developments in technology.

Case Study - 7

As Ford Motor Company's lead logistics provider (LLP), Penske quality associates, each trained in Six Sigma practices, worked closely with Ford to streamline operations and to create and maintain an optimised central logistics network. Together, we, Penske Quality Associates, uncovered areas for real cost savings. We decreased inbound carrier discrepancies, eliminated unnecessary premium costs and reduced shipment overages. Plus, we implemented accountability procedures and advanced logistics management technologies to gain more visibility of Ford's overall supply network.

Summary

Ford Motor Company, one of the world's largest automotive manufacturers, has worked with Penske on several Six Sigma initiatives. As its lead logistics provider (LLP), Penske's quality team of associates are trained in Six Sigma practices and work closely with Ford to streamline operations and create and maintain a more centralised logistics network. Together, they uncovered several areas for real cost savings as a result of reducing inbound carrier discrepancies, eliminating unnecessary premium costs and reducing shipment overages. Plus, Penske implemented accountability procedures and advanced logistics management technologies to gain more visibility of its overall supply network.

Challenges	Solutions / Results
• To develop, implement and operate a centralised logistics network for Ford	• Penske established 10 Order Dispatch Centers (ODCs) and consolidated shipments to plants. Approximately 1,200 trailers now ship to and from Ford's ODCs per day, with most trucks at 95 percent capacity. Penske has reduced plant inventory by 15 percent.
• To streamline supplier and carrier operations for improved performance and accountability	• Penske trained more than 1,500 suppliers on a uniform set of procedures and logistics technologies. Stringent carrier requirements and a Carrier Rating System were implementted to measure carrier performance.
• To provide Ford with real-time supply chain and financial visibility	• Penske implemented strict accountability procedures and advanced logistics management technologies to gain real-time visibility of delivery status, routing schedules and productivity. A new freight billing system was designed to immediately capture logistics costs.

Getting Started

Today, Ford owns and produces automobiles under several major brands : Ford, Lincoln, Mercury, Mazda, Land Rover, Aston Martin and Volvo. They maintain one of the automotive industry's most complex manufacturing, transportation and distribution networks.

Penske Logistics began its relationship with Ford as lead logistics provider (LLP) for Ford's assembly plant in Norfolk, Va. At the time, each of Ford's 20 North American assembly plants managed its own logistics operations. A decentralised approach provided total control of logistics at the plant level, but presented costly redundancies in materials handling and transportation.

Ford conducted studies to determine the benefits of transitioning the company's decentralised logistic operations to a centralised approach. The decision was quickly apparent centralisation of the company's logistics operations would increase both velocity and visibility throughout the network, as well as reduce supply chain costs.

Shortly thereafter, Ford selected Penske as its North American LLP. Under the contract, Penske would centralise and manage all inbound materials handling for 19 assembly plants and seven stamping plants.

Consolidating Logistics Operations

Penske immediately developed an aggressive logistics transition programme with Ford. Penske would provide Ford with a single point of contact for all logistics operations.

By working with individual plants and corporate management, Penske established a baseline of current operations and outlined the proposed solutions. The new logistics programme would establish a Penske Logistics Center that included the following core functions :

- **Network Design Optimisation:** Implement a more efficient inbound materials strategy through order dispatching centers (ODC).
- **Carrier and Premium Freight Management:** Manage all carriers and logistics companies, while reducing premium freight costs.
- **Information Technology System Integration:** Achieve real-time visibility of supply chain shipments, schedules and orders.
- **Finance Management:** Improve freight bill payment, claim processing and resolution throughout the supply chain.

Upon development of this new plan, the Penske/Ford team began evaluating Ford's existing network design. Under the plant-centric approach, suppliers would make multiple deliveries of the same parts to different plants. A supplier would pick up a small load, deliver it to one plant, pick up another small load of the same parts and deliver it to another plant. Carriers with half-empty trucks would often cross routes with each other en route to the same plant. Aside from being highly inefficient, this design allowed for excessive inventory and storage costs at the plant level.

To centralise transportation and distribution operations, Penske implemented a new network design consisting of 10 new ODCs. The ODCs would be a central delivery point for suppliers. Different supplier shipments going to the same plant would now be cross-docked into trailers at the ODC. Loads would be consolidated and delivered on a scheduled basis to reduce the amount of milkruns, less than truckload shipments (LTL) and premium freight charges. To meet Penske's new transportation and distribution standards, more than 1,500 suppliers were trained on new uniform procedures.

For carrier and premium freight management, Penske's goal was simply stated as maximise carrier service, minimise carrier costs. Penske refined Ford's carrier bidding process by placing more stringent requirements on carrier partners. Carriers were now required to meet specific safety, equipment and technological specifications; provide experienced and certified drivers; and show proven experience of on-time delivery/pickups.

Penske's new procedures required carriers to meet established route pick-up and delivery windows within 15 minutes of the scheduled time. Additionally, carriers would supervise loading and unloading operations to verify order accuracy, adequate packaging and labeling, and freight damage.

With new stringent carrier requirements in place, Penske closed the accountability loop by implementing a Carrier Rating System. All incidents would be recorded and reported. Carriers would issue corrective action reports for actions that negatively impacted Ford's operations. If a carrier accumulated an excessive amount of incidents on their "scorecard," Penske would issue a low carrier rating, thus jeopardising the carrier's ability to participate in future bids.

Penske also implemented several information technology solutions throughout the logistics network, including its proprietary Logistics Management System and Route Assist, an advanced routing tool. Other programmes included a Web-based metric reporting system and order tracking software. Drivers were provided with PDA scanners and an electronic driver log. Carriers were now required to have satellite communications and engine monitoring systems on all trucks for load tracking. ODCs were provided with integrated RF cross-dock scanners that tracked the delivery of individual parts.

Prior to implementing a centralised approach, Ford was unable to gain a clear view of the financial status of logistics operations. With approximately 1,500 suppliers handling more than 20,000 shipments per week, freight billing was complicated. As part of its carrier management system, Penske would now provide drivers with a single set of paperwork procedures to ensure delivery documentation was collected and submitted to accounting. Penske developed a new freight billing system that would capture freight costs and allocate those costs by plant. As a result, Ford could see which plants had the highest and lowest freight costs and which carriers were most cost effective.

Penske and Ford :Entering a New Century of Automotive Achievement

In approximately 18 months, Penske had completely transitioned Ford's logistics operations to a centralised network design. More than 700 inbound and 500 outbound trailers now move to and from Ford's ODCs per day, with most loads carrying at 95 percent capacity. Shipments are consolidated at the ODC and previously unused cross-docking space is now in high demand. Fourteen million pounds of freight are cross-docked each day, resulting in an inventory reduction of 15 percent.

Suppliers and carriers currently operate under a single set of transportation and distribution procedures, enabling better service throughout the supply chain. The level of accountability established with Penske's Carrier Rating System has enabled Ford to rid its distribution network of costly, ineffective carriers.

With uniform technologies, ODCs are able to monitor shipments, identify inefficiencies and address materials handling issues in a real-time environment. Furthermore, logistics costs now enter the supply chain immediately. This allows Ford to see overall supply chain costs and per plant allocations at any given point in time.

Penske met its logistics programme objectives six months ahead of schedule - a testament to the joint-team approach established between Penske and Ford. More importantly, as Ford continues to evolve, the Penske Logistics Center provides Ford with a single point of contact for all logistics operations.

"Having a single point of contact delivers more than cost benefits. Penske allows us to clearly understand how our logistics operations impact the entire company. From the assembly line to the end-consumer, the efficiencies provided by Penske are realised at virtually every level throughout Ford." Grant Belanger, director of material planning and logistics, Ford Motor Company

Penske continues to deliver significant cost savings to Ford by continuous process improvement. And, to keep pace with assembly plant requirements, Penske closed six of its ODCs due to a change in shipping frequency strategy. With four ODCs operating at full capacity, Penske once again streamlined its logistics strategy to reduce costs for Ford.

Ford has honoured Penske with several awards, including the Q1award, its highest recognition of superior supplier quality. Today, with a century of automotive achievement behind them, Ford and Penske continue to redefine the highest standards for logistics and operational efficiency.

Questions:
1. Give a summary of the challenges faced by the Ford Company and its solutions.
2. Analyse the consolidating logistics operations developed by Penske and the Ford company.

Numericals

- **EOQ**
- **Stock Levels**
- **Inventory Turnover Ratio**

EOQ

It is also termed as "**Re-ordering Quantity**" or "**Economic Lot Size**". It is the most economical quantity to be ordered under normal conditions. This is one of the important decision-making area. The Purchase Department has to decide about the number of units of each type of required raw materials to be purchased at a time. For this purpose, it has to consider two important items of costs pertaining to material. They are : Ordering or acquisition costs and carrying costs.

Ordering Costs are those which pertain to the acquisition of materials. They are the costs of placing a purchase order. Usually, these costs are constant per order irrespective of the number of units for which an order is placed. Buying in large quantities, therefore, ensures lower unit cost of acquisition.

On the other hand, **Carrying Costs** represent the costs which relate to the carrying of materials from one point of time to another. Rent and insurance of storage, interest on capital blocked, clerical costs, cost of pilferage, normal loss, risk of obsolescence, etc. fall into this category. The cost of carrying and the number of units to be carried from one point to another point of time move in the same direction and more or less, in the same proportion. In order to minimise these costs, it is necessary to order most economical size (EOQ) so that the aggregate of ordering costs and carrying costs is minimum per period. EOQ is therefore, the optimum or the most desirable quantity for which order should be placed for purchase every time when the materials are to be purchased.

Purchase of large quantities and the resultant overstocking increases the cost of carrying the stores. On the other hand, if purchases are made in small quantities and also frequently, the ordering cost will increase. It is therefore, necessary to strike out a balance between the two extremes, and maintain the optimum level of investment in inventory.

The exact quantity to be ordered at a time so as to achieve this objective is known as the "**Economic Order Quantity**" (EOQ). EOQ is thus, the size of the order which produces the lowest cost of the material ordered. In other words, it is the order quantity which minimises the balance of the cost between carrying costs and ordering costs.

Assumptions underlying EOQ or (Limitations of EOQ) :

(i) Ordering costs and carrying costs are known and they are fixed per unit.

(ii) Anticipated usage is known.

(iii) Cost per unit is known and it is constant.

(iv) Quantity ordered is delivered immediately.

(v) It assumes that demand is uniform.

(vi) It is applied without considering the possibility of a falling demand and can lead to a high value of inventory obsolescence.

Approaches to Determination of Economic Order Quantity :

In order to determine the Economic Order Quantity, the following methods are normally used. Dependence on any one of the following methods depends upon the nature of the problem.

1. Tabular Approach to EOQ i.e. (Tabular Method) :

Under this approach which is also called **Trial and Error Approach**, a table showing the Annual Ordering Costs, Carrying Costs and the aggregate of these two at different order sizes is prepared. By looking at the column showing the aggregate of carrying and ordering costs, one will be able to determine the Economic Order Quantity. Because, the EOQ corresponds to the order size having the lowest annual cost of ordering and carrying. At this order size, the Total Carrying Costs will normally be equal to the Total Ordering Cost. While dealing with EOQ, the following indications should be kept in mind.

(i) Annual Usage (U) = Number of units of a material required for consumption during the year;

(ii) Order Size (Q) = Number of units of the material for which Purchase Order is to be placed;

(iii) Number of Orders (N) = Number of Purchase Orders to be placed in a year
$(N = U/Q)$

(iv) Average Inventory = $\frac{\text{Order Size}}{2}$ $\left(\text{i.e. } \frac{Q}{2}\right)$

(v) Total, Annual Carrying Cost = $\left[\left(\frac{Q}{2}\right) \times \text{Carrying Cost per unit per year}\right]$

i.e. $\left[\left(\frac{Q}{2}\right) \times \text{Unit Purchase Price} \times \text{Carrying Cost}\right.$

as a percentage of Unit Purchase Price]

$\left[\text{i.e. } \left(\frac{Q}{2}\right) \times P \times C\right]$

(vi) Total Ordering Cost = N × Ordering Cost per order (i.e. N × A).

The one advantage of this method is that, it is valid for both simple and complex function in a situation of multivariability. Problems of graded quantity discount can also be integrated into this method. The following illustration clarifies these important points.

Example

Novelty Ltd., Nagpur carries a wide assortment of items for customers. One item, Gaylook, is very popular. Desirous of keeping its inventory under control, a decision is taken to order only the optimum economic quantity, for this item, each time. You have the following information. Make your recommendation. Annual Demand : 1,60,000 units; Price per unit : ₹ 20; Carrying Cost : ₹ 1 per unit or 5 percent per rupee of Inventory Value; and Cost per order : ₹ 50. Determine the optimum or Economic Order Quantity by developing the following table.

Size of Order   :
Number of Order   : 1   10   20   40   80   100
Average Inventory   :
Carrying Costs   :
Order Costs   :
Total Costs   :

Answer

Annual Demand ... 1,60,000 units
Price per unit ... ₹ 20
Cost per order ... ₹ 50
Carrying Cost ... ₹ 1 per unit or 5% of Inventory Value

In the books of Novelty Ltd., Nagpur

Statement showing Determination of Economic Order Quantity (EOQ)

Number of Orders N	Size of Order (U / N) Q	Average Inventory Q/2	Total Carrying Cost $\frac{5}{100} \times ₹20 \times \frac{Q}{2}$	Total Ordering Cost N × ₹ 50	Total of Carrying and Ordering Costs
	Units	Units	₹	₹	₹
1	1,60,000	80,000	80,000	50	80,050
10	16,000	8,000	8,000	500	8,500
20	8,000	4,000	4,000	1,000	5,000
40	4,000	2,000	2,000	2,000	4,000
80	2,000	1,000	1,000	4,000	5,000
100	1,600	800	800	5,000	5,800

At the order size of 20 orders as the Total Carrying Cost (i.e. ₹ 2,000) equals to the Total Ordering Costing (i.e. ₹ 2,000), hence, 4,000 units will be the optimum or economic order quantity.

2. Graphical Approach to EOQ i.e. Graphical Method :

The two cost components are plotted for the Carrying Cost and Ordering Cost as well as the corresponding Total Cost, C for different values of q, the ordering quantity. The point on the quantity axis (X-axis), for which the combination of the two costs gives the least value of C shows the EOQ point. It should be noted that in a situation of certaining (Fixed Lead Time and Fixed Demand) the point of intersection of the two curves for Carrying Costs and Ordering Costs determines the EOQ. The following example clarifies these important points.

Example

From the following information relating to Binaca Ltd., Badalapur using Graphical Approach, determine the Economic Order Quantity :

Annual Requirement of a Material = 80,000 units; Carrying Cost = 5% of Average Inventory Value; Ordering Cost = ₹ 20,000 and Price per unit = ₹ 40.

Answer

Annual Requirement ... 80,000 units

Carrying Cost ... 5% of Average Inventory Value

Total Ordering Cost ... ₹ 20,000

Price per unit ... ₹ 40

In the books of Binaca Ltd., Badalapur

Statement showing determination of Economic Ordering Quantity

No of Orders	Order Size	Total Ordering Cost	Carrying Cost $\left(H = \frac{Q}{2} \times ₹\,40 \times \frac{5}{100}\right)$	Total of Ordering and Carrying Costs
	Q	₹	₹	₹
1	80,000	20,000	80,000	1,00,000
2	40,000	40,000	40,000	80,000
4	20,000	80,000	20,000	1,00,000
5	16,000	1,00,000	16,000	1,16,000
8	10,000	1,60,000	10,000	1,70,000

From the above, it is observed that the Total of Carrying Cost and Ordering Cost is minimum at 40,000 units and therefore, 40,000 units is the EOQ. Further, it may be noticed from the graph that the Total Ordering Cost is equal to the Total Carrying Cost. The graph also shows the behaviour of Carrying and Ordering Costs with respect to the order sizes.

3. Algebraic or Equational Approach to EOQ i.e. Formulae Method :

This method is highly useful if the purchase price of material does not fluctuate from one order size to another. Under this approach, EOQ is computed by using a mathematical formula.

The Economic Order Quantity can be calculated by the simple mathematical formula introduced by **Simpson** which is as follows :

$$EOQ = \sqrt{\frac{2AO}{C}}$$

where,

EOQ = Economic Order Quantity
A = Annual Consumption or Usage in units or in Value
O = Ordering and Receiving Cost per order
C = Cost of Carrying one unit of Inventory for one year

This formula is based on three assumptions.

(i) Price will remain constant throughout the year and quantity discount is not involved.

(ii) Pattern of consumption, variable ordering costs per order and variable inventory carrying charge per unit per annum will remain the same throughout and

(iii) EOQ will be delivered each time the stock balance, excluding safety stock is just reduced to nil.

The following example clarifies these important points :

Example

Calculate Economic Order Quantity from the following information.
- Annual Consumption ... 60,000 units
- Ordering Cost per order ... ₹ 1,200
- Carrying Cost ... 20% of Inventory Value
- Price per unit ... ₹ 2,000

Answer

$$EOQ = \sqrt{\frac{2AO}{C}}$$

where,

EOQ = Economic Order Quantity

A = Annual Consumption in units i.e. 60,000 units

O = Ordering Cost per Order i.e. ₹ 1,200

C = Inventory Carrying Cost i.e. 20% of ₹ 2,000 = ₹ 400

$$= \sqrt{\frac{2 \times 60{,}000 \text{ units} \times ₹1{,}200}{₹400}}$$

$$= \sqrt{3{,}60{,}000} \text{ units}$$

$$= 600 \text{ units}$$

4. Cost Comparison Approach to EOQ i.e. Cost Comparison Method :

Suppliers offer quantity discounts to encourage the buyer companies to place order for large quantities. In this type of situation, the price per unit of raw materials varies from one range to another range. For instance, upto 200 units, he may charge ₹ 2 per unit; and for 200 units and above at a time, he may charge ₹ 1.95 per unit. In this type of situation, total costs (i.e. the aggregate of Carrying Costs, Ordering Costs and Cost of Materials) at different order sizes are to be computed and compared to find out the most economical order quantity. The following example clarifies these important points.

Example

The annual requirement of an item is 12,000 units, each costing ₹ 6. Every order costs ₹ 200 to release and Inventory Carrying Charges are 20 percent of the Average Inventory per annum. Find out :

(a) Economic Order Quantity and Corresponding Total Inventory Cost (including Item Costs).

(b) Whether the item should be purchased in lots of 6,000 units at a time, if the price per unit is reduced by 5 percent of this quantity.

Answer

$$EOQ = Q = \sqrt{\frac{2UA}{PC}}$$

where, U = 12,000 units

A = ₹ 200

P = ₹ 6

C = 20%

$$Q = \sqrt{\frac{2 \times 12{,}000 \text{ units} \times ₹\,200}{20\% \text{ of } ₹\,6}}$$

$$= \sqrt{\frac{48{,}00{,}000 \text{ units}}{₹\,1.2}}$$

$$= \sqrt{40{,}00{,}000}$$

$$= 2{,}000 \text{ units}$$

Total (Annual) Inventory Costs when order size is 2,000 units.

$$= (\text{Total Purchase Price} + \text{Total Ordering Cost} + \text{Total Carrying Cost})$$

$$= (U \times P) + \left(A \times \frac{U}{Q}\right) + \left(C \times P \times \frac{Q}{2}\right)$$

$$= (12{,}000 \text{ units} \times ₹\,6) + \left(₹\,200 \times \frac{12{,}000 \text{ units}}{2{,}000 \text{ units}}\right)$$

$$+ \left(\frac{20}{100} \times ₹\,6 \times \frac{2{,}000 \text{ units}}{2}\right)$$

$$= ₹\,72{,}000 + ₹\,1{,}200 + ₹\,1{,}200$$

$$= ₹\,74{,}400$$

Evaluation of the Offer :

Total Annual Inventory Costs when order size is 6,000 units.

$$= (U \times P) + \left(A \times \frac{U}{Q}\right) + \left(C \times P \times \frac{Q}{2}\right)$$

$$= 12{,}000 \text{ units} \,(₹\,6 - 5\% \text{ of } ₹\,6) + \left(₹\,200 \times \frac{12{,}000 \text{ units}}{6{,}000 \text{ units}}\right)$$

$$+ \left(\frac{20}{100} \times ₹\,5.7 \times \frac{6{,}000 \text{ units}}{2}\right)$$

$$= ₹\,68{,}400 + ₹\,400 + ₹\,3{,}420$$

$$= ₹\,72{,}220$$

The above calculations clearly indicates that the Inventory Costs can be reduced by ₹ 2,180 by purchasing materials in lots of ₹ 6,000 units. Hence, it is economical to place order for 6,000 units at a time and to take the benefit of quantity discount.

FORMULAE TO REMEMBER

STOCK LEVELS

1) Reorder Level = MX · C × MX · RP

   = Maximum rate of consumption × Maximum reorder period

2) Maximum Level = RL + RQ − (MN · C × MN · RP)

   = Reorder Level + Reorder Quantity − (Minimum rate of consumption × Minimum reorder period)

3) Minimum Level = RL − (A · C × A · RP)

   = Reorder Level − (Average rate of consumption × Average reorder period)

4) Average Level = MN · L + ½ RQ

   = Minimum Level + ½ of Reorder quantity

   OR

   Average Level = MN · L + MX · L / 2

   = Minimum Level + Maximum Level / 2

5) Danger Level = A · C × MX · RP for EP

   = Average rate of consumption × Maximum reorder period for emergency purchases

where,

C = Rate of consumption of material or rate of usage which is ascertained by dividing quantity of materials issued on a certain date by the number of days which elapse between this date and the date of subsequent issue.

RP = Reorder period or delivery period or lead time or time lag for procurement of materials or period for receiving the goods, which indicates time lapse elapsing between the date of placing an purchase order and the date of the receipt of corresponding material.

RQ = Reorder quantity or ordering quantity or economic order quantity or standard ordering quantity

A = Average or Normal

MX = Maximum

MN = Minimum

L = Level

EP = Emergency purchases

ECONOMIC ORDER QUANTITY

1. $$EOQ = \sqrt{\frac{2AO}{C}}$$

where,

EOQ = Economic Order Quantity or Standard Ordering Quantity or Optimum Ordering Quantity or Reorder Quantity

A = Annual or monthly consumption or usage or needs or demand or requirements or production rate in terms of units.

O = Cost of placing one purchase order or order placing and receiving cost or procurement cost or buying cost.

C = Cost of carrying one unit in inventory or inventory carrying cost.

2. Number of orders to be placed in a year or month or order schedule.

$$= \frac{A}{EOQ}$$

where,

A = Total consumption of material during the year or month

EOQ = Economic Order Quantity

ILLUSTRATIONS

ILLUSTRATION 1

From the following information calculate: (a) Reordering Level, (b) Maximum Level, (c) Minimum Level, (d) Average stock Level, (e) Danger Level.

Lead Times : Average 10 days

Maximum 15 days

Minimum 6 days

Maximum for emergency purchases 4 days

Rate of consumption : Average 15 units per day

Maximum 20 units per day

Minimum 10 units per day

Ordering Quantity : 200 units

SOLUTION

(a) Reordering Level = MX · C × MX · RP
 = Maximum rate of consumption per day × Maximum lead times in days
 = 20 units × 15 days = 300 units.

(b) Maximum Level = RL + RQ − (MN · C × MN · RP)
 = Reordering Level + Ordering Quantity − (Minimum rate of consumption per day × Minimum lead time in days)
 = 300 units + 200 units − (10 units × 6 days)
 = 500 units − 60 units = 440 units.

(c) Minimum Level = RL − (A · C × A · RP)
 = Reordering Level − (Average rate of consumption per day × Average lead time in days)
 = 300 units − (15 units × 10 days) = 300 units − 150 units
 = 150 units.

(d) Average Stock Level = MN · L + ½ RQ
 = Minimum Level + ½ of Ordering Quantity
 = 150 units + ½ × 200 units = 150 units + 100 units
 = 250 units.

(e) Danger Level = A · C × MX · RP for EP
 = Average rate of consumption per day × Maximum lead time for emergency purchases in days
 = 15 units × 4 days = 60 units.

ILLUSTRATION 2

Two components 'A' and 'B' are used in Swastic Industries, Pune as follows :

Normal Usage	:	150 units per week each
Minimum Usage	:	75 units per week each
Maximum Usage	:	225 units per week each
Re-order Quantity	:	A − 900 units
		B − 1,500 units
Re-order Period	:	A − 4 to 6 weeks
		B − 2 to 4 weeks

Calculate for each component.

(a) Reorder Level, (b) Maximum Level, (c) Minimum Level, (d) Average Stock Level.

SOLUTION

(a) Reorder Level = MX · C × MX · RP

= Maximum usage per week × Maximum re-order period in weeks

Component A' = 225 units × 6 weeks = 1,350 units

Component B' = 225 units × 4 weeks = 900 units

(b) Maximum Level = RL + RQ − (MN · C × MN · RP)

= Reorder Level + Reorder Quantity − (Minimum Usage per week × Minimum reorder period in weeks)

Component A' = 1,350 units + 900 units − (75 units × 4 weeks)

= 2,250 units − 300 units = 1,950 units

Component B' = 900 units + 1,500 units − (75 units × 2 weeks)

= 2,400 units − 150 units = 2,250 units.

(c) Minimum Level = RL − (A · C × A · RP)

= Reorder Level − (Normal usage per week × Normal reorder period in weeks)

Component A' = 1,350 units − (150 units × 5 weeks)

= 1,350 units − 750 units = 600 units

Component B' = 900 units − (150 units × 3 weeks)

= 900 units − 450 units = 450 units.

(d) Average Stock Level = MN · L + ½ RQ

= Minimum Level + ½ of Reorder Quantity

Component A' = 600 units + $\frac{1}{2}$ × 900 units

= 600 units + 450 units = 1,050 units

Component B' = 450 units + $\frac{1}{2}$ × 1,500 units

= 450 units + 750 units = 1,200 units

ILLUSTRATION 3

The following particulars are furnished by Casio Ltd., Cochin for 12 months ended 31-03-2009.

Month in 2008-2009	Budget consumption in units
April	300
May	400
June	500
July	600
August	800
September	1,000
October	1,000
November	900
December	800
January	700
February	600
March	800
Total Yearly Consumption	8,400

Delivery period : 2 to 4 months

Reorder Quantity : 1,000 units

Calculate : (1) Reorder Level, (2) Maximum Level, (3) Minimum Level, (4) Average Stock Level using reorder quantity.

SOLUTION

(1) Reorder Level = MX · C × MX · RP
 = Maximum rate of consumption per month × Maximum Delivery period in months
 = 1,000 units × 4 months
 = 4,000 units.

(2) Maximum Level = RL + RQ − (MN · C × MN · RP)
 = Reorder Level + Reorder Quantity − (Minimum rate of consumption per month × Minimum delivery period in months)
 = 4,000 units + 1,000 units − (300 units × 2 months)
 = 5,000 units − 600 units
 = 4,400 units

(3) Minimum Level = RL − (A · C × A · RP)

= Reorder Level − (Average rate of consumption per month × Average delivery period in months)

= 4,000 units − (700 units × 3 months)

= 4,000 units − 2,100 units

= 1,900 units.

(4) Average Stock Level = MN · L + ½ RQ

= Minimum Level + ½ of Reorder Quantity

= 1,900 units + ½ × 1,000 units

= 1,900 units + 500 units

= 2,400 units.

Working Notes :

1. Calculation of rate of consumption per month
   (a) Maximum = 1,000 units (i.e. September and October)
   (b) Minimum = 300 units (i.e. April)
   (c) Average = 700 units (i.e. 8,400 units / 12 months)

ILLUSTRATION 4

The following information is available in respect of a material.

Economic Ordering Quantity :   900 units

Rate of consumption per week :
  1) Normal   25 units
  2) Maximum   35 units
  3) Minimum   15 units

Delivery period :
  1) Minimum   20 weeks
  2) Normal   25 weeks
  3) Maximum   30 weeks

Calculate : (i) Reorder Level, (ii) Maximum Level, (iii) Minimum Level, (iv) Average Stock Level.

SOLUTION

(1) Reorder Level = MX · C × MX · RP

		=	Maximum rate of consumption per week × Maximum delivery period in weeks
		=	35 units × 30 weeks = 1,050 units
(2)	Maximum Level	=	RL + RQ − (MN · C × MN · RP)
		=	Reorder Level + Economic Order Quantity − (Minimum rate of consumption per week × Minimum delivery period in weeks)
		=	1,050 units + 900 units − (15 units × 20 weeks)
		=	1,950 units − 300 units = 1,650 units.
(3)	Minimum Level	=	RL − (A · C × A · RP)
		=	Reorder Level − (Normal rate of consumption per week × Normal delivery period in weeks)
		=	1,050 units − (25 units × 25 weeks) = 1,050 units − 625 units
		=	425 units
(4)	Average Stock Level	=	MN · L + $\frac{1}{2}$ RQ
		=	Minimum Level + $\frac{1}{2}$ of Economic Ordering Quantity
		=	425 units + $\frac{1}{2}$ × 900 units = 425 units + 450 units
		=	875 units

ILLUSTRATION 5

Find out Reorder Level, Maximum Level, Minimum Level and Average Stock Level from the following particulars:

Normal consumption : 300 units per day
Maximum consumption : 420 units per day
Minimum consumption : 240 units per day
Reorder Quantity : 3,600 units
Minimum perod for receiving the goods – 10 days
Maximum period for receiving the goods – 15 days
Normal period for receiving the goods – 12 days.

SOLUTION

(a)	Reorder Level	=	MX · C × MX · RP
		=	Maximum rate of consumption per day × Maximum period for receiving the goods in days
		=	420 units × 15 days = 6,300 units

(b) Maximum Level = RL + RQ − (MN · C × MN · RP)

= Reorder Level + Reorder Quantity − (Minimum consumption per day × Minimum period for receiving the goods in days)

= 6,300 units + 3,600 units − (240 units× 10 days)

= 9,900 units − 2,400 units = 7,500 units

(c) Minimum Level = RL − (A · C × A · RP)

= Reorder Level − (Normal consumption per day ×Normal period for receiving the goods in days)

= 6,300 units − (300 units × 12 days) = 6,300 units − 3,600 units

= 2,700 units

(d) Average Stock Level= MN · L + ½ RQ

= Minimum Level + ½ of Reorder Quantity

= 2,700 units + $\frac{1}{2}$ × 3,600 units = 2,700 units + 1,800 units

= 4,500 units

ILLUSTRATION 6

(a) The availability of an imported machinery component is irregular and consequently the consumption pattern also varies during the year. Show how should the 'Reorder level' be ascertained for this component.

(b) From the following annual data, compute the 'Average Stock Level' for the said component.

Particulars	Consumption
(i) Maximum usage in a month	300 Nos.
(ii) Minimum usage in a month	200 Nos.
(iii) Average usage in a month	225 Nos.

Time lag for procurement of material :

(i) Maximum − 6 months

(ii) Minimum − 2 months

Reordering quantity − 750 Nos.

SOLUTION

(a) Reorder Level = MX · C × MX · RP
  = Maximum usage per month × Maximum time lag for procurement of material in months
  = 300 Nos. × 6 months
  = 1,800 Nos.

(b) Average Stock Level = MN · L + ½ RQ

Here, Minimum Level of Stock is not given in the problem, hence,

Minimum Level = RL − (A · C × A · RP)
  = Reorder Level − (Average usage per month × Average time lag for procurement of materials in months)
  = 1,800 Nos. − $\left(225 \text{ Nos.} \times \left(\frac{6+2}{2}\right) \text{ i.e. 4 months}\right)$
  = 1,800 Nos. − 900 Nos.
  = 900 Nos.

Now Average Stock Level = Minimum Level + $\frac{1}{2}$ of Reordering Quantity

  = 900 Nos. + $\frac{1}{2}$ × 750 Nos.
  = 900 Nos. + 375 Nos.
  = 1,275 Nos.

ILLUSTRATION 7

A Company uses certain raw material for a particular product for which the following information is available.

Usage per unit of product	: 10 kgs
Reorder Quantity	: 10,000 kgs.
Delivery period in weeks	:
• Minimum	− 1
• Average	− 2
• Maximum	− 3

The weekly production varies from 175 to 225 units averaging 200 units of the said product.

You are required to calculate, (i) Reorder Level, (ii) Maximum Level, (iii) Minimum Level, (iv) Average Stock Level.

SOLUTION

(i) Reorder Level = MX · C × MX · RP
= Maximum usage of production per week × Maximum delivery period in weeks
= (225 units × 10 kgs) × 3 weeks = 2,250 kgs. × 3 weeks
= 6,750 kgs.

(ii) Maximum Level = RL + RQ − (MN · C × MN · RP)
= Reorder Level + Reorder Quantity − (Minimum usage of production per week × Minimum delivery period in weeks)
= 6,750 kgs + 10,000 kgs − (175 units × 10 kgs) × 1 week
= 16,750 kgs. − (1,750 kgs × 1 week) = 16,750 kgs − 1,750 kgs.
= 15,000 kgs.

(iii) Minimum Level = RL − (A · C × A · RP)
= Reorder Level − (Average usage of production per week × Average delivery period in weeks)
= 6,750 kgs − (200 units × 10 kgs. × 2 weeks)
= 6,750 kgs. − (2,000 kgs × 2 weeks) = 6,750 kgs. − 4,000 kgs.
= 2,750 kgs.

(iv) Average Stock Level = MN · L + MX · L / 2
= Minimum Level + Maximum Level /2
= $\dfrac{2{,}750 \text{ kgs.} + 15{,}000 \text{ kgs.}}{2} = \dfrac{17{,}750 \text{ kgs.}}{2}$ = 8,875 kgs.

ILLUSTRATION 8

In manufacturing certain products, a company uses three raw materials viz. A, B and C in respect of which the following data is made available.

Raw Material	Usage per unit of product	Re-order Quantity	Price per	Delivery period in weeks			Re-order level	Minimum level
				Minimum	Average	Maximum		
	kgs.	kgs.	kgs.				kgs.	kgs.
A	10	10,000	0.10	1	2	3	8,000	−
B	4	5,000	0.30	3	4	5	4,750	−
C	6	10,000	0.15	2	3	4	−	2,000

Weekly production varies from 175 to 225 units, averaging 200 units. What would you expect the quantities of the following to be?

i) Minimum level of A'
ii) Maximum level of B'
iii) Reorder level of C'
iv) Average stock level of A'

SOLUTION

i) Minimum Level of A' = RL − (A · C × A · RP)
= Reorder level − (Average rate of consumption per week × Average delivery period in weeks)
= 8,000 kgs. − (2,000 kgs × 2 weeks) = 8,000 kgs. − 4,000 kgs. = 4,000 kgs.

Working Notes:

a) Calculation of average rate of consumption per week −

Average production per week × Usage per unit = Average consumption
200 units × 10 kgs = 2,000 kgs.

ii) Maximum Level of B = RL + RQ − (MN · C × MN · RP)
= Reorder Level + Reorder Quantity − (Minimum rate of consumption per week × Minimum delivery period in weeks)
= 4,750 kgs. + 5,000 kgs. − (700 kgs × 3 weeks)
= 9,750 kgs. − 2,100 kgs. = 7,650 kgs.

Working Notes:

i) Calculation of Minimum rate of consumption per week −

Minimum production per week × Usage per unit = Minimum consumption
175 units × 4 kgs = 700 kgs.

ii) Reorder Level of C = MX · C × MX · RP
= Maximum rate of consumption per week × Maximum delivery period in weeks
= 1,350 kgs. × 4 weeks = 5,400 kgs.

Working Notes:

a) Calculation of Maximum rate of consumption per week −

Maximum production per week × Usage per unit = Maximum consumption
225 units × 6 kgs. = 1,350 kgs.

(iv) Average Stock Level of A' = MN · L + ½ RQ
= Minimum Level + $\frac{1}{2}$ of Reorder Quantity
= 4,000 kgs. + $\frac{1}{2}$ × 10,000 kgs. = 4,000 kgs + 5,000 kgs.
= 9,000 kgs.

ILLUSTRATION 9

From the following information made available in respect of a component, you are required to calculate reorder level and reorder quantity.

Maximum stock level : 8,400 units

Budgeted consumption per month :
    i)   Maximum : 1,500 units
    ii)   Minimum : 800 units

Estimated delivery period :
    i)   Maximum : 4 months
    ii)   Minimum : 2 months

SOLUTION

1) Reorder Level = MX · C × MX · RP
   = Maximum budgeted consumption per month × Maximum estimated delivery period in months
   = 1,500 units × 4 months
   = 6,000 units

2) Reorder Quantity = Reorder quantity can be found out by using the formula for maximum level, hence

   Maximum Level = RL + RQ − (MN · C × MN · RP)
   = Reorder level + Reorder Quantity − (Minimum budgeted consumption per month × Minimum estimated delivery period in months)

   ∴ 8,400 units = 6,000 units + Reorder Quantity − (800 units × 2 months)
   ∴ Reorder Quantity = 8,400 units + 1,600 units − 6000 units
   ∴ Reorder Quantity = 10,000 units − 6,000 units = 4,000 units

ILLUSTRATION 10

Amit Enterprises manufactures a special product 'Sumit'. The following are the particulars collected for the year 2008-2009.

(i) Monthly demand of Sumit :   1,000 units
(ii) Cost of placing an order :   ₹ 100
(iii) Annual carrying cost per unit :   ₹ 15
(iv) Rate of usage per week :
    Normal - 50 units, Maximum - 75 units, Minimum - 25 units
(v) Reorder period : 4 to 6 weeks

From the above information compute Average Stock Level.

SOLUTION

Average Stock Level can be computed only after calculating Reorder Quantity, Reorder Level, Maximum Level and Minimum Level.

(i) Reorder Quantity i.e. Economic Order Quantity

$$EOQ = \sqrt{\frac{2AO}{C}}$$

where,

EOQ = Economic Order Quantity
A = Annual demand in units i.e. 1,000 units × 12 months = 12,000 units
O = Cost of placing an order i.e. ₹ 100
C = Annual carrying cost per unit i.e. ₹ 15

$$= \sqrt{\frac{2 \times 12,000 \text{ units} \times ₹ 100}{₹ 15}}$$

$$= \sqrt{\frac{24,00,000 \text{ units}}{₹ 15}}$$

$$= \sqrt{1,60,000} \text{ units}$$

= 400 units

(ii) Reorder Level = MX · C × MX · RP
= Maximum rate of usage per week × Maximum reorder period in weeks
= 75 units × 6 weeks = 450 units

(iii) Maximum Level = RL + RQ − (MN · C × MN · RP)
= Reorder Level + Reorder Quantity − (Minimum rate of usage per week × Minimum reorder period in weeks)
= 450 units + 400 units − (25 units × 4 weeks)
= 850 units − 100 units = 750 units.

(iv) Minimum Level = RL − (A · C × A · RP)
= Reorder Level − (Normal rate of usage per week × Normal reorder period in weeks)
= 450 units − (50 units × 5 weeks) = 450 units − 250 units
= 200 units

(v) Average Stock Level = MN · L + ½ RQ
= Minimum Level + ½ of Reorder Quantity
= 200 units + ½ × 400 units = 200 units + 200 units
= 400 units

OR

$$\text{Average Stock Level} = MN \cdot L + MX \cdot L / 2$$

$$= \text{Minimum Level} + \text{Maximum Level} / 2$$

$$= \frac{200 \text{ units} + 750 \text{ units}}{2}$$

$$= \frac{950 \text{ units}}{2}$$

$$= 475 \text{ units}$$

ILLUSTRATION 11

From the following relevant details calculate (i) Reorder Quantity, (ii) Reorder Level, (iii) Maximum Level, (iv) Minimum Level, (v) Average Stock Level, (vi) Danger Level.

Total cost of purchasing relating to the order : ₹ 20

Number of units to be produced during the year : Units 5,000

Purchase price including transport cost : ₹ 50 per unit

Annual carrying cost per unit : ₹ 5

Maximum lead time for emergency purchases : 4 days

Lead times :

(i) Average - 10 days, (ii) Maximum - 15 days, (iii) Minimum - 5 days,

Rate of consumption per day

(i) Average - 15 units, (ii) Maximum - 20 units, (iii) Minimum - 10 units

SOLUTION

(i) Reorder Quantity i.e. Economic Order Quantity

$$EOQ = \sqrt{\frac{2AO}{C}}$$

where,

EOQ = Economic Order Quantity

A = Number of units to be purchased during the year i.e. 5,000 units

O = Total Cost of purchasing i.e. ₹ 20

C = Annual carrying cost i.e. ₹ 5

$$= \sqrt{\frac{2 \times 5,000 \text{ units} \times ₹ 20}{₹ 5}}$$

$$= \sqrt{\frac{2,00,000 \text{ units}}{₹5}}$$

$$= \sqrt{40,000 \text{ units}}$$

$$= 200 \text{ units}$$

(ii) Reorder Level = MX · C × MX · RP
 = Maximum rate of consumption per day × Maximum lead time in days
 = 20 units × 15 days
 = 300 units.

(iii) Maximum Level = RL + RQ − (MN · C × MN · RP)
 = Reorder Level + Reorder Quantity − (Minimum rate of consumption per day × Minimum lead time in days)
 = 300 units + 200 units − (10 units × 5 days) = 500 units − 50 units
 = 450 units

(iv) Minimum Level = RL − (A · C × A · RP)
 = Reorder Level − (Average rate of consumption per day × Average lead times in days)
 = 300 units − (15 units × 10 days) = 300 units − 150 units
 = 150 units

(v) Average Stock Level = MN · L + ½ RQ
 = Minimum Level + ½ of Reorder Quantity
 = 150 units + ½ × 200 units = 150 units + 100 units
 = 250 units

6) Danger Level = A · C × MX · RP for EP
 = Average rate of consumption per day × Maximum lead times for emergency purchases
 = 15 units × 4 days
 = 60 units.

ILLUSTRATION 12

Calculate the Economic Order Quantity from the following particulars :

Annual Consumption :	675 units
Cost of Material :	₹30 per unit
Cost of placing an order :	₹18
Annual carrying cost of one unit :	10% of inventory value

SOLUTION

$$EOQ = \sqrt{\frac{2AO}{C}}$$

where, EOQ = Economic Order Quantity
A = Annual consumption in units i.e. 675 units
O = Cost of placing an order i.e. ₹ 18
C = Inventory carrying cost i.e. 10% of ₹ 30 = ₹ 3

$$= \sqrt{\frac{2 \times 675 \text{ units} \times ₹18}{10\% \text{ of } ₹30}}$$

$$= \sqrt{\frac{24{,}300 \text{ units}}{₹3}}$$

$$= \sqrt{8{,}100 \text{ units}}$$

$$= 90 \text{ units}$$

ILLUSTRATION 13

A manufacturer buys certain equipments from outside suppliers at ₹ 30 per unit. Total annual needs are 1,600 units. The following further data are available –

Annual return on investment :	10%
Rent, Insurance, Tax per unit per year :	₹ 1
Cost of placing an order :	₹ 50

Calculate the Economic Order Quantity

SOLUTION

$$EOQ = \sqrt{\frac{2AO}{C}}$$

where, EOQ = Economic Order Quantity
A = Annual need in unit i.e. 1,600 units
O = Cost of placing an order i.e. ₹ 50
C = Inventory carrying cost including Rent, Insurance, Tax per unit per year i.e. 10% of ₹ 30 = ₹ 3 + ₹ 1 = ₹ 4

$$= \sqrt{\frac{2 \times 1{,}600 \text{ units} \times ₹50}{10\% \text{ of } ₹30 + ₹1}}$$

$$= \sqrt{\frac{1{,}60{,}000 \text{ units}}{₹3 + ₹1}}$$

$$= \sqrt{\frac{1,60,000 \text{ units}}{₹4}}$$

$$= \sqrt{40,000 \text{ units}}$$

$$= 200 \text{ units}$$

Illustration 14

A Company uses 10,000 units per year of an item costing ₹ 25 each. The cost of processing a purchase order is ₹ 10 and the stock holding cost amounts to 20% per year of the money value of inventory. How much should the company buy at a time in a single order, in order to minimise the inventory cost ?

SOLUTION

$$EOQ = \sqrt{\frac{2AO}{C}}$$

where, EOQ = Economic Order Quantity
A = Annual usage in terms of units i.e. 10,000 units
O = Cost of processing a purchase order i.e. ₹ 10
C = Stock holding cost i.e. 20% of ₹ 25 = ₹ 5

$$= \sqrt{\frac{2 \times 10,000 \text{ units} \times ₹10}{₹5}}$$

$$= \sqrt{\frac{2,00,000 \text{ units}}{₹5}}$$

$$= \sqrt{40,000 \text{ units}}$$

$$= 200 \text{ units}$$

Conclusion : The Company should buy 200 units in a single order at a time, to minimise the inventory cost.

ILLUSTRATION 15

Given the annual consumption of material is 1,800 units, ordering cost are ₹ 2 per order, price per unit of material is 32 ps. and storage cost are 25% p.a. of stock value, find the Economic Order Quantity.

SOLUTION

$$EOQ = \sqrt{\frac{2AO}{C}}$$

where, EOQ = Economic Order Quantity
A = Annual consumption of material in units i.e. 1,800 units
O = Ordering cost per order i.e. ₹ 2
C = Storage cost per unit i.e. 25% of 32 ps. = ₹ 0.08

$$= \sqrt{\frac{2 \times 1{,}800 \text{ units} \times ₹\, 2}{25\% \text{ of } 32 \text{ ps.}}}$$

$$= \sqrt{\frac{7{,}200 \text{ units}}{₹\, 0.08}}$$

$$= \sqrt{7{,}200 \text{ units} \times \frac{100}{8}}$$

$$= \sqrt{90{,}000 \text{ units}}$$

$$= 300 \text{ units}$$

ILLUSTRATION 16

Calculate Economic Order Quantity from the following particulars by using Simpson's Mathematical formula:

Annual requirement:	1,600 units
Cost of material per unit:	₹ 40
Cost of placing and receiving one order:	₹ 200
Annual carrying cost of inventory: 10% of inventory value	

SOLUTION

- Calculation of EOQ by Simpson's Mathematical formula

$$EOQ = \sqrt{\frac{2AO}{C}}$$

where, EOQ = Economic Order Quantity
A = Annual requirements in units i.e. 1,600 units
O = Cost of placing and receiving one order i.e. ₹ 200
C = Inventory carrying cost i.e. 10% of ₹ 40 = ₹ 4

$$= \sqrt{\frac{2 \times 1{,}600 \text{ units} \times ₹\, 200}{10\% \text{ of } ₹\, 40}}$$

$$= \sqrt{\frac{6{,}40{,}000 \text{ units}}{₹\, 4}}$$

$$= \sqrt{1{,}60{,}000 \text{ units}}$$

$$= 400 \text{ units}$$

ILLUSTRATION 17

From the following particulars calculate Economic Order Quantity

Annual Demand	:	4,000 units
Rate of Interest	:	6% p.a.
Unit Price	:	₹ 2
Ordering Cost per order	:	₹ 5
Storage cost	:	2% p.a.

SOLUTION

$$EOQ = \sqrt{\frac{2AO}{C}}$$

where,

EOQ = Economic Order Quantity
A = Annual demand in units i.e. 4,000 units
O = Ordering cost per order i.e. ₹ 5
C = Inventory carrying cost i.e. 8% of ₹ 2 = ₹ 0.16

$$= \sqrt{\frac{2 \times 4,000 \text{ units} \times ₹5}{8\% \text{ of } ₹2}}$$

$$= \sqrt{\frac{40,000 \text{ units}}{Re. \ 0.16}}$$

$$= \sqrt{40,000 \text{ units} \times \frac{100}{16}}$$

$$= \sqrt{2,50,000} \text{ units}$$

= 500 units

ILLUSTRATION 18

The annual requirement of an item is 12,000 units, each costing ₹ 6, every order costs ₹ 200 to release and inventory carrying charges are 20% of the average inventory per annum.

Find out Economic Order Quantity.

SOLUTION

$$EOQ = \sqrt{\frac{2AO}{C}}$$

where,

EOQ = Economic Order Quantity

A = Annual requirements in units i.e. 12,000 units
O = Order cost i.e. ₹ 200
C = Inventory carrying charges i.e. 20% of ₹ 6 = ₹ 1.20

$$= \sqrt{\frac{2 \times 12{,}000 \text{ units} \times ₹\,200}{20\% \text{ of } ₹\,6}}$$

$$= \sqrt{\frac{48{,}00{,}000 \text{ units}}{₹\,1.20}}$$

$$= \sqrt{40{,}00{,}000} \text{ units}$$

$$= 2{,}000 \text{ units}$$

ILLUSTRATION 19

You are required to calculate Economic Order Quantity from the following information.

Annual consumption :	15,000 kg.
Cost of placing an order :	₹ 48
Cost of Raw Materials :	₹ 2 per kg.
Storage cost : 8% of average inventory	

SOLUTION

$$EOQ = \sqrt{\frac{2AO}{C}}$$

where, EOQ = Economic Order Quantity
A = Annual consumption in kg. i.e. 15,000 kg.
O = Cost of placing an order i.e. ₹ 48
C = Storage cost i.e. 8% of ₹ 2 = ₹ 0.16

$$= \sqrt{\frac{2 \times 15{,}000 \text{ kg.} \times ₹\,48}{8\% \text{ of } ₹\,2}}$$

$$= \sqrt{\frac{14{,}40{,}000 \text{ kg.}}{Re.\,0.16}} = \sqrt{14{,}40{,}000 \text{ kg.} \times \frac{100}{16}}$$

$$= \sqrt{90{,}00{,}000} \text{ kg.}$$

$$= 3{,}000 \text{ kg}$$

ILLUSTRATION 20

A Company uses annually 50,000 units of an item each costing ₹ 1.20. Each order costs ₹ 45 and carrying cost 15% of the annual average inventory value. Calculate Economic Order Quantity.

SOLUTION

$$EOQ = \sqrt{\frac{2AO}{C}}$$

where, EOQ = Economic Order Quantity
A = Annual usage in units i.e. 50,000 units
O = Order placing cost i.e. ₹ 45
C = Inventory carrying cost i.e. 15% of ₹ 1.20 = ₹ 0.18

$$= \sqrt{\frac{2 \times 50,000 \text{ units} \times ₹ 45}{15\% \text{ of } ₹ 1.20}}$$

$$= \sqrt{\frac{45,00,000 \text{ units}}{\text{Re. } 0.18}}$$

$$= \sqrt{45,00,000 \text{ units} \times \frac{100}{18}}$$

$$= \sqrt{2,50,00,000} \text{ units}$$

$$= 5,000 \text{ units}$$

ILLUSTRATION 21

Calculate the Economic Order Quantity from the following information. Also state the number of orders to be placed in a year.

Consumption of material per annum :	10,000 kg.
Order placing cost per order :	₹ 50
Storage costs :	8% on average inventory
Cost per kg. of raw materials :	₹ 2

SOLUTION

(i) Calculation of Economic Order Quantity :

$$EOQ = \sqrt{\frac{2AO}{C}}$$

where,

EOQ = Economic Order Quantity
A = Annual consumption of material in kg. i.e. 10,000 kg.
O = Order placing cost per order i.e. ₹ 50
C = Storage cost i.e. 8% of ₹ 2 = ₹ 0.16

$$= \sqrt{\frac{2 \times 10,000 \text{ kg.} \times ₹ 50}{8\% \text{ of } ₹ 2}}$$

$$= \sqrt{\frac{10,00,000 \text{ units}}{\text{Re. } 0.16}}$$

$$= \sqrt{10,00,000 \text{ kg.} \times \frac{100}{16}}$$

$$= \sqrt{62,50,000 \text{ kg.}}$$

$$= 2,500 \text{ kg.}$$

(ii) **Calculation of number of orders to be placed in a year :**

$$= \frac{A}{EOQ}$$

where,

    A = Annual consumption of material in kg. i.e. 10,000 kg.

    EOQ = Economic Order Quantity i.e. 2,500 kg.

$$= \frac{10,000 \text{ kg.}}{2,500 \text{ kg.}}$$

= 4 orders in a year.

ILLUSTRATION 22

Find out the Economic Order Quantity and order schedule for raw materials and packaging materials with the following data given to you -

1) Cost of ordering :
   Raw Materials - ₹ 1,000 per order
   Packaging Materials - ₹ 5,000 per order
2) Cost of holding inventory :
   Raw Materials - 1 ps. per unit per month
   Packaging Materials 5 ps. per unit per month
3) Production rate : 2,00,000 units per month

SOLUTION

(i) **Calculation of Economic Order Quantity :**

$$EOQ = \sqrt{\frac{2AO}{C}}$$

where,

    EOQ = Economic Order Quantity

    A = Monthly consumption in units i.e. production rate per month i.e. 2,00,000 units per month

O = Cost of ordering i.e.
    (i)   Raw Materials - ₹ 1,000 per order
    (ii)   Packaging Materials - ₹ 5,000 per order

C = Cost of holding inventory per month i.e.
    (i)   Raw Materials - 1 ps. per unit per month
    (ii)   Packaging Materials - 5 ps. per unit per month

(a) Raw materials -

$$= \sqrt{\frac{2 \times 2,00,000 \text{ units} \times ₹ 1,000}{1 \text{ Ps}}}$$

$$= \sqrt{40,00,00,000 \text{ units} \times \frac{100}{1}}$$

$$= \sqrt{40,00,00,00,000 \text{ units}}$$

$$= 2,00,000 \text{ units}$$

(b) Packaging Materials -

$$= \sqrt{\frac{2 \times 2,00,000 \text{ units} \times ₹ 5,000}{5 \text{ Ps.}}}$$

$$= \sqrt{2,00,00,00,000 \text{ units} \times \frac{100}{5}}$$

$$= \sqrt{40,00,00,00,000 \text{ units}}$$

$$= 2,00,000 \text{ units.}$$

(ii) Calculation of order schedule i.e. number of orders to be placed in a month :

$$= \frac{A}{EOQ}$$

where,

    A = Monthly consumption in units i.e. production rate per month i.e. 2,00,000 units

    EOQ = Economic Order Quantity i.e. (i) Raw Materials - 2,00,000 units, (ii) Packaging Materials - 2,00,000 units.

(a) Raw Materials –

$$= \frac{2,00,000 \text{ units}}{2,00,000 \text{ units}}$$

$$= 1 \text{ order in a month}$$

(b) Packaging Materials –

$$= \frac{2,00,000 \text{ units}}{2,00,000 \text{ units}}$$

= 1 order in a month.

ILLUSTRATION 23

Find out the Economic Ordering Quantity from the following particulars and also show a graph identifying Economic Ordering Quantity.

Annual usage : 6000 units

Cost of material per unit : ₹ 20

Cost of placing and receiving one order : ₹ 60

Annual carrying cost of one unit : 10% of inventory value

SOLUTION

(i) Formula Method :

$$EOQ = \sqrt{\frac{2AO}{C}}$$

where,

EOQ = Economic Order Quantity

A = Annual usage in units i.e. 6,000 units

O = Cost of placing and receiving one order i.e. ₹ 60

C = Annual carrying cost i.e. 10% of ₹ 20 = ₹ 2

$$= \sqrt{\frac{2 \times 6{,}000 \text{ units} \times ₹\, 60}{10\% \text{ of } ₹\, 20}}$$

$$= \sqrt{\frac{7{,}20{,}000 \text{ units}}{₹\, 2}}$$

$$= \sqrt{3{,}60{,}000} \text{ units}$$

= 600 units

(ii) Tabular Method :

Annual Average	Orders per year	Units per order Col. 1 ÷ 2	Value per order @ ₹ 20 per unit Col. 3 ×₹ 20	Average Inventory value Col. 4 ÷ 2	Carrying Cost 10% of Col. 5	Ordering Cost @ ₹ 60 per order	Total Cost Col. 6 + 7
1	2	3	4	5	6	7	8
6,000 units		₹	₹	₹	₹	₹	₹
	1	6,000	1,20,000	60,000	6,000	60	6,060
	2	3,000	60,000	30,000	3,000	120	3,120
	3	2,000	40,000	20,000	2,000	180	2,180
	4	1,500	30,000	15,000	1,500	240	1,740
	5	1,200	24,000	12,000	1,200	300	1,500
	6	1,000	20,000	10,000	1,000	360	1,360
	7	857	17,140	8,570	857	420	1,277
	8	750	15,000	7,500	750	480	1,230
	9	667	13,340	6,670	667	540	1,207
	10	600	12,000	6,000	600	600	1,200
	11	545	10,900	5,450	545	660	1,205
	12	500	10,000	5,000	500	720	1,220
	13	462	9,240	4,620	462	780	1,242
	14	429	8,580	4,290	429	840	1,269
	15	400	8,000	4,000	400	900	1300

The above table shows that the cost of placing and receiving order and the carrying cost are equal when order is of 600 units. Total cost of ₹ 1,200 is minimum when the ordering quantity is 600 units. Thus, this is the Economic Order Quantity.

ILLUSTRATION 24

The following data pertain to a component part no. 06280 :

Purchase price per unit ₹ 60

Purchase order cost ₹ 240

Total requirement for a 45-weekly year 9,000 units

Carrying cost 20% of average inventory value

What is the Economic Order Quantity ?

SOLUTION

(i) Formula Method :

$$E.O.Q. = \sqrt{\frac{2AO}{C}}$$

where,

EOQ = Economic Order Quantity
A = Annual requirement i.e. 9,000 units.
O = Ordering and receivng cost per order i.e. ₹ 240
C = Cost of carrying of inventory per year i.e. 20% of ₹ 60 = ₹ 12.

$$= \sqrt{\frac{2 \times 9{,}000 \text{ units} \times ₹240}{20\% \text{ of } ₹60}}$$

$$= \sqrt{\frac{43{,}20{,}000 \text{ units}}{₹12}}$$

$$= \sqrt{3{,}60{,}000} \text{ units}$$

$$= 600 \text{ units}$$

(ii) Tabular Method :

No. of Units Procured per order (q)	100	200	400	600	800	1,000	2,000	4,000
Average Inventory (q ÷ 2)	50	100	200	300	400	500	1,000	2,000
No. of Order (A ÷ q)	90	45	22.50	15	11.25	9	4.50	2.25
Annual Carrying Cost	600	1,200	2,400	3,600	4,800	6,000	12,000	24,000
Annual Ordering Cost	21,600	10,800	5,400	3,600	2,700	2,160	1,080	540
Total Annual Cost	22,200	12,000	7,800	7,200	7,500	8,160	13,080	24,540

∴ E.O.Q. is 600 units which gives the least total cost. At this point carrying cost and ordering cost are equal.

II. Practical Problems :

1. From the following particulars calculate :
   a) Re-order Level, b) Minimum Level and   c) Maximum Level

Normal usage	100 units per day
Minimum usage	60 units per day
Maximum usage	130 units per day
E.O.Q.	4,000 units
Re-order period	25 to 30 days

2. The components A and B are used as follows :

Re-ordering Quantity	A : 3,000 units
	B : 4,000 units
Re-ordering period	A : 4 to 6 weeks
	B : 2 to 4 weeks
Normal usage	3,000 units per week each
Minimum usage	1,500 units per week each
Maximum usage	4,500 units per week each

   You are required to calculate for each of the components :

   a) Maximum Level, b) Minimum Level c) Average stock level
   d) Re-ordering Level.

3. From the following particulars, calculate the minimum stock level, maximum stock level and reorder level :

a)	Maximum consumption	150 units per day
b)	Minimum consumption	100 units per day
c)	Normal consumption	120 units per day
d)	Re-order quantity	1,500 units
e)	Re-order period	10 - 15 days
f)	Normalre-order period	12 days

4. Two components A and B are used as follows :

Normal usage	50 per week each
Minimum usage	25 per week each
Maximum usage	75 per week each
Re-order quantity	A : 300 ; B : 500
Re-order period	A : 4 to 6 weeks; B : 2 to 4 weeks

   Calculate for each component
   a) Re-order Level
   b) Minimum Level
   c) Maximum Level and
   d) Average stock level

5. From the following data, Calculate,
   a) Re-order Level,

b) Minimum stock level
c) Maximum stock level

Re-order quantity	1,500 units
Re-order period	4 to 6 weeks
Maximum consumption	400 units per week
Normal consumption	30 units per week
Minimum consumption	250 units per week

6. From the following particulars, Calculate,
    a) Re-order Level
    b) Minimum Level
    c) Maximum Level and
    d) Average Level

Normal usage	100 units per day
Minimum usage	60 units per day
Maximum usage	130 units per day
E.O.Q.	5,000 units
Re-order period	25 to 30 days

7. You have been asked to calculate the following levels for Part No. 'T' from the following information.

    a) Re-ordering level, b) Maximum level, c) Minimum level, d) Danger stock level, e) Average stock level

    The re-ordering quantity is to be calculated from the following data :

    Total costs of purchasing relating to the order are ₹ 20.

    No. of units to be purchased during the year is 5000.

    Purchase price per unit including transportation costs is ₹ 50.

    Annual cost of storage of one unit is ₹ 5.

Lead Times		Rate of Consumption	
Average	10 days	Average	15 units per day
Maximum	15 days	Maximum	20 units per day
Minimum	6 days	Minimum	10 units per day
Maximum for emergency purchases	4 days		

8. Calculate the stock levels for an item of material from the following information :

Normal usage	200 units per day
Maximum usage	250 units per day
Minimum usage	120 units per day
Re-order period	5 to 15 days
Economic Order Quantity	4,000 units

9. From the following particulars, calculate the economic order quantity.

Annual requirements	:	1,600 units
Cost of materials per unit	:	₹ 40
Cost of placing and receiving one order	:	₹ 50
Annual carrying cost of inventory	:	10% of inventory value.

10. A unit of article A costs ₹ 50 and the annual consumption is 2,000 units. The cost of placing an order is ₹ 40 and the interest is 10% per annum. Find the economic order quantity.

11. From the following figures, you are required to calculate Economic Order Quantity and No. of orders to be placed per year.

Total consumption of material per year	1,000 kg.
Procurement cost per order	₹ 5
Unit price of material	₹ 2
Storage and carrying cost	8%

12. If the annual usage of a component is 4,000 pieces, set up and order processing cost ₹ 50, annual rate is 10% and cost of manufacturing a unit is ₹ 100. Calculate the Economic Order Quantity.

13. Find out the economic order quantity from the following particulars :

Annual usage	:	6,000 units
Cost of materials per unit	:	₹ 20
Cost of placing and receiving one order	:	₹ 60
Annual carrying cost of one unit	:	10% of inventory value

14. From the following information determine E.O.Q.

Annual usage	:	90,000 units
Cost per unit	:	₹ 50
Buying cost per order	:	₹ 10
Cost of carrying Inventory	:	10% of cost

15. Given : Annual usage of a material 600 units, ordering costs are ₹ 12 per one order, price of material is ₹ 20 per unit, and cost of storage is 20% of inventory value, find out EOQ.

16. Suppose the annual consumption is 675 units, 10% is the interest and cost of storing an article ₹ 30 per unit, cost of placing an order is ₹ 18. Calculate the Economic Order Quantity.

17. A factory requires 15,000 units of a certain material for the year. Cost of carrying one unit of material is calculated to be ₹ 20 per annum, and it is estimated that the expenses of placing an order and receiving would amount to ₹ 375. Calculate Economic Order Quantity.

18. From the following particulars determine the E.O.Q.

Cost of materials per unit	₹ 5
Demand per month	500 units
Cost of placing each order	₹ 15
Inventory carrying cost	20%

This is also one of the useful methods of exercising material control. The inventory ratios can be calculated by the following formula :

(i) **Turnover of Stores Materials :** Inventory Turnover Ratio i.e. Stock Turnover is usually measured in terms of the ratios of the value of materials consumed to the average stock held during the period.

$$\text{Stock Turnover} = \frac{\text{Value of Materials Consumed during the period}}{\text{Cost of Average Stock held during the period}}$$

(ii) **Inventory Turnover in days** $= \dfrac{\text{Number of Days during the period}}{\text{Stock Turnover Ratio}}$

$$\text{Average Stock} = \frac{\text{Opening Stock} + \text{Closing Stock}}{2}$$

$$\text{Inventory Performance Index} = \frac{\text{Actual Stock Turnover Ratio}}{\text{Standard Stock Turnover Ratio}} \times 100$$

A high ratio indicates fast-moving stock whereas a low ratio indicates slow-moving stock. It is, therefore, advantageous to compare the stock turnover of the different grades and kinds of materials in order to find out the slow-moving items thus, enabling the management to avoid blocking up of capital in such slow-moving stocks. If stock turnover ratio for a particular item is zero, it means that the item had not been used during the period.

FORMULAE TO REMEMBER

(i) Inventory Turnover Ratio expressed in Number of Times :

$$= \frac{\text{Cost of Materials Consumed during the period}}{\text{Cost of Average Stock held during the period}}$$

(ii) Inventory Turnover Ratio expressed in Number of Days :

$$= \frac{\text{Number of Days during the period}}{\text{Inventory Turnover Ratio}}$$

where,

- Inventory Turnover = Material Turnover = Turnover of Stores Material
- Cost of Materials Consumed = Opening Stock + Purchases − Closing Stock
- Cost of Average Stock = Average Inventory = $\dfrac{\text{Opening Stock + Closing Stock}}{2}$

Indications :

(i) Inventory Turnover Ratio expressed in Number of Times :

(a) Low Ratio indicates slow moving stock, accumulation of obsolete stock, carrying of too much stock, i.e. those items of stores which are not issued frequently, their issue is irregular and at large intervals. It leads to the disadvantages arising out of over-stocking. Hence, every attempt should be made to reduce the amount of capital locked up and prevent over stocking of slow moving items. Losses and costs arising from slow moving stocks can be reduced by reducing their quantity in the store. Smaller quantity of such material should be purchased keeping in view their consumption rate and lead period. To reduce the quantity of such stores, efforts should be made to increase their consumption by finding out their alternative uses and increasing the production by creating more demand in the market.

(b) High Ratio indicates fast moving stock and less investment in stock i.e. those items of stock which are issued frequently and their issue is very regular.

(c) Zero Ratio means the item of stock had not been used at all during the period and hence it should be disposed off immediately, otherwise the quality and value of such item will be deteriorated. Such dormant stocks are very rarely issued from the store and their consumption is almost nil. Losses and costs arising from these stocks can be reduced by purchasing only those items which are very much necessary for the continuous production.

(ii) Inventory Turnover Ratio expressed in Number of Days :

Inventory turnover ratio can also be expressed in terms of number of days for which the inventory will be sufficient. This period should be as minimum as possible. Shorter the period better is the management.

ILLUSTRATIONS

ILLUSTRATION 1

Calculate Inventory Turnover Ratio from the following for Material 'X'.

Particulars	₹
Stock on hand 1-4-2007	20,000
Closing Stock on 31-3-2008	15,000
Purchases during year 2007-2008	70,000

SOLUTION

(i) Calculation of Inventory Turnover Ratio (in times):

$$= \frac{\text{Cost of Materials Consumed}}{\text{Cost of Average Stock}}$$

$$= \frac{\text{Opening Stock + Purchases} - \text{Closing Stock}}{\frac{\text{Opening Stock + Closing Stock}}{2}}$$

$$= \frac{₹20,000 + ₹70,000 - ₹15,000}{\frac{₹20,000 + ₹15,000}{2}}$$

$$= \frac{₹75,000}{₹17,500}$$

= 4.3 i.e. 4 times.

(ii) Calculation of Inventory Turnover Ratio (in days):

$$= \frac{\text{Number of Days during the year}}{\text{Inventory Turnover Ratio}}$$

$$= \frac{366 \text{ days}}{4.3 \text{ times}}$$

= 85.12 i.e. 85 days

Working Notes:

(i) 2007-2008, being a Leap Year, the number of days during the year are 366.

ILLUSTRATION 2

The following information is available from the books of Xansa Ltd., Pimpri for the year 2008. Calculate Material Turnover Ratio and determine which of the material is **fast moving**.

Particulars	Material 'A' ₹	Material 'B' ₹
Opening Stock	1,400	2,000
Purchases	23,000	3,600
Closing Stock	1,000	2,400

SOLUTION

(i) Calculation of Material Turnover Ratio (in times):

$$= \frac{\text{Cost of Materials Consumed}}{\text{Cost of Average Stock}}$$

$$= \frac{\text{Opening Stock + Purchases − Closing Stock}}{\frac{\text{Opening Stock + Closing Stock}}{2}}$$

Material 'A' $= \dfrac{₹1,400 + ₹23,000 − ₹1,000}{\dfrac{₹1,400 + ₹1,000}{2}}$

$= \dfrac{₹23,400}{₹1,200}$

= 19.5 i.e. 19 times

Material 'B' $= \dfrac{₹2,000 + ₹3,600 − ₹2,400}{\dfrac{₹2,000 + ₹2,400}{2}}$

$= \dfrac{₹3,200}{₹2,200}$

= 1.45 i.e. 1 time

(ii) Calculation of Material Turnover Ratio (in days):

$$= \frac{\text{Number of Days during the year}}{\text{Inventory Turnover Ratio}}$$

Material 'A' $= \dfrac{366 \text{ days}}{19.5 \text{ times}} = 18.77$ i.e. 19 days

Material 'B' $= \dfrac{366 \text{ days}}{1.45 \text{ times}} = 252.41$ i.e. 252 days

Working Notes:

(i) 2008, being the Leap Year, the number of days during the year are 366.

Conclusion:

In case of Material 'A', the Material Turnover Ratio of 19 times shows that an Average Stock is being held for 19 days, on the other hand in case of Material 'B', the Material Turnover Ratio of 1 time shows that an Average Stock is being held for 252 days. As Material Turnover Ratio of Material 'A' (i.e. 19 times) is high as compared to Material 'B' (i.e. 1 times), Material 'A' is a fast moving material.

ILLUSTRATION 3

From the following data, calculate the Inventory Turnover Ratio for 2008-2009.

Particulars	₹
Purchases during the year 2008-2009	1,10,000
Stock as on 31-3-2009	15,000
Stock as on 01-4-2008	25,000

Also comment upon the **inventory position**.

SOLUTION

(i) Calculation of Cost of Materials Consumed :

= Opening Stock + Purchases − Closing Stock

= ₹ 25,000 + ₹ 1,10,000 − ₹ 15,000

= ₹ 1,35,000 − ₹ 15,000

= ₹ 1,20,000.

(ii) Calculation of Cost of Average Stock :

$$= \frac{\text{Opening Stock + Closing Stock}}{2}$$

$$= \frac{₹ 25,000 + ₹ 15,000}{2}$$

$$= \frac{₹ 40,000}{2}$$

= ₹ 20,000

(iii) Calculation of Inventory Turnover Ratio :

$$= \frac{\text{Cost of Materials Consumed}}{\text{Cost of Average Stock}}$$

$$= \frac{₹ 1,20,000}{₹ 20,000}$$

= 6 times

Comment :

The Inventory Turnover Ratio is 6 times, it means that the stock has been turned over six times during the year 2008-2009 or on an average the stock has been held for two months.

ILLUSTRATION 4

From the following information in respect of Material 'A' calculate Inventory Turnover Ratio.

Issue of Material 'A' during the year 2008-2009 - 8,000 units
Re-order Quantity – 3,000 units
Minimum Level of Stock – 500 units

Also put forward your comments upon the **inventory position**.

SOLUTION

(i) **Calculation of Material Consumed i.e. Issue of Material during the year – 8,000 units**

(ii) **Calculation of Average Stock** = $MN \cdot L + \frac{1}{2} RQ$

    = Minimum Level of Stock + $\frac{1}{2}$ of Re-order Quantity
    = 500 units + $\frac{1}{2}$ × 3,000 units
    = 500 units + 1,500 units
    = 2,000 units.

(iii) **Calculation of Inventory Turnover Ratio :**

$$= \frac{\text{Material Consumed in units}}{\text{Average Stock in units}}$$

$$= \frac{8,000 \text{ units}}{2,000 \text{ units}}$$

= 4 times

(iv) **Comment :**

The Inventory Turnover Ratio of Material 'A' is 4 times it means that the stock has been turned over 4 times during the year 2008-2009 or on an average, the stock has been held for three months.

ILLUSTRATION 5

The following information is available from the books of M/s Royal Traders, Sholapur, for the year 2008-2009.

Particulars	Material	
	X ₹	Y ₹
Stock as on 31-3-2009	3,000	3,500
Purchases	26,000	7,000
Stock as on 1-4-2008	2,000	3,000

Calculate Inventory Turnover Ratio and determine which material is **fast moving**.

SOLUTION

(i) **Calculation of Cost of Materials Consumed:**

= Opening Stock + Purchases − Closing Stock

X = ₹ 2,000 + ₹ 26,000 − ₹ 3,000

= ₹ 28,000 − ₹ 3,000

= ₹ 25,000

Y = ₹ 3,000 + ₹ 7,000 − ₹ 3,500

= ₹ 10,000 − ₹ 3,500

= ₹ 6,500

(ii) **Calculation of Cost of Average Stock:**

$$= \frac{\text{Opening Stock + Closing Stock}}{2}$$

$$X = \frac{₹\,2{,}000 + ₹\,3{,}000}{2}$$

$$= \frac{₹\,5{,}000}{2}$$

= ₹ 2,500

$$Y = \frac{₹\,3{,}000 + ₹\,3{,}500}{2}$$

$$= \frac{₹\,6{,}500}{2}$$

= ₹ 3,250

(iii) **Calculation of Inventory Turnover Ratio:**

$$= \frac{\text{Cost of Materials Consumed}}{\text{Cost of Average Stock}}$$

$$X = \frac{₹\,25{,}000}{₹\,2{,}500}$$

= 10 times

$$Y = \frac{₹\,6{,}500}{₹\,3{,}250}$$

= 2 times

(iv) **Conclusion:** As Inventory Turnover Ratio of Material 'X' (i.e. 10 times) is high as compared to Material 'Y' (i.e. 2 times), Material X is a Fast Moving Material.

Operations & Supply Chain Management   Numericals

ILLUSTRATION 6

Calculate the Inventory Turnover Ratio expressed in Number of Times and in Number of Days separately for the year ended 31-03-2008 and determine which of the two materials is **fast moving**.

Particulars	Material	
	M	N
	₹	₹
Opening Balance of Stock as on 1-4-2007	20,000	30,000
Average Stock	16,000	25,000
Purchases during the year 2007-2008	72,000	90,000

SOLUTION

(i) Calculation of Value of Closing Stock :

$$\text{Average Stock} = \frac{\text{Opening stock} + \boxed{\text{Closing Stock}}}{2}$$

∴   2 × Average Stock = Opening Stock + $\boxed{\text{Closing Stock}}$

∴ $\boxed{\text{Closing Stock}}$ = (2 × Average Stock) − Opening Stock

M = (2 × ₹ 16,000) − ₹ 20,000
= ₹ 32,000 − ₹ 20,000
= ₹ 12,000

N = (2 × ₹ 25,000) − ₹ 30,000
= ₹ 50,000 − ₹ 30,000
= ₹ 20,000

(ii) Calculation Cost of Materials Consumed :

= Opening Stock + Purchases − Closing Stock

M = ₹ 20,000 + ₹ 72,000 − ₹ 12,000
= ₹ 92,000 − ₹ 12,000
= ₹ 80,000

N = ₹ 30,000 + ₹ 90,000 − ₹ 20,000
= ₹ 1,20,000 − ₹ 20,000
= ₹ 1,00,000

(iii) Calculation of Inventory Turnover Ratio expressed in number of times :

$$= \frac{\text{Cost of Materials Consumed}}{\text{Cost of Average Stock}}$$

$$M = \frac{₹\,80{,}000}{₹\,16{,}000}$$

= 5 times

$$N = \frac{₹\,1{,}00{,}000}{₹\,25{,}000}$$

= 4 times

(iv) Calculation of Inventory Turnover Ratio expressed in Number of Days :

$$= \frac{\text{Number of Days during the year}}{\text{Inventory Turnover Ratio}}$$

$$M = \frac{366 \text{ days}}{5 \text{ times}} = 73.2 \text{ i.e. 73 days,}$$

$$N = \frac{366 \text{ days}}{4 \text{ times}} = 91.50 \text{ i.e. 91 days.}$$

Working Notes :

(i) 2007-2008, being a Leap Year, the number of days during the year are 366.

Conclusion :

In case of material M, the Inventory Turnover Ratio of 5 times shows that an Average Stock is being held for 73 days, on the other hand in case of Material N, the Inventory Turnover Ratio of 4 times shows that an Average Stock is being held for 91 days. As Inventory Turnover Ratio of Material M (i.e. 5 times) is high as compared to Material N (i.e. 4 times), Material M is a Fast Moving Material.

ILLUSTRATION 7

From the following data for the year 2007-2008 calculate the Inventory TurnoverRatio and determine which material is **Slow-Moving**.

Particulars	Material A ₹	Material B ₹
Stock of Material as on 1-4-2007	40,000	60,000
Stock of Material as on 31-3-2008	24,000	20,000
Yearly Purchases	2,08,000	2,00,000

Solution:

(i) Calculation of Cost of Materials Consumed :

$$= \text{Opening Stock + Purchases − Closing Stock}$$

A = ₹ 40,000 + ₹ 2,08,000 − ₹ 24,000
  = ₹ 2,48,000 − ₹ 24,000
  = ₹ 2,24,000

B = ₹ 60,000 + ₹ 2,00,000 − ₹ 20,000
  = ₹ 2,60,000 − ₹ 20,000
  = ₹ 2,40,000

(ii) Calculation of Cost of Average Stock :

$$= \frac{\text{Opening Stock + Closing Stock}}{2}$$

A $= \dfrac{₹\,40{,}000 + ₹\,24{,}000}{2}$

  $= \dfrac{₹\,64{,}000}{2}$

  = ₹ 32,000

B $= \dfrac{₹\,60{,}000 + ₹\,20{,}000}{2}$

  $= \dfrac{₹\,80{,}000}{2}$

  = ₹ 40,000

(iii) Calculation of Inventory Turnover Ratio :

$$= \frac{\text{Cost of Materials Consumed}}{\text{Cost of Average Stock}}$$

A $= \dfrac{₹\,2{,}24{,}000}{₹\,32{,}000}$

  = 7 times

B $= \dfrac{₹\,2{,}40{,}000}{₹\,40{,}000}$

  = 6 times

(iv) Conclusion : As Inventory Turnover Ratio of Material B (i.e. 6 times) is low as compared to Material A (i.e. 7 times), Material B is a Slow Moving Material.

ILLUSTRATION 8

From the following information calculate Inventory Turnover Ratio and Inventory Turnover period for the year 2007-2008 and determine which of the materials is **fast moving**.

Particulars	Material C ₹	Material D ₹
Materials in Hand on -		
(i) 1-4-2007	50,000	50,000
(ii) 31-3-2008	30,000	1,00,000
Materials Purchased during the year 2007-2008	3,80,000	3,50,000

SOLUTION

(i) Calculation of Cost of Materials Consumed :

$$= \text{Opening Stock + Purchases – Closing Stock}$$

$$C = ₹\,50,000 + ₹\,3,80,000 - ₹\,30,000$$
$$= ₹\,4,30,000 - ₹\,30,000$$
$$= ₹\,4,00,000$$

$$D = ₹\,50,000 + ₹\,3,50,000 - ₹\,1,00,000$$
$$= ₹\,4,00,000 - ₹\,1,00,000$$
$$= ₹\,3,00,000$$

(ii) Calculation of Cost of Average Stock :

$$= \frac{\text{Opening Stock + Closing Stock}}{2}$$

$$C = \frac{₹\,50,000 + ₹\,30,000}{2}$$
$$= \frac{₹\,80,000}{2}$$
$$= ₹\,40,000$$

$$D = \frac{₹\,50,000 + ₹\,1,00,000}{2}$$
$$= \frac{₹\,1,50,000}{2}$$
$$= ₹\,75,000$$

(iii) Calculation of Inventory Turnover Ratio :

$$= \frac{\text{Cost of Materials Consumed}}{\text{Cost of Average Stock}}$$

$$C = \frac{₹\,4,00,000}{₹\,40,000}$$

= 10 times

$$D = \frac{₹\,3,00,000}{₹\,75,000}$$

= 4 times

(iv) Calculation of Inventory Turnover Period :

$$= \frac{\text{Number of Days during the year}}{\text{Inventory Turnover Ratio}}$$

$$C = \frac{366 \text{ days}}{10 \text{ times}}$$

= 36.6 i.e. 37 days

$$D = \frac{366 \text{ days}}{4 \text{ times}}$$

= 91.50 i.e. 91 days

Working Notes :

(i) 2007-2008, being a Leap Year, the number of days during the year are 366.

(iv) Conclusion :

In case of material C, the Inventory Turnover Ratio of 10 times shows that an Average Stock is being held for 37 days, on the other hand in case of Material 'D', the Inventory Turnover ratio of 4 times shows that an Average Stock is being held for 91 days. As Inventory Turnover Ratio of Material C (i.e. 10 times) is high as compared to Material D (i.e. 4 times), Material 'C' is a Fast Moving Material.

ILLUSTRATION 9

From the following information relating to two materials C and D for the year 2008-2009, determine which of the two materials **is to be disposed off immediately**.

Particulars	Material	
	C ₹	D ₹
Material in Hand on 1-4-2008	25,000	20,000
Materials Purchased during the year 2008-2009	50,000	40,000
Material in Hand on 31-3-2009	75,000	20,000

SOLUTION

(i) Calculation of Cost of Materials Consumed:

$$= \text{Opening Stock + Purchases − Closing Stock}$$

$$C = ₹25,000 + ₹50,000 − ₹75,000$$
$$= ₹75,000 − ₹75,000$$
$$= \text{NIL.}$$

$$D = ₹20,000 + ₹40,000 − ₹20,000$$
$$= ₹60,000 − ₹20,000$$
$$= ₹40,000$$

(ii) Calculation of Cost of Average Stock:

$$= \frac{\text{Opening Stock + Closing Stock}}{2}$$

$$C = \frac{₹25,000 + ₹75,000}{2}$$
$$= \frac{₹1,00,000}{2}$$
$$= ₹50,000$$

$$D = \frac{₹20,000 + ₹20,000}{2}$$
$$= \frac{₹40,000}{2}$$
$$= ₹20,000$$

(iii) Calculation of Inventory Turnover Ratio:

$$= \frac{\text{Cost of Materials Consumed}}{\text{Cost of Average Stock}}$$

$$C = \frac{\text{Nil}}{₹50,000}$$
$$= \text{Nil}$$

$$D = \frac{₹40,000}{₹20,000}$$
$$= 2 \text{ times}$$

(iv) Conclusion: As Material 'C' indicates Zero Inventory Turnover Ratio, it is to be disposed off immediately.

ILLUSTRATION 10

The following information is available from the books of Utkal Enterprises, Nashik for the year 2007-2008.

Particulars	Material A ₹	Material B ₹	Material C ₹
Opening Stock on 1-4-2007	10,000	10,000	25,000
Material Consumption Cost	40,000	90,000	60,000
Closing Stock on 31-3-2008	30,000	20,000	15,000

You are required to calculate,
(i) Cost of Materials Consumed,
(ii) Cost of Average Stock,
(iii) Inventory Turnover Ratio
(iv) Inventory Turnover Period and
(v) Determine which of the three materials is **Fast Moving**.

SOLUTION

(i) **Calculation of Cost of Material Consumed i.e. Material Consumption Cost :**

$$A = ₹ 40,000$$
$$B = ₹ 90,000$$
$$C = ₹ 60,000$$

(ii) **Calculation of Cost of Average Stock :**

$$= \frac{\text{Opening Stock + Closing Stock}}{2}$$

$$A = \frac{₹ 10,000 + ₹ 30,000}{2}$$
$$= \frac{₹ 40,000}{2}$$
$$= ₹ 20,000$$

$$B = \frac{₹ 10,000 + ₹ 20,000}{2}$$
$$= \frac{₹ 30,000}{2}$$
$$= ₹ 15,000$$

$$C = \frac{₹25,000 + ₹15,000}{2}$$

$$= \frac{₹40,000}{2}$$

$$= ₹20,000$$

(iii) **Calculation of Inventory Turnover Ratio :**

$$= \frac{\text{Cost of Materials Consumed}}{\text{Cost of Average Stock}}$$

$$A = \frac{₹40,000}{₹20,000}$$

$$= 2 \text{ times}$$

$$B = \frac{₹90,000}{₹15,000}$$

$$= 6 \text{ times}$$

$$C = \frac{₹60,000}{₹20,000}$$

$$= 3 \text{ times}$$

(iv) **Calculation of Inventory Turnover Period :**

$$= \frac{\text{Number of Days during the year}}{\text{Inventory Turnover Ratio}}$$

$$A = \frac{366 \text{ days}}{2 \text{ times}}$$

$$= 183 \text{ days}$$

$$B = \frac{366 \text{ days}}{6 \text{ times}}$$

$$= 61 \text{ days}$$

$$C = \frac{366 \text{ days}}{3 \text{ times}}$$

$$= 122 \text{ days}$$

Working Notes :

(i) 2007-2008, being a Leap Year, the number of days during the year are 366.

(v) **Conclusion :**

As Inventory Turnover Ratio of Materials B (i.e. 6 times) is higher as compared to Material A (i.e. 2 times) and Material C (i.e. 3 times), and Inventory Turnover Period of

Material B (i.e. 61 days) is Shorter as compared to Material A (i.e. 183 days) and Material C (i.e. 122 days), Material B is a Fast Moving Material. The control has to be exercised more stricly over purchases of Material A.

ILLUSTRATION 11

The following information is available from the books of Vanita Enterprises, Varanasi for the year ended 31st March, 2008.

Particulars	Material	
	X ₹	Y ₹
Stock of Material in hand on 1-4-2007	10,000	9,000
Stock of Material in hand on 31-3-2008	6,000	11,000
Purchases during the year 2003-2008	52,000	32,000

Which material requires **Strict Control over the Purchases** ?Comment.

SOLUTION

(i) **Calculation of Cost of Materials Consumed :**

$$= \text{Opening Stock + Purchases − Closing Stock}$$

$$X = ₹10,000 + ₹52,000 − ₹6,000$$
$$= ₹62,000 − ₹6,000$$
$$= ₹56,000$$

$$Y = ₹9,000 + ₹32,000 − ₹11,000$$
$$= ₹41,000 − ₹11,000$$
$$= ₹30,000$$

(ii) **Calculation of Cost of Average Stock :**

$$= \frac{\text{Opening Stock + Closing Stock}}{2}$$

$$X = \frac{₹10,000 + ₹6,000}{2}$$
$$= \frac{₹16,000}{2}$$
$$= ₹8,000$$

$$Y = \frac{₹9,000 + ₹11,000}{2}$$
$$= \frac{₹20,000}{2}$$
$$= ₹10,000$$

(iii) Calculation of Inventory Turnover Ratio :

$$= \frac{\text{Cost of Material Consumed}}{\text{Cost of Average Stock}}$$

$$X = \frac{₹\,56{,}000}{₹\,8{,}000}$$

= 7 times

$$Y = \frac{₹\,30{,}000}{₹\,10{,}000}$$

= 3 times

(iv) Calculation of Inventory Turnover Period :

$$= \frac{\text{Number of Days in a year}}{\text{Inventory Turnover Ratio}}$$

$$X = \frac{366 \text{ days}}{7 \text{ times}}$$

= 52.29 i.e. 52 days

$$Y = \frac{366 \text{ days}}{3 \text{ times}}$$

= 122 days

Working Notes :

(i) 2007-2008 being a Leap Year, the number of days during the year are 366.

(v) Comment :

As Inventory Turnover Ratio of Material Y (i.e. 3 times) is lower as compared to Material X (i.e. 7 times) and Inventory Turnover Period of Material Y (i.e. 122 days) is longer as compared to Material X (i.e. 52 days), Material Y is a Slow Moving Material which requires strict control over their purchases.

II. Practical Problems :

1. Calculate the material turnover ratio for the year 2008-2009 from the following information and determine which of the two materials is fast moving.

Particulars	Material X ₹	Material Y ₹
Material in hand :		
On 1-4-2008	40,000	30,000
On 31-3-2009	20,000	50,000
Material purchases during the year	4,50,000	3,60,000

2. Calculate the material turnover ratio for the year 2008-2009 from the following information and determine which of the two materials is the slow moving.

Particulars	Material A ₹	Material B ₹
Material in Hand :		
On 1-4-2008	1,00,000	1,50,000
On 31-3-2009	2,30,000	1,70,000
Material purchased during the year	5,00,000	3,40,000

3. Calculate the material turnover ratio for the year 2008-2009 from the following information and determine which of the three materials is to be immediately disposed off.

Particulars	Material X ₹	Material Y ₹	Material Z ₹
Material in Hand :			
On 1-4-2008	1,00,000	1,50,000	1,25,000
On 31-3-2009	5,00,000	1,40,000	75,000
Material purchased during the year	4,00,000	3,60,000	2,50,000

4. Calculate the material turnover ratio for the year 2008-2009 from the following information and determine which of the four materials is fast moving.

Particulars	A ₹	B ₹	C ₹	D ₹
Material in hand :				
On 1-4-2008	5,000	10,000	15,000	20,000
On 31-3-2009	20,000	15,000	10,000	5,000
Cost of material consumed	1,00,000	1,50,000	40,000	25,000

1. A furniture manufacturer requires 25 nos. of a certain size of wooden plank everyday. Each wooden plank is priced at ₹ 120. The buyer company's inventory carrying cost is ₹0.10 per unit per day and the procurement cost per order is ₹80. Determine (a) the optimal order size, (b) the optimal period of coverage, (c) the expected relevant cost per annum. (The company works 25 days per month.)

2. Economic order quantity of an item 'X' is three times that of item 'Y'. If the annual usage of item 'Y' is ₹800, what would be the annual usage of item 'X'?

Operations & Supply Chain Management
Numericals

3. A company's annual requirement of an item which costs ₹6 each is 36,000 nos. The acquisition cost amounts to ₹150 per order. The carrying cost is estimated at 20% per year. Assume the following order sizes : (i) 30,000 (ii) 15,000 (iii) 6,000 (iv) 3,000 (v) 1,500 (vi) 750. Calculate (a) annual procurement cost (b) average inventory (c) annual carrying cost (d) economic order quantity.

4. Impellers are procured by a pneumatic compressor manufacturer from a local firm and are consumed at an average rate of 1000 nos. per month. If the procurement cost is ₹64 per order and the cost of handling it in stock is ₹2.40 per unit per year, determine the quantity that should be procured at a time to optimise the costs involved. If the consumption of the above item increases to 1250 nos. per month and the inventory carrying cost reduces to 1.60 per unit per year, what is the revised EOQ? Also calculate the total cost of inventory in both the cases.

5. Economic order quantity of an item which costs ₹4 each is half of its annual consumption. If the procurement cost is ₹36 per order and the inventory carrying cost is 1.5 percent per month, find the economic order quantity.

6. Precision Tools Ltd. requires annually 4,000 bolts costing ₹3 each. It has been estimated to cost ₹60 to place an order and execute the delivery.

(a) If the carrying cost is 25 percent of the value of inventory held, what would be the optimum size of each order? How many orders are placed per year?

(b) Calculate annual total cost from effecting economic lot size purchases.

(c) If the order quantity is raised by 25 percent above the quantity calculated under (a), what would be the effect on the annual total cost?

(d) If the order quantity is lowered by 25 percent below the quantity calculated under (a), what would be the effect on the annual total cost?

(e) Comment on the costs obtained under (a), (b) and (c).

7. A chemical firm buys 2500 units annually of a particular item from a vendor at a cost of ₹3 per unit. It has now received a revised price schedule from the vendor which is as follows :

Order quantity	Price per unit
Less than 500 units	₹3
Between 500 and 1250 units	₹2.90
1250 units or more	₹2.85

The cost of placing an order and executing the delivery once is ₹25, Inventory carrying cost as a percentage of average inventory investment is 20 percent. Determine economic order quantity of the item.

8. A trading company buys and sells 10,000 bottles of pain balm every year. The cost per bottle is ₹2 and the cost of placing an order is ₹100. The company's standard rate of return on working capital funds is 1and 1/3% per month. The cost of physical storage of pain balm is fixed.

   (a) Determine the optimal order quantity and inventory cycle duration for the pain balm.

   (b) How many orders are placed each year?

   (c) What is minimum yearly inventory cost?

9. A manufacturer buys an item in lots of 500 units which is three months requirements. The cost per unit is ₹90 and the ordering cost is ₹180 per batch order. The inventory carrying cost is estimated at 20% of the average inventory investment.

   (a) What is the annual inventory cost of the existing policy?

   (b) How much can be saved using EOQ policy?

10. The company that you are working for uses a certain type of item in its final assembly. The company uses 100 units of this item per month. Each unit costs the company ₹3. The cost of putting through each order and inventory carrying charges are computed to be ₹28 and 14% of the average investment respectively.

    (i) Calculate EOQ of the above item.

    (ii) The supplier offers you 3% discount if you increase your order size to one and half times, should you do it?

Multiple Choice Questions

Chapter 1

1. The term supply chain management (SCM) was developed to express the need to integrate the key business processes in the year:
   (a) 1975
   (b) 1980
   (c) 1962
   (d) 1991

2. Supply Chain and Logistics are the same terms and can be used interchangeably.
   (a) True
   (b) False

3. The term _____ is employed in manufacturing and commerce to describe the broad range of activities (like freight, warehousing, material handling, protective packing, inventory control, selection of site for various activities, marketing, forecasting) concerned with the efficient movement of finished products from the end of production line to the consumer and in some cases, includes the movement of raw materials from the sources of supply to the beginning of the production line.
   (a) Supply Chain
   (b) Logistics
   (c) Physical Distribution
   (d) Production Process

4. Supply Chain is a broader concept than Logistics.
   (a) True
   (b) False

5. The factors which move the goods from one production point to the other are a part of _____.
   (a) Production
   (b) Process
   (c) Capacity
   (d) Logistics

6. Services are _____.
   (a) Tangible
   (b) Inseparable
   (c) Constant
   (d) Non Perishable

7. Fitness for purpose is a notion used for
   (a) Supply Chain
   (b) Logistics
   (c) Process
   (d) Quality

8. Quality = Tangible + Intangible (esteem) value
   (a) True
   (b) False

9. Inspection and Quality Control are one and the same.
   (a) True
   (b) False

10. The concept of Internal Customer has developed out of a need to build quality into the product rather than inspect the product for quality.
    (a) True
    (b) False

11. Total Quality Management and Lean Management are the same concepts.
    (a) True
    (b) False
12. Lean Management is an approach linked towards efficient inventory management.
    (a) True
    (b) False
13. As a result of the many business scandals that have been in the news in recent years, more academic attention is being given to the role of _____ in business.
    (a) Processes
    (b) Controls
    (c) Ethics
    (d) Quality
14. _____ Management is an area of management concerned with overseeing, designing, and controlling the process of production and redesigning business operations in the production of goods or services.
    (a) Supply Chain
    (b) Operations
    (c) Quality
    (d) Design
15. A _____ is the network of organisations that are involved through upstream and downstream linkages in the different processes and activities that produce value in the form of products and services in the hands of ultimate customers. It is also called as a value chain.
    (a) Process
    (b) Supply Chain
    (c) Flow
    (d) Capacity Plan

Answer Key

1. (b)	2. (b)	3. (c)	4. (a)	5. (d)	6. (b)	7. (d)
8. (a)	9. (b)	10. (a)	11. (b)	12. (a)	13. (c)	14. (b)
15. (b)						

Chapter 2

1. Designing of processes is an important and early step in operations management.
   (a) True
   (b) False
2. Volume, Variety and Flow are the three aspects which must be considered in the process of _____.
   (a) Operations
   (b) Process Design
   (c) Product design
   (d) Logistics
3. _____ indicates the quantity of products produced in a manufacturing system.
   (a) Variety
   (b) Flow
   (c) Volume
   (d) Capacity

4. _____ refers to the number of subcategories of products and variants of each product produced in a manufacturing system.
   (a) Variety
   (b) Flow
   (c) Volume
   (d) Capacity
5. A _____ flow system is characterised by a streamlined flow of products in the operating system.
   (a) Intermittent
   (b) Continuous
   (c) Jumbled
6. The mass production system in the discrete manufacturing industry is an example of continuous and streamlined flow in the manufacturing system.
   (a) True
   (b) False
7. _____ Production helps ensure that the product or service matches the customer's exact needs, as closely as the firm is able, because it is literally 'custom-made'.
   (a) Batch
   (b) Mass
   (c) Job
   (d) Flow
8. _____ Production is the method pioneered by Henry Ford for his Model T car, and the efficiencies he gained enabled him to produce large numbers of cars at low cost.
   (a) Flow
   (b) Mass
   (c) Job
   (d) Batch
9. Designing operations systems excludes making choices with respect to the location, technology, capacity, and layout of the system.
   (a) True
   (b) False
10. Service blueprinting is a method by which the service delivery process is broken down into individual elements through a step-by-step mapping of the process.
    (a) True
    (b) False

Answer Key

| 1. (a) | 2. (b) | 3. (c) | 4. (a) | 5. (b) | 6. (a) | 7. (c) |
| 8. (a) | 9. (b) | 10. (a) | | | | |

Chapter 3

1. Production Planning and Control is a tool which is used to coordinate all manufacturing activities in a production system.
   (a) True
   (b) False
2. Production planning is an activity that is performed before the actual production process takes place.
   (a) True
   (b) False

3. Demand forecasting does not seek to investigate and measure the forces that determine sales for existing and new products.
   (a) True
   (b) False
4. Businesses buy inventory based upon demand forecasts.
   (a) True
   (b) False
5. _____ Systems provide data to the organisations regarding forecasting.
   (a) Point of Sale
   (b) Supply Chain
   (c) Logistics
   (d) Market
6. _____ is a planning exercise done for production using data at an aggregate level.
   (a) Aggregate Production Planning
   (b) Operations Planning
   (c) Supply Chain Designing
   (d) Process Designing
7. _____ represents the critical linking between planning and execution of operations.
   (a) Master Production Schedule (MPS)
   (b) Materials Resource Planning
   (c) MRP II
   (d) CRP
8. _____ is the process of determining what personnel and equipment capacities (times) are needed to meet the production objectives embodied in the master schedule and the material requirements plan.
   (a) Capacity Requirements Planning (CRP)
   (b) Master Production Schedule (MPS)
   (c) Materials Resource Planning
   (d) MRP II

Answer Key						
1. (a)	2. (a)	3. (b)	4. (a)	5. (a)	6. (a)	7. (a)
8. (a)						

Chapter 4

1. The word _____ means the total of goods and services that businesses hold in stock.
   (a) Physical Distribution
   (b) Inventory
   (c) Store
   (d) Warehouse
2. The word 'inventory' can refer to both the total amount of goods and the act of counting them.
   (a) True
   (b) False
3. _____ is the method and procedures companies use to determine the amount of products they should have on hand for meeting consumer demand.
   (a) Logistics
   (b) Storing
   (c) Process Control
   (d) Inventory planning

4. The first step of inventory planning is to estimate future sales.
   (a) True
   (b) False
5. Inventory control is the process of managing an inventory so that the business derives the most overall benefit from the existence of the inventory.
   (a) True
   (b) False
6. In case of Intermittent Demand Systems, organisations do not work exactly opposite the structure of Continuous Demand Systems.
   (a) True
   (b) False
7. _____ systems enjoy very irregular flow of demand and hence anticipating the demand forecast becomes a substantially difficult task.
   (a) Continuous demand
   (b) Intermittent demand
   (c) Mass Flow
   (d) Job Flow
8. When the demand for some products is identified at regular intervals and in uniform quantities, they are termed to fall under the category of _____.
   (a) Decoupling Inventory
   (b) Cyclic inventory
   (c) Reverse Logistics
   (d) Intermittent System
9. Economic Order Quantity formula established under the basic EOQ model is based on the assumption that the price per unit is fixed irrespective of the quantity ordered.
   (a) False
   (b) True
10. GOLF Analysis is maintaining inventory based on:
    (a) Usage Value
    (b) Unit Price
    (c) Source of Procurement
    (d) Seasonality
11. ABC Analysis is maintaining inventory based on:
    (a) Usage Value
    (b) Unit Price
    (c) Source of Procurement
    (d) Seasonality
12. Inventory Turns Ratios are calculated to exercise material control.
    (a) True
    (b) False
13. Continuous demand system is a practice of inventory management and inventory control which is executed by organisations where there is a regular and consistent demand for the manufactured finished products in the market.
    (a) True
    (b) False
14. Excess inventory or inventory shortage - both cause financial impact and they affect the business opportunities.
    (a) True
    (b) False
15. _____ Inventory also understood as pipeline stock is used to refer such goods which have left the firm's warehouse but are still in company's distribution chain as they are yet to be bought by ultimate consumers.
    (a) Cyclic
    (b) Safety
    (c) Decoupling
    (d) Pipeline

Operations & Supply Chain Management **Multiple Choice Questions**

Answer Key

1. (b)	2. (a)	3. (d)	4. (a)	5. (a)	6. (b)	7. (b)
8. (b)	9. (b)	10. (c)	11. (a)	12. (a)	13. (a)	14. (a)
15. (d)						

Chapter 5

1. A supply chain is a system of organisations, people, activities, information, and resources involved in moving a product or service from supplier to customer.
   (a) True
   (b) False

2. The framework of an integrated supply chain is a multi-firm relationship management within the framework characterised by capacity limitations, information management, core competencies, capital, and human resource constraints.
   (a) True
   (b) False

3. The concept of _____ implies the expansion of managerial influence and control beyond the ownership boundaries of a single enterprise to facilitate joint planning and operations with customers and suppliers.
   (a) Collaboration
   (b) Enterprise Extension
   (c) Integrated Service Providers
   (d) Logistics

4. The _____ measures the time in days that it takes for a company to convert resource inputs into cash flows.
   (a) Responsiveness
   (b) cash conversion cycle (CCC)
   (c) Integrated Service Providers
   (d) Logistics

5. Customer satisfaction is defined as "the number of customers, or percentage of total customers, whose reported experience with a firm, its products, or its services (ratings) exceeds specified satisfaction goals.
   (a) True
   (b) False

6. Facilities or Location refers to the geographical sitting of supply chain facilities.
   (a) True
   (b) False

7. _____ is the stock of any item or resource used in an organisation.
   (a) Logistics
   (b) Capacity
   (c) Inventory
   (d) Process

Answer Key

1. (a)	2. (a)	3. (b)	4. (b)	5. (a)	6. (a)	7. (c)

UNIVERSITY QUESTION PAPER
April 2014

Time : 2 ½ Hours   Maximum Marks : 50

Instructions ...
(i) Answer any five questions.
(ii) All questions carry equal marks.

1. State the meaning basis of master production schedule. Explain in brief raw of master production schedule in MRP system.

2. What is importance of maintenance management in an organization ? Discuss its connection with spare part management in detail by giving example.

3. What is operation and supply chain management ? Describe operation process in detail.

4. Discuss the objective and function of production, planning and control ? Explain the input and output of CRP.

5. Explain the functions of operation management in detail ? What are the elements of TQM discuss.

6. How are internal customers ? Discuss the steps for retaining internal customer ?

7. Write short notes on (Any Two) :

    (a) Lean Manufacturing.

    (b) Golf Analysis.

    (c) Purchase Cycle.

    (d) Zero Inventory Concept.

April 2015

Time : 2 ½ Hours　　　　　　　　　　　　　　　　　　　　　　　　　　Maximum Marks : 50

Instructions ...
  (i)　All questions are compulsory.
  (ii)　Each question has an internal option.
  (iii)　Each question carries 10 marks.
  (iv)　Figures to the right indicate marks for that question/sub question.
  (v)　Draw neat diagrams and illustrations supportive to your answer.
  (vi)　Your answer should be specific and to the point.

1. (a) What is Supply Chain Management ? Explain scope, objective and significance of supply chain management. [10]

OR

   (b) Discuss the types of processes and operation. Explain the process product mix with help of diagram. Also discuss its advantages. [10]

2. (a) (i) Define production planning and control. [5]
       (ii) Explain the objectives and functions of MPS. [5]

OR

   (b) Explain important three flows in Supply Chain Management. [10]

3. What is reorder point ? Explain inventory control system with various control techniques. Discuss [10]

OR

Explain the elements of customer service. Discuss globalization and information technology in operation and supply chain management. [10]

4. (a) Explain EQO with quantity discounts also discuss single and multiple price breaks. Explain various inventory control technique. [10]

OR

   (b) (i) Batch Production and Job Production. [5]
       (ii) Note on SDE Analysis. [5]

5. (a) (i) Explain T.Q.M. [5]
       (ii) Explain PERT and CPM. [5]

OR

   (b) Explain - "Forecasting is a planning tool". [10]

www.ingramcontent.com/pod-product-compliance
Lightning Source LLC
Chambersburg PA
CBHW080438230426
43662CB00015B/2315